Contents of the Other Volumes
in Street's Cruising Guide to the
Eastern Caribbean

D1735072

Books by Donald M. Street, Jr.

Cruising Guide to the Lesser Antilles (1966, 1974)
A Yachting Guide to the Grenadines (1970)
The Ocean Sailing Yacht, Volume I (1973)
The Ocean Sailing Yacht, Volume II (1978)
Seawise (1980)
Street's Cruising Guide to the East Caribbean (1980) in five volumes

Street's Cruising Guide to the Eastern Caribbean

Venezuela

Donald M. Street, Jr.

Sketch Charts by Imray, Laurie,
Norie & Wilson

First Edition.

ISBN 0-393-03345-7

W. W. Norton & Company, Inc., 500 Fifth Avenue, New York, N.Y. 10110
W. W. Norton & Company, Ltd., 10 Coptic Street, London-WC1A 1PU

1 2 3 4 5 6 7 8 9 0

Dedication

The idea for this cruising guide was conceived in 1963, and it was only through the hard work, perseverance, courage, and self-sacrifice of my late wife, Marilyn, that the original book got off the ground.

Fortunately for myself and my daughter, Dory, I met Patricia Boucher, now my wife, on the beach in Tyrell Bay. She has presented me with three active sons yet has had time to help in business, sailing *Iolaire*, and exploring. Although she had hardly sailed before our marriage, she has taken to sailing like a duck to water. Her love of sailing was largely instrumental in my decision to keep *Iolaire* when I was thinking of selling her to reduce expenses.

It is only because of Trich's hard work keeping our various enterprises going in my absence that I have been able to keep the third love of my life, *Iolaire*.

Iolaire has been my mistress for thirty-three years; at age eighty-five, she is still the type of boat Michel Dufour would appreciate: She is "fast, beautiful, and responsive." She first arrived in the islands in 1947, remained for a few years, and cruised back to Europe in 1949, directly from Jamaica to England. In 1950, under the ownership of R.H. Somerset, she won her division's RORC Season's Points Championship at the age of forty-five, returned to the islands in 1951, cruised there during the winter of 1951-52, sailed in the Bermuda Race in 1952, then cruised back to Europe and the Mediterranean. In 1954, she returned to the islands, where I purchased her in 1957.

In 1975, we celebrated *Iolaire*'s seventieth birthday by cruising to Europe via Bermuda, New London, New York, Boston, Halifax, and then a fifteen-day passage to Ireland. We cruised on to Cowes, took part in the fiftieth anniversary of the first Fastnet Race, and then raced to La Rochelle, La Trinité, Benodet, and back to the Solent—four races, totaling 1,300 miles, in twenty-one days.

After Calais, we went up the Thames to St. Katherine's Dock in the Pool of London under Tower Bridge, then back down the Thames and up the Colne River in Essex, where we lay alongside the dock in Rowhedge, where *Iolaire* had been built seventy years earlier. Then we went to Plymouth, Glandore (Ireland), Madeira, the Canaries, and back across the Atlantic in eighteen-and-a-half days to Antigua.

We arrived in Antigua seven months and seven days after our departure, having sailed 13,000 miles and raced 1,300 miles—all without an engine—and having visited all the places people had said we would never get to except under power.

We decided that *Iolaire* should celebrate her eightieth birthday in 1985 by retiring from round-the-buoys racing. Her swan song in Antigua Week of 1985 was wonderful—third in the cruising division (seventeen boats), first in the boats twenty years old or older.

Then we took *Iolaire* on a 12,000-mile double-transatlantic jaunt. In seven months, we visited Bermuda, five of the Azores islands, Ireland, Vigo (Spain), the Salvage Islands and the Madeiran archipelago, five of the Canary Islands, and three of the Cape Verde Islands. Then we rolled on home in fourteen days and four hours from the Cape Verdes to Antigua—not a record but a good, fast passage for a heavy-displacement cruising boat.

We spent the winter of 1989-90 exploring Venezuela and crisscrossing the Caribbean, finalizing update information for all volumes of this guide. After that, we sailed from Antigua directly to the Azores, then on to Ireland, down to Vigo, the Canaries, and the Cape Verdes—visiting all the islands we had not visited before in order to eliminate all secondhand information from the *Transatlantic Crossing Guide*. Again we did 12,000 miles in twelve months, without the aid of an engine. We did the Cape Verdes-to-Antigua leg of the trip in fourteen days and twelve hours—with the spinnaker up the last five-and-a-half days. Not bad for an old girl of eighty-five!

In 1990, *Iolaire* came out of retirement to sail in the new Classic Regatta and won her division! She is not ready to race against her younger sisters, but she is still ready, willing, and able to take on the classic boats.

Iolaire has eleven transatlantic passages under her belt. I have sailed her at least 140,000 miles. Who knows how many miles she has sailed during her lifetime? There is little of the Caribbean that has not been furrowed by her hull—and as some of my good friends will point out, there are few rocks that have not been dented by her keel!

To my three loves—Marilyn, Trich, and *Iolaire*—I dedicate this book.

Contents: Venezuela

	Dedication	*v*
	Publisher's Preface	*xvi*
	Foreword	*xvii*
	Acknowledgments	*xxi*
	Charts	*xxiv*
	List of Sketch Charts	*xxvii*
	Introduction to Venezuela	*xxix*
1	Sailing Directions	*1*
2	The Golfo de Paria	*8*
3	North Side: The Peninsula de Paria to Ensa Esmeralda	*20*
4	Isla Margarita and Adjacent Islands	*37*
5	The Peninsula de Araya and the Golfo de Cariaco	*52*
6	Cumaná to El Morro de Barcelona	*58*
7	Carenero to Puerto Tucacas	*77*
8	Puerto Tucacas and Chichiriviche Westward	*95*
9	Eastern Offshore Islands: Los Testigos, La Blanquilla, La Tortuga, La Orchila	*105*
10	Western Offshore Islands: Los Roques, Las Aves	*119*
11	Aruba, Bonaire, Curaçao	*138*
	Bibliography	*149*
	Index	*151*

Contents of the Other Volumes in Street's Cruising Guide to the Eastern Caribbean

Contents: Transatlantic Crossing Guide

List of Sketch Charts
Publisher's Note
Preface
Foreword
Acknowledgments
Charts
1 The Eastern Caribbean—a General Description
2 Preparations
3 Charts
4 Getting There
5 Wind, Weather, and Tides
6 Sailing Directions
7 Entry and Communications
8 Provisions and Services
9 Chartering
10 Yacht Clubs and Racing
11 Boats of the Eastern Caribbean
12 Leaving
Appendices
    Principal Navigational Aids
    Principal Radio Aids
    Principal Commercial Radio Stations
    Principal Holidays
    Chart Number Conversion Table
Bibliography
Index

Contents: Puerto Rico, The Passage Islands, The U.S. and British Virgin Islands

List of Sketch Charts

Publisher's Note

Preface

Foreword

Acknowledgments

Charts

U.S. Chart Number Conversion Table

1 Sailing Directions

2 Puerto Rico

3 Passage Islands

4 U.S. Virgin Islands

5 British Virgin Islands

Bibliography

Index

Contents: Anguilla to Dominica

List of Sketch Charts
Publisher's Note
Preface
Foreword
Acknowledgments
Charts
U.S. Chart Number Conversion Table
1   *Anguilla*
2   *St. Martin*
3   *St. Barthélemy*
4   *Saba, Sint Eustatius (Statia), St. Kitts, and Nevis*
5   *Antigua and Barbuda*
6   *Montserrat and Redonda*
7   *Guadeloupe*
8   *Dominica*

Contents: Martinique to Trinidad

   List of Sketch Charts
   Publisher's Note
   Preface
   Foreword
   Acknowledgments
   Charts
1 Sailing Directions
2 Martinique
3 St. Lucia
4 St. Vincent
5 Barbados
6 Northern Grenadines
7 Southern Grenadines
8 Grenada
9 Trinidad and Tobago
   Chart Number Conversion Table
   Bibliography
   Index

Publisher's Preface

Donald M. Street, Jr., a veteran Caribbean sailor, is also known as an author and the compiler of Imray-Iolaire charts of that area, and as a worldwide yacht insurance broker who places policies with Lloyd's of London.

Mr. Street also serves as a design consultant on new construction, most notably recently on *Lone Star*, a 54-foot wooden ketch built by Mashford Brothers of Plymouth, England. He also acts as design consultant on rerigging existing yachts and finding good cruising boats for people who want a proper yacht. His latest project is a sailing and seamanship video series with *Sailing Quarterly*.

Street is known mainly as a cruising skipper, but he has raced successfully on *Iolaire* and other boats. *Iolaire*, now eighty-five, has retired from round-the-buoys racing, but her skipper has not. He still races in the various Caribbean regattas as an elder statesman—usually as "rock pilot." It is said he knows all the rocks, as he has hit most of them while exploring the Caribbean.

His contributions to sailing in the Eastern Caribbean consist of his five-volume cruising guide and the Imray-Iolaire charts. Forty-seven Imray-Iolaire charts have replaced roughly 200 French, US, British, Dutch, and a few Spanish charts and are all that are needed to cruise the Eastern Caribbean.

As an author, Street is prolific. His original *Cruising Guide to the Lesser Antilles* was published in 1966, *A Yachting Guide to the Grenadines* in 1970, and an updated and expanded *Cruising Guide to the Eastern Caribbean* in 1974, with continual expansions and updates during the 1980s. This has now become *Street's Cruising Guide to the Eastern Caribbean*, a five-volume work that covers a 1,000-mile-long arc of islands.

Street has also written *The Ocean Sailing Yacht, Volume I* (1973) and *Volume II* (1978). *Seawise*, a collection of articles, came out in 1976. He is also working on a series of books—*Street on Sails, Street on Seamanship and Storms*, and *Street on Small-Boat Handling*—as well as *Iolaire and I*, the story of *Iolaire* and Street's lifetime of adventures and misadventures in the yachting world.

Street writes regularly for *Sail, Cruising World, Sailing, WoodenBoat, Telltale Compass, Yachting, Yachting World*, and *Yachting Monthly*, as well as for publications in Sweden, Germany, Italy, Ireland, Australia, and New Zealand.

For more than twenty years, Street owned land and two houses in Grenada, but, unfortunately, the houses are no more. They were taken over by the People's Revolutionary Army (PRA) in May 1979 to be used as part of its military base. The houses did not survive the United States liberation in 1983, when helicopter gunships destroyed both of them. He hopes someday to rebuild on the old site. During the winter, he crisscrosses the Caribbean.

Since Street's main occupation is yacht insurance, he and *Iolaire* appear at all the major gatherings of yachts in the Eastern Caribbean. In the fall, he is always at the St. Thomas and Tortola charterboat shows. Then he proceeds eastward via St. Martin and St. Barts en route to the Nicholsons Agents Week. Spring finds him at the Rolex and BVI regattas, after which he heads to Antigua for the Classic Regatta and Antigua Week. Then it is south to lay up *Iolaire* beyond the hurricane belt. Formerly, *Iolaire* was laid up in Grenada, but her berth has been moved south and west to Centro Marina de Oriente in Puerto La Cruz, Venezuela. In July and August, Street is usually in Glandore, County Cork, Ireland, skippering the family's fifty-nine-year-old Dragon, *Gypsy*, or trimming her sheets for his sons.

As mentioned, Street is an insurance broker—and, in fact, it is his main source of income. He has pointed out that many boats are having trouble obtaining insurance coverage while in Venezuela, so if you are having such difficulties, contact the author, c/o David Payne, B and C Marine Brokers, Ltd., 6 Alie Street, London E1 8DD, England.

Foreword

The Lesser Antilles stretch southward from St. Thomas to Grenada in a great crescent 500 miles long, offering the yachtsman a cruising ground of unequaled variety. Some of the islands are flat, dry, and windswept, their shores girded by coral reefs and their land barely arable. Others are reef-less, jagged peaks jutting abruptly from the sea, where they block the ever-present trade winds and gather rain clouds year round; water cascades in gullies down their sides and their slopes are well cultivated. The character of their peoples likewise varies—from the charming and unspoiled though desperately poor Dominican to the comparatively well-to-do and worldly wise Frenchman of Martinique.

Unless you have a whole season at your disposal, it is foolhardy to attempt all the islands in a single cruise. Not only will you not make it, but you will fail to enjoy the slow, natural, and relaxed pace of life in these tropical islands. The first measure of a successful cruise is how soon your carefully worked-out timetable gets thrown away.

Rule number 1 in the Antilles is: Don't make any plan more than a day in advance, since you will frequently—in fact, constantly—alter your intentions to suit the pace and attractions of the locale.

Rule number 2: Each night before going to bed, read the sailing directions to the next proposed anchorages so that plans can be made for departure at the appropriate hour.

Rule number 3: Read the detailed description of the next anchorage the night before, since in some cases it will affect the next day's plans—particularly the hour of departure. Remember that when you are on the east coast of Martinique, Guadeloupe, Antigua, or Grenada, you must be in the anchorage by 1400. Otherwise, the sun is in the west, directly in your line of vision, making it impossible to see any reefs until it is too late.

It should be left to the gazetteers to squabble over whether Puerto Rico to the north or Trinidad and Tobago to the south should be considered members of the Lesser Antilles. For the purposes of this book, we welcome all three into the fellowship of proximity. Taken as such, the Antilles conveniently break up into a number of areas suitable for two- or three-week cruises. The starting and ending points of a cruise will be governed by your own tastes and the availability of air transportation. The air services into San Juan and Trinidad, for example, are excellent, but neither of these places is a particularly good spot to begin a cruise. San Juan is dead to leeward of the rest of the chain—and who wants to start out with a hard slog into the wind against a strong current? Trinidad is not much better, the anchorage at the Trinidad Yacht Club being a poor lee. It is probably the only yacht-club anchorage in the world where you can get seasick lying to a mooring. The anchorage at the main commercial harbor is a gloomy alternative. Pilferage is so out of control that if you have gold fillings, you are advised to sleep with your mouth closed. The Trinidad Yachting Association has taken a lease in the old U.S. Navy Chaguaramas Base, just west of the seaplane hangar and ramp. Visiting yachtsmen are welcomed, and here, at least, the anchorage is excellent.

Air communications throughout the area have improved over the years, making the entire area readily available to the yachtsman not only from Canada and the United States but also from Europe. Direct international flights arrive at San Juan, Antigua, St. Lucia, Martinique, Guadeloupe, Barbados, and Trinidad, as well as at Maiquetía, the airport for Caracas. Favorite starting points for cruises are St. Thomas, Tortola, Grenada, Barcelona, and Puerto La Cruz in the El Morro area of Venezuela.

One must often rely on secondary local airlines with shuttle services. These vary from being fairly good from San Juan to St. Thomas and Tortola and the Venezuelan airlines to downright disastrous with LIAT. LIAT's aircraft, pilots, and maintenance personnel are first class, but the office staff has developed to an exact science the art of losing baggage and double-booking reservations.

The starting point you choose should relate to your tastes in cruising. If you prefer gunkholing and short jaunts between many little islands a few miles apart, if you like snorkeling and little in the way of civilization, then it should be the Virgins or the Grenadines for you. But you'd best hurry down, because real-estate developers are fast making this a thing of the past. Mustique, for one example, was until recently a private estate in the hands of the Hazel family. But it was sold to a developer, who has worked it over at a pretty fast rate. Well-to-do Europeans have bought land and built houses, creating many new jobs for local labor but depriving the yachtsman of a wonderful hideaway.

For those of you who want to give boat and crew a good tune-up for offshore racing, set out from St. Thomas up through the Virgins, then work your way across Anegada Passage to St. Martin or Anguilla and finish with a final leg up to Antigua. In doing so, you will gain a fair sampling of island diversity and of French, Dutch, and British colonial temperaments. The Anegada Passage is a nice, hard drive to windward, which should uncover any weak points in rig or crew.

Those interested exclusively in the pursuits of diving, treasure hunting, or snorkeling should steer for the low-lying islands of Anguilla, Barbuda, Anegada, Los Roques, and Las Aves. The reefs in these areas are vast and inexhaustible. Fortune hunters still flock to these islands, where innumerable offlying wrecks date back hundreds of years, some presumably undiscovered. Consult the source books—but remember that these islands are low, flat, encircled by reefs, and hard to spot. The charts are based on surveys done mainly in the middle of the nineteenth century. Coral grows, and hurricanes have moved through the area a number of times; earthquakes have shaken the islands and sand bars have moved. In short, you must be extremely careful. Do not let your boat become the next curiosity for inquisitive divers!

Saba and Statia (Sint Eustatius) are two attractive islands that are too seldom visited. Their anchorages are exceptionally bad, but when the conditions are right, they certainly are worth a go. Their close neighbors, St. Kitts and Nevis, are of historical interest, figuring as they do in the lives of Alexander Hamilton, Admirals Nelson and Rodney, and Generals Shirley and Frazer.

If you like longer sails, the bright lights of civilization, and a variety of languages and customs, the middle islands—from Antigua to St. Lucia—should keep you happy. The French islands of Guadeloupe and Martinique afford the finest cuisine in the Antilles. The local merchants offer an excellent selection of cheeses and meats from Europe and the best wines available outside of France. The tourist shops are a woman's delight, and the perfumes are at about half the price in the States. Up until a few years ago, bikinis were so inexpensive (two for $5 US) that the women bought them by the dozen. Regrettably, those days are gone—probably forever. There is still a fabulous collection of bikinis in Martinique, but the prices have gone up so much in France that the savings for an American no longer are substantial. Rough rule of thumb: The smaller the bikini, the more expensive it is. The string has arrived: its size—minuscule; its price—astronomical. One solution frequently used by the always economical French women was to buy only half the string at half the price. Others even felt that was too expensive and sailed *au naturel*—not really showing off, just economizing!

The universal pastime of watching members of the opposite sex is alive and well in Martinique, and the visiting seafarer soon gets into the spirit of things. This pastime can be enjoyed in many ways, but the two most popular methods are strolling around the streets of Fort-de-France and rowing around in Anse Mitan (which today is likely to have forty or fifty boats in it) and pretending to admire the boats while admiring the crews. An added bonus here is that at Anse Mitan, going topless seems to be *de rigeur*.

The women in Fort-de-France may not be the prettiest in the Caribbean, but they are far and away the most stylish. And the men, sitting at sidewalk cafés sipping their coffee or *punch vieux*, cut figures worthy of the *boulevardiers* of Paris. Newcomers, however, should take note: The punch will make a strong man weak-kneed and the coffee tastes not unlike battery acid.

The French and their chicory-laced coffee have distressed visiting foreigners for many decades. A story is told of Count von Bismarck touring France after the Franco-Prussian War. At the close of a fine meal in a country inn, he called for the maître d'hôtel and offered to buy all his chicory at 10 percent over the market price; the maître d' agreed and sold him what he claimed was all he had. Again the count offered to buy any remaining chicory, this time at 50 percent over the market price; the maître d' managed to produce a second quantity of the plant. For a third time, the count offered to buy any that remained—at *twice* the market price—and the maître d' surrendered an additional small amount, insisting that this was indeed all that remained. Satisfied at last, the count concluded,

"Very well, now you may prepare me a cup of coffee!"

Dominica is for the adventurous. A ride into the mountains by Jeep and horseback will take you to the last settlement of the Carib peoples. Here the natives fashion the distinctive Carib canoes that are also seen in Guadeloupe, Martinique, and St. Lucia. With nothing but a flour sack for a sail and a paddle for a rudder, the islanders set out in these boats against the wind to fish in the open Atlantic. Not an easy way to earn a living.

St. Lucia provides some superb anchorages at Pigeon Island, Marigot, and Vieux Fort, and the truly unbelievable one beneath the Pitons at Soufrière. The volcano and sulfur baths are an impressive spectacle, and it is well worth the expense to explore the island by car or Jeep, an adventure vividly recounted by George Eggleston in *Orchids on the Calabash Tree*.

St. Vincent, just north of the Grenadines, is a high, lush island richly and diversely cultivated. The island has an intriguing history, highlighted by the almost continual warfare among French, English, and Caribs that lasted from 1762 until 1796, when the Caribs were expelled to Central America.

Bequia is the home of fishermen and whalers, an island where any sailor can explore, relax, and "gam" for days on end. The harbor is beautiful and life is relaxed.

After cruising the entire Caribbean and getting to know all the islands intimately, many experienced yachtsmen declare Grenada to be "the loveliest of the islands." The highlands produce enough rain to allow the farmers to grow a large quantity of fresh fruit and vegetables, but the south coast is dry enough to allow the yachtsman to live and work on his boat. The island also has a dozen different harbors, providing sixty separate anchorages. Most of these harbors are only short, one- or two-hour sails from each other.

The town of St. George's is picturesque; the main anchorage, in the lagoon, is only a short dinghy ride from supermarkets, cable and telephone offices, banks, and other services. The island has two yacht yards and a yacht club, providing three completely separate slipways, a good stock of marine supplies, and—most important—a large stock of friendly people. In short, the island should, in years to come, reassert itself as the capital of Eastern Caribbean yachting.

Barbados is relatively remote and seldom visited by yachts, except those that are coming downwind from Europe. If your plane stops there en route to another island, arrange for a layover of a day or two.

It is undoubtedly the best-run island in the entire Caribbean. Everything is clean and neat (by West Indian standards); the people are charming and speak with the most wonderful accent. They are solicitous and helpful to visitors. The old carenage in Bridgetown should not be missed, nor should the screw-lift dock.

It is a shame that Tobago is seldom visited by yachtsmen. It is dead to windward of Trinidad, and from Grenada it is 90 miles hard on the port tack. Even if you manage to lay the rhumb line from Grenada, it will be a long slog, hard on the wind. Current and sea will drive you off to the west. It is fairly inaccessible except from Barbados, from where it is an easy reach southwestward.

The American and British Virgin Islands have been laboriously described in the various tourist guides, but whatever the evaluation of shoreside life, a sailor can pass a very pleasant month cruising this area.

The character of the various island peoples is apt to vary broadly within a very small area. Even among the former British islands, each has its own peculiar flavor, its own outlook and accent. (In fact, natives are known to complain that they can't understand the English spoken on neighboring islands.) For the most part, the people are quiet and law-abiding. Actually, the sort of racially inspired violence that periodically has troubled St. Croix and St. Thomas has been far less a problem in the islands farther south.

As the years go by, the Eastern Caribbean becomes more crowded; hence, yachtsmen are beginning to head west to Venezuela. In the 1950s and 1960s, cruising in Venezuela was looked on as a dangerous occupation—not because of unfriendliness to yachtsmen but rather because Castro was smuggling guerrillas ashore in small fishing boats. The Guardia Nacional and the Navy frequently were guilty of shooting first and asking questions later, with the result that a number of yachts were ventilated by Venezuelan government agencies. All that is now a thing of the past. Although you may have to fill out a lot of documents, everyone is extremely friendly and, to the best of my knowledge, there have been no nasty incidents involving yachts in Venezuela for many years.

We hope that with the aid of this book, you will enjoy the islands and the Venezuelan coast as much as I have for more than two decades. (For a more detailed summary of the coast, the offshore islands, and the ABC islands of Aruba, Bonaire, and Curaçao, see the Introduction to Venezuela.)

Anyone contemplating a cruise aboard a charter

boat is well advised to read the supplementary chapters, which will give you much background information. Not only will they explain why your charter skipper might look tired (he probably spent the last two days fixing his generator under sail while he was deadheading to pick you up), but you also will have a better idea of what to expect upon your arrival in the islands. I trust that you will find in this book a host of important tips and facts that are not included in the average tourist or charter-boat broker's brochure. And, needless to say, anyone planning to bring his or her boat to the Eastern Caribbean should read this whole book carefully with pencil in hand to make notes on what is applicable.

To repeat, chapter 1—"Sailing Directions"— probably is the most important chapter. It needs to be read and studied. It should be consulted regularly before you finalize each day's plans. While the navigational features and anchorages of individual islands are described in the chapters concerned with those islands, the routes *between* the islands are described in the sailing directions—so be sure to consult them each day.

Please remember that the sketch charts are just that—drawings meant only to update and supplement the standard navigational charts; be sure you have an overlapping section of the latter on board.

Finally, be cautious. Almost every place in the Eastern Caribbean where a yacht can anchor has been described or at least mentioned in this series, but not all are easy to enter. Many of these anchorages can be used only in good weather and perfect visibility. Besides, some boats are handier than others, and some sailors are better than others. Thus, you must evaluate each anchorage for yourself before entering. The time of day, the weather, your skills, the weatherliness of your boat—all influence the final decision.

As an addendum to this, here's some advice to readers who operate bareboat charter fleets: Carefully study this book (as well as the other volumes in the series), make your judgments, and mark on the sketch charts of each boat's copy the anchorages you want your charterers to avoid.

Fair sailing to all!

—D.M.S.

Acknowledgments

Yachtsmen who cruise the Caribbean should be thankful to Phelps Platt of Dodd, Mead, who saw my original draft of what was then going to be a privately printed guide to the Virgin Islands and liked it enough to encourage me to write a complete guide to the other islands. Yachtsmen should also thank Bernard Goldhirsh, founder of *Sail* magazine, who published the 1974 updated and expanded cruising guide.

Thanks are now due to Eric Swenson of W.W. Norton and Company, who not only agreed to publish a completely updated guide but also agreed that it should be expanded to include Venezuela, its offlying islands, and Aruba, Bonaire, and Curaçao, plus tremendously enlarged sections on "Getting There" and "Leaving." The guide has become so comprehensive that we have produced it in several volumes.

Special thanks should go to Harvey Loomis—a good literary editor and an excellent sailor. Finally, I have an experienced editor who has cruised in the Caribbean and understands the problems of sailing—and racing—in the Caribbean. For eight years he has labored hard as editor of these guides, and he has been a tremendous help in rewriting the sailing and piloting directions to make them clear to the reader. Both I, the author, and you, the reader, owe Harvey a vote of thanks.

I must also thank the many yachtsmen who have helped me with valuable information. Augie Hollen (the only person I know who cruises in a genuine Block Island Cowhorn), Carl Powell of *Terciel*, and Ross Norgrove, formerly of *White Squall II*, all deserve a special vote of thanks for helping me update the Virgin Islands section. Jon Repke of Power Products—a refrigeration expert, electrician, mechanic, sailor, and pilot—solved many of the mysteries of St. Martin/St. Barts/Anguilla by spending the better part of a day flying me through that area. Carl Kaushold supplied an excellent chart and information on the Salt River. Ray Smith of Grenada was most helpful in his suggestions on tides and weather patterns in the Caribbean, and in compiling the list of radio stations and radio beacons. His brother, Ron, solved the mystery of the whereabouts of Tara Island, on the south coast of Grenada, which is marked improperly on the chart. Carl Amour of the Anchorage Hotel solved the great mystery of the rocks off Scotts Head, Dominica. Dr. Jack Sheppard of *Arieto*, the late Dick Doran of *Laughing Sally*, and Carlos Lavendero of several boats made possible the inclusion of the Puerto Rico and Passage Islands information. Gordon Stout of *Shango* and Peter Lee of *Virginia Reel* made possible the inclusion of Tobago. Jerry Bergoff of *Solar Barque* and Sylver Brin of St. Barts were most helpful in clearing up some of the mysteries of the eastern end of St. Barts.

Pieter van Storn, formerly of Island Waterworld, and Malcolm Maidwell and Peter Spronk, both of Caribbean Catamaran Centre, were most helpful in the Sint Maarten area. Hans Hoff, from the 90-foot ketch *Fandango*, is one of the few people who has won a bet from me on anchorages. The standing bet is that I will buy a drink for anyone who can find a good, safe anchorage with 6 feet of water in it that has not been mentioned in this cruising-guide series. I expect to be nabbed once in a while by a small boat, but not by the skipper of a 90-foot ketch! Hans found an anchorage inside the reef on the north coast of Anguilla. Where the chart showed nothing but solid reef, Hans managed to find himself inside the reef with 40 feet of water!

John Clegg, formerly of *Flica II*, Dave Price, formerly of *Lincoln*, and Gordon Stout have popped up continually with wonderful odd bits of information that they have gleaned on their cruises from one end of the Lesser Antilles to the other.

Numerous other skippers have, over the years, given me a tremendous amount of help. They include, in the Antigua area, Desmond Nicholson, of V.E.B. Nicholson and Sons, English Harbour, and Joel Byerley, skipper of *Morning Tide* (and former charter skipper on *Ron of Argyll*, *Mirage*, *Étoile de Mer*, and *Lord Jim*), to name but two. For finer points on the exploration of the east coast of

Antigua, I am deeply indebted to David Simmons of the little cruising/racing sloop *Bacco*. David is also head of Antigua Slipways and the senior marine surveyor in the Eastern Caribbean. Thanks should also go to Simon Cooper and David Corrigan, both of whom unfortunately have left the islands; Morris Nicholson of *Eleuthera*; Simon Bridger of *Circe* and other boats; Peter Haycraft and George Foster, harbor pilots and yachtsmen based in Tortola; Martin Mathias of the sportfisherman *Bihari*; Bert Kilbride, diver extraordinary of Saba Rock, Virgin Islands; and the Trinidadians Doug and the late Hugh ("Daddy") Myer of *Rosemary V* and *Huey II*. I want also to thank Arthur Spence of *Dwyka*, Marcy Crowe of *Xantippe*, Andy Copeland of various boats, Mike Smith of *Phryna*, and Ken McKenzie of *Ti*. The Venezuelan yachtsmen Humberto Contazano of *Boomerang*, Pedro Glaecksman of *Bayola*, Rolly Edmonds of various boats, Dr. Daniel Camejo of *Caribana*, Otto Castillo, Port Captain of Sinclair Oil, and the Curaçao yachtsman Dick Nebbling were most helpful with the Venezuela and Netherlands Antilles section of the books. And in the last five years, a number of other people also have helped us tremendously in updating the information on Venezuela and the Netherlands Antilles. Particular thanks must go to Peter Bottome of *Socrates*, who not only loaned us his boat to do a video with *Sailing Quarterly* but also flew me and Willie Wilson, of Imray, twice around the Los Roques area and also over Isla La Blanquilla and Isla Tortuga. These flights gave us a great deal of information that we were able to obtain from the air because of the clarity of the water. The pilots of Aereotuy, Peter's airline, were extremely helpful. Other valuable assistance came from the late Alex Dearden of *Chubasco*, Paul Adamthwaite of *Stormy Weather*, Billy Wray of *Indalo*, Glen Smith and Helena Henderson of *Hornpipe*, John Vieverich and Myra Rauchbaar of the Curaçao yacht *Jomy*, and Peter York, the marina builder, who supplied us with the plans of the marinas he had engineered. (He also found for us the plans of marinas he had not built.) His partner in the marina business, Daniel Shaw of *Selina*, deserves thanks for efforts above and beyond the call of duty in obtaining topo maps from the topographic division of the Venezuelan government. These maps enabled us to solve many mysteries about the small, uncharted harbors along the north coast of Venezuela. Daniel's son, Enrique, also was tremendously helpful in driving us to the airport, flying with us, and acting as interpreter while we explored Los Roques from the air. And there are no doubt others whose names I have unintentionally left out. It is only with the help of experienced yachtsmen such as these that a book of this type can be written.

A special vote of thanks must go to my nephew Morgan B. MacDonald III, who labored hard for three months in Grenada putting together the sketch charts contained in volumes II and III of this series. Thanks to the staff of Imray, Laurie, Norie & Wilson, especially the late Tom Wilson, who decided to produce the Imray-Iolaire charts; his son, Willy Wilson, who is carrying on his efforts; and Alan Wilkinson, their cartographer, who has labored long and hard to draw the charts for all five volumes of Street's guides and who also draws all the Imray-Iolaire charts of the Eastern Caribbean. Thanks to Jim Mitchell, who has done a superb job of drawing the local watercraft and preparing topographical views.

Thanks should also go to Patricia Street, and to my sister Elizabeth Vanderbilt, her husband Peter, and their son Jay, for their help in rechecking many facts.

I am also grateful to my Irish typists—Maria MacCarthy (summer 1978), Mary Teresa Ronan (summer 1979), and Mary Walch (summer 1980)—who labored hard typing, clipping, and gluing. During the winters, three successive secretaries combined sailing on *Iolaire* with the secretarial duties involved in keeping the guides progressing, articles written, and the insurance and design consulting business functioning. My thanks also to Audrey Semple, Geraldine Hickey, and Rosemary Jennings.

Particular appreciation goes to Aileen Calnan, who sailed and raced with us on *Iolaire* from 1984 to 1988 and filled in whenever needed as secretary, crew, babysitter, and sometimes even cook. In 1989, we had a disaster: Our new secretary fell in love with our Venezuelan interpreter and departed with one day's notice. Luckily, we found, on the beach, Nick Pearson, an ex-British Army telegrapher, who became our "hairy-legged secretary" and labored hard throughout the winter of 1989. Not only did he bang away on the typewriter, but he also was our number-one man for jumping overside in shoal water, grabbing the anchor, carrying it up on the beach, and burying it. Finally, Cheryl Tennant, who came aboard in January 1990, has worked extremely hard in putting together the final sections of this book.

The help of all these devoted friends of the Street family and of *Iolaire* has been invaluable to the production of this book.

During the summer of 1985, *Iolaire* visited and

explored the Azores, the Madeiran archipelago, the Canaries, and the Cape Verde Islands. In 1989, we again did a double-transatlantic—*Iolaire*'s tenth and eleventh, my eighth and ninth—visiting the Azores, the Canaries, and the Cape Verdes and stopping at all the islands we had not visited on previous expeditions. All this information has been included in *Street's Transatlantic Crossing Guide*.

Now I feel my exploring days are over—the "Old Tiger" has retired—and it is time that one of the "Young Tigers" (daughter Dory or one of her three brothers, Donald, Richard, and Mark) should take over *Iolaire* and explore new fields.

It is impossible for any one yachtsman to describe absolutely every cove, find every rock, and ascertain everything to be known about the currents for such a vast area as is covered by these five volumes, so I would greatly appreciate any help that yachtsmen can give. If any yachtsman has suggestions for corrections, additions, or deletions, I would request that the information be sent to: D.M. Street, Jr., c/o David Payne, B and C Marine Brokers, Ltd., 6 Alie Street, London E1 8DD, England. (Needless to say, this address is also valid for anyone requiring marine insurance.)

Charts

REMEMBER: DO NOT ENTER STRANGE HARBORS AT NIGHT!

I formerly carried on board *Iolaire* about 200 United States, British, French, Dutch, and a few Spanish charts—all of which were out of date; that is, even though they were new charts, the various government offices had not accurately corrected and updated them. The British Admiralty will correct charts of a foreign area only if the government concerned officially notifies the BA. Much worse, US charts are corrected *only* when a whole plate is corrected; if you buy a new chart of Puerto Rico and it is a twelve-year-old edition, no corrections will have been made on that chart since the date of the edition twelve years earlier!

Furthermore, BA and US charts are often on the wrong scale for inshore navigation by a yacht. The charts covering Grenada, the Grenadines, and St. Vincent are 1:72,000, while the famous old Virgin Islands chart is 1:100,000, which is even worse. One needs a magnifying glass to find small anchorages and coves. In addition, it cuts Virgin Gorda in half. Several of the US and British charts break up the St. Vincent and Grenadines area in odd splits not conducive to use by the average yachtsman. The US chart of the Grenadines has an excellent enlarged insert for the Tobago cays, but it does not have tidal reference points. The British chart does have this valuable information. Furthermore, the US and BA charts are based on surveys made in the 1890s. The latest NOAA and Admiralty charts have new deep-water information but retain the old inshore errors.

As a result of all these difficulties, I signed a contract with Imray, Laurie, Norie & Wilson (usually known simply as Imray), which traces its ancestry back to 1670, to do updated and accurate charts specifically tailored to the needs of the yachtsman. Our information has been gathered from United States NOS and DMA charts, British Admiralty charts, French and Dutch charts, plus unpublished US and British Admiralty surveys, topographical maps, and aerial photography, backed up by the information I have gathered in more than thirty years of exploring the Eastern Caribbean. Information also has been supplied to me by other experienced yachtsmen. Although it may be that I know the Eastern Caribbean as a whole better than any other yachtsman, there are individuals who know individual islands and areas much better than I do. These yachtsmen have been tremendously helpful in supplying me with their information.

Our charts come in one standard size, 25" x 35 1/2", and three colors: blue denotes deep water; white denotes water 5 fathoms or less; and yellow indicates 1 fathom or less. Detailed harbor charts are inserted in the margins of the general charts. Useful ranges (transits) are shown to guide the mariner clear of dangers. Various overlapping coverages and often contradictory information found in the various French, US, Dutch, and British Admiralty charts have been eliminated.

Imray-Iolaire charts are kept up to date through careful attention to the British Notices to Mariners, my own observations, and comments sent by users of these charts and readers of these cruising guides. Important corrections are inserted by hand at Imray prior to shipment; all corrections are logged in on the master sheet so that even minor corrections are included in new editions. Seldom do we go more than six months between printings of a chart. (The most popular Imray-Iolaire charts—those of the US and British Virgin Islands, and Anguilla, St. Barthélemy, St. Martin, and Antigua—are available on waterproof paper.)

As of this writing, forty-seven Imray-Iolaire charts cover the entire Eastern Caribbean, except for Tobago, which will be along in due course.

The Imray-Iolaire charts have become the accepted standard; the US Coast Guard, as well as the St. Vincent and Grenadian Coast Guards, use

Imray-Iolaire charts rather than government charts. Very few chart agents in the Eastern Caribbean continue to stock the government charts.

The charts of Venezuelan waters have been updated as a result of nine cruises in that area. We have been aided by the Venezuelan Hydrographic Office, which has made unpublished Venezuelan charts available to us.

In short, I strongly recommend that yachtsmen use the Imray-Iolaire charts instead of British Admiralty or US government charts.

The Atlantic islands are well covered by Spanish and Portuguese charts, except that when new harbors are built, they are seldom included on the charts. For the average yachtsman, there is also the disadvantage of trying to find the Spanish and Portuguese charts, which are extremely difficult to obtain. Therefore, the Imray-Iolaire charts eventually will be expanded to cover the Atlantic islands. In the meantime, virtually all harbors in the Atlantic islands either appear as harbor charts or in some areas (where we are working from minimal information) as sketch charts. Sketch charts must be used with EXTREME caution. Most of the harbor charts in this volume have been taken from the relevant Imray-Iolaire charts. However, the sketch charts included here are just that—sketches. They are as accurate as I can make them, but they are *not* official publications, so they should be used only in conjunction with reliable navigational charts, common sense, and eyeball observations.

The sea level is roughly 12 to 18 inches lower in May, June, and July than it is the rest of the year. Imray-Iolaire chart soundings are based on this low, low datum. Other charts may not be.

Warning regarding all Venezuelan charts of islands off the coast of Venezuela: Almost all the lights on the north coast of Venezuela and on to Bonaire are flashing lights. When bouncing up and down in a swell, it is extremely difficult to distinguish whether a light is flashing six seconds or eight seconds. Augie Hollen points out that the best way to time a light—and in fact the only sure way—is to time how long it takes for the light to go through ten full sequences; then divide by ten and you will come up with the correct answer. However, it must be remembered that the lights are not very reliable. Frequently they are out, and at other times the timing mechanism is off, so what is reported on the chart and the light list may not be correct. *View all lights with extreme suspicion.*

No chart can be absolutely accurate, but I feel that the Imray-Iolaire charts are the most accurate charts available. They can be kept that way only if experienced yachtsmen continue to feed information and corrections to us to correct the small errors that may still exist or to update charts where the topography has been changed by hurricanes, earthquakes, or dredging.

Please send any chart correction information to: D.M. Street, Jr., c/o David Payne, B and C Marine Brokers, Ltd., 6 Alie Street, London E1 8DD, England.

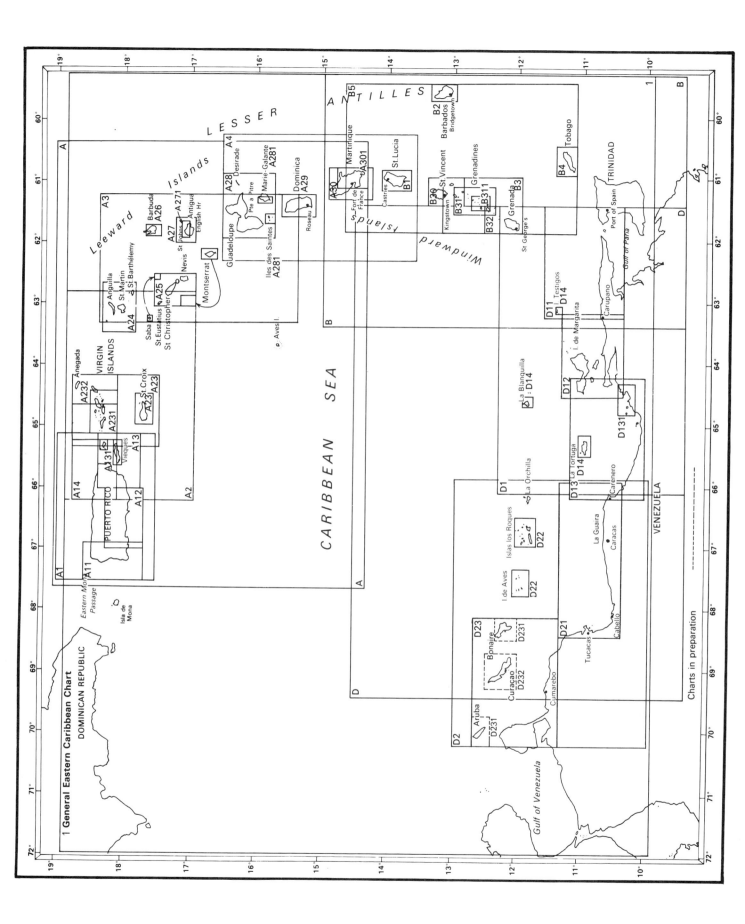

List of Sketch Charts

V-1	Monjes del Sur	V-36	Paseo Colón Marina, Puerto La Cruz
V-2	Ensa Cariaquita	V-37	Américo Vespucio Marina, El Morro
V-3	Ensa Macuro/Cristóbal Colón	V-38	Marina El Morro de Barcelona
V-4	Ensa Yacua	V-39	Islas de Píritu
V-5	Ensa Patao and Ensa Uquirito	V-40	Puerto Carenero
V-6	Güiria	V-41	Higuerote
V-7	Eastern End, Peninsula de Paria	V-42	Ensenada de Corsarios/Rondón
V-8	Boca de la Serpiente	V-43	Puerto Azul
V-9	Orinoco Delta and River	V-44	Caraballeda Yacht Club and Marina
V-10	North Coast, Peninsula de Paria (Uquire to Mejillones)		Mar
		V-45	Puerto La Guaira
V-11	North Coast, Peninsula de Paria (Ensa Unare to Puerto Santos)	V-46	Puerto Calera
		V-47	Puerto La Cruz
V-12	North Coast, Peninsula de Paria (Carúpano to Punta Manzanillo)	V-48	Isla Larga
		V-49	Puerto Cabello
V-13	Ensenada Uquire	V-50	Puerto Cabello (Street Plan)
V-14	Ensenada Pargo	V-51	Puerto Tucacas and Morrocoy
V-15	Ensenada Mejillones	V-52	Puerto Chichiriviche
V-16	Playa Cacao	V-53	Islas Los Testigos
V-17	San Juan de Unare	V-54	Isla La Blanquilla
V-18	Ensa Medina	V-55	Isla Tortuga (East End)
V-19	Río Caribe	V-56	Islas Los Tortuguillos and Cayo Heradura, Tortuga
V-20	Bahías Puerto Santos		
V-21	Carúpano	V-57	Boca de Cangrejo and Boca Palo, Tortuga
V-22	Punta Patilla to Punta de Lande		
V-23	Ensenada Esmeralda	V-58	Los Roques
V-24	Pampatar, Isla Margarita	V-59	Puerto El Roque, Los Roques
V-25	Porlamar, Isla Margarita	V-60	Cayo de Agua, Los Roques
V-26	Punta de Piedras (Bahía Guamache), Isla Margarita	V-61	Las Aves de Barlovento
		V-62	Las Aves de Sotavento
V-27	Boca del Río, Isla Margarita	V-63	Lighthouse Island, Sotavento
V-28	Chacachacare, Isla Margarita	V-64	Round Island, Sotavento
V-29	Juangriego, Isla Margarita	V-65	Long Island, Sotavento
V-30	El Saco, Isla Coche	V-66	Kralendijk Town Dock, Bonaire
V-31	Ensa El Rincon and Puerto Réal	V-67	Kralendijk Yacht Harbor, Bonaire
V-32	Laguna Chica	V-68	Lac Baai, Bonaire
V-33	Laguna Grande del Obispo	V-69	Willemstad, Curaçao
V-34	Cumaná	V-70	Spanish Water, Curaçao
V-35	Puerto Mochima	V-71	Oranjestad, Aruba

Introduction to Venezuela

Venezuela is the new cruising ground for the yachtsman who, having sailed in the relatively crowded waters of the Lesser Antilles, wants to continue cruising in tropical waters that are totally unspoiled and uncrowded.

Yachtsmen began to arrive in Venezuelan waters in fair-sized numbers after my *Guide to Venezuela* came out in 1980. For the next few years, more and more yachts came to Venezuela, but then the influx stabilized for a number of years when the Venezuelan bolívar was very high, making Caracas the most expensive city in the world.

With the decline in oil prices came devaluation of the bolívar, and suddenly Venezuela became incredibly inexpensive. Yachtsmen flooded the area in the late 1980s. Then, unfortunately, a couple of days of rioting following the 1989 elections scared them off. The rioting occurred in a very few locations in major cities, and everything quieted down rather quickly. The Perez government now is working very hard to revitalize the economy, but it is a tough uphill struggle that has caused a lot of drastic belt-tightening. Venezuela in 1990 is not as inexpensive as it was in 1988, but it is still, in comparison with the rest of the Eastern Caribbean, incredibly reasonable. The exchange rate has gone from 4.5 bolívars (Bs.) to the dollar in 1980, 22.5 to the dollar in 1987, 32 to the dollar in 1988, and 48 to the dollar in 1990.

Yachtsmen also worry about piracy and drug smugglers, but these problems do not affect Venezuela; they appear to be a peculiarly Colombian phenomenon, and the law in Colombia is the gun. Anyone visiting the Colombian coast in a yacht has got to be out of his mind: His chances for survival are minimal. But the western portion of Venezuela, near the Colombian border, is so lacking in harbors, and so rough, that you're not missing anything by avoiding that area. Chichiriviche, about 80 miles from the Colombian border, is about the farthest west you'd want to go. Thus, for the average yacht, the chances of running into drug smugglers in Venezuelan waters is absolutely nil. Further, to make sure the drug lords never get the upper hand, and to keep smugglers from using the islands off the coast of Venezuela as drug transfer points, the Venezuelan government has established a military presence on all of the offshore islands. This varies from a naval base with an airstrip on Blanquilla to two or three members of the Guardia Nacional on Islas de Aves and Los Testigos. As a result of all this, the drug smugglers have avoided the Venezuelan islands and coast.

One reason why Venezuela is relatively undiscovered is that yachtsmen beating their way from Panamá to the Lesser Antilles usually stop only once or twice. Similarly, yachtsmen heading from the Lesser Antilles to Panamá and the Pacific have tended to hurry on through without pausing to explore this extremely fine cruising area.

Venezuela is completely different from the Eastern Caribbean in language, customs, weather, terrain—everything. The language, of course, is Spanish, although many middle-class and upper-class people speak a second language—usually English, Italian, or French. However, the man in the street with whom you usually will come in contact has no second language. Before you go, you should try to memorize some basic Spanish phrases, and plan to carry a Spanish-English phrase book.

Venezuelans are friendly and hospitable. In all the times I have cruised there, I have never experienced anything but superb hospitality and assistance from the local people—from the wealthy yachtsmen at Puerto Azul to the fishermen of the offshore islands or the ladies in the market. There is absolutely no feeling of racial prejudice or evidence of the "chip on the shoulder" that one occasionally finds in the Eastern Caribbean.

Historically, Venezuela is much older than the rest of the Caribbean, the Margarita and Cumaná areas having been settled in the opening years of the sixteenth century. Thus, many buildings and forts predate the earliest buildings in the Eastern Caribbean.

Venezuela is a land of contrasts. The coast, with its mountains that rise directly from the sea to 9,000 feet, in some parts is dry and desolate like a desert; other sections, like the eastern end of the Peninsula de Paria, are covered with dense jungle. The easternmost tip of the peninsula rises 5,000 feet, with vertical slopes spilling into the Caribbean on one side and the Golfo de Paria on the other. From the Golfo de Paria, one can visit Angel Falls and the Orinoco Delta, take excursions into the jungle, and see unbelievable wildlife right from the boat. This area is the original primeval jungle, occasionally visited by powerboats but seldom by sailing yachts. The windswept offshore islands provide some of the finest fishing, snorkeling, and diving in the Eastern Caribbean. They have not been fished out and they are generally uninhabited. (Before spearfishing in Venezuela, however, check local regulations carefully, as some of the offshore islands have become national parks, and spearfishing is absolutely prohibited. This, by the way, makes for great snorkeling, as the fish are not gun-shy.)

The north coast of Venezuela, as one progresses westward, begins with heavy jungle that tapers out to brush and ends up finally in Laguna Grande del Obispo. In the Golfo de Cariaco, one finds a fantastic harbor—the scenery ashore is like a lunar landscape. One has the impression that it has not rained here in twenty years!

Continuing westward, the mountains of Venezuela are always close to the coastline and always barren. The cities are exploding rather than simply growing. Side by side are sophisticated new marinas and tiny fishing villages. Offshore are low, deserted reefs and uninhabited islands. After Puerto Cabello, you can pretty much forget the rest of the Venezuelan coast and head for Bonaire, Aruba, and Curaçao.

Los Roques, a 355-square-mile cruising area off the north coast, is almost as large as the American and British Virgin Islands, and at least 50 percent of it is unsurveyed. Venezuelan yachtsmen and a few Americans (such as Gordon Stout) have crisscrossed this wonderful place and spent as long as a week cruising here. This area would be ideal for a bareboat organization, and perhaps one will expand into this area. It will be interesting to see what develops here in years to come.

Yachting facilities have improved considerably in recent years, and almost all of the major ports of Venezuela and the ABC islands have yacht clubs. Racing is not as intensive and widespread as in the Eastern Caribbean, but it is active. (For more information on this, see *Street's Transatlantic Crossing Guide*.) As for hauling, Venezuela now offers the cheapest hauling facilities in the Eastern Caribbean. There are marinas at Cumaná, Puerto La Cruz (three), Caracas area (five), Puerto Cabella, and in the Morrocoy National Park. The yards in the Cumaná area are capable of hauling even the largest yachts, while fifty-ton travel lifts can be found all along the coast. Paint, varnish, and bottom paint are available and inexpensive in Venezuela, but no one seems to have decided how good the paint is.

More and more yachts are heading down to Venezuela for their summer refits for two reasons: (1) Labor charges are a fraction of what they are elsewhere in the Caribbean. In 1990, yards were charging $2 US per hour for gut labor, $11 per hour for the highest skilled labor. (2) Venezuela is south of the hurricane belt. After the 1989 disaster of Hurricane Hugo in the northern part of the Caribbean, I suspect that the number of boats heading south for the summer will increase exponentially! Admittedly, yachting facilities are practically nonexistent east of Cumaná, but it's not that far from there to Grenada. And just because of its relative lack of facilities, this area is a place where you can really get away from it (and them) all.

Once you get away from the major population areas, you will seldom have more than one or two other yachts in your anchorage—and the only time you are likely to find many boats in the anchorages is on the weekends.

One cruising technique used by some yachts is to arrive at a major marina on Friday night as the Venezuelans are departing and berths are available. You can do your sightseeing and shopping on Saturday, have a night on the town Saturday night, sleep late Sunday morning, and depart Sunday afternoon prior to the return of the Venezuelan yachts.

A word of warning: Mail to Venezuela is hopeless, so do not write to reserve hauling dates; it's more expedient to telephone. The good yards have more business than they can handle, so the waiting list may be three or four weeks if you haven't made prior arrangements.

Where the mail in Venezuela goes, no one

knows. The only way to get mail there is to have it sent via courier service. Various courier post services operate better than their agents abroad realize. The courier post is sent to major distribution centers and then distributed from there via taxi. For instance, our mail came into Puerto La Cruz (we were in Cumaná), and two hours after we found out which courier service had it (it seems there are six, and most of them are not listed in the telephone directory), it was placed in a taxi and sent on to us in Cumaná. The extra cost of delivery was something like $3 US. Before you go to Venezuela, make sure to decide which courier service you are going to use, and then obtain the phone numbers of the various offices of that service.

Telephone service in Venezuela makes you virtually incommunicado unless you are staying in a hotel or can use a friend's phone. There are pay phones everywhere; some take coins and others take phone cards. However, the largest coin that will fit in a pay phone is 1 bolívar, about 5 cents US. If you have 1B coins, you can make calls, but only inside the country, as it is impossible to assemble enough of these coins to make an overseas call. The second problem is that coins have almost disappeared from circulation, as paper has replaced them. There are even 1B and 2B notes! Thus, you can only use coin phones with difficulty. Using a phone card, you can direct-dial almost anywhere in the world, but as of 1990, the cards for these phones virtually ceased to exist! Result: hotel or friend, or go to the main local exchange and stand in line!

Regarding money in Venezuela, the best thing to do is to carry a MasterCard or Visa card. With that and your passport, you can obtain money from the various banks. (Rather than always carrying their passports, some people just photocopy the first two pages.) Having money transferred into Venezuela by the banks is nearly impossible.

A good English-language reference to Venezuela and some of the offshore islands is the 945-page *Guide to Venezuela*, by Janice Bauman and Leni Young, published by Ernesto Armitano in Caracas.

For those who wish to join friends cruising the area, Maiquetía Airport, which services Caracas, is connected to the entire international network with direct jet flights that include the supersonic Concorde. Within Venezuela, air transportation is good, even though reservations are somewhat unreliable; but they're no worse than dear old LIAT. But unlike flying in other areas of the Eastern Caribbean, flying within Venezuela is incredibly cheap. You can buy a three-week excursion ticket with unlimited

mileage that allows you to fly anywhere in Venezuela for an incredibly low price. Some yachtsmen locate a safe place to leave their boats and then go skiing in the Andes. Wonderful tours to Angel Falls can be arranged through Peter Bottome's Aereotuy airlines.

Access to the area for the yachtsman coming from the north and east is extremely easy. From Puerto Rico or St. Thomas down to Margarita is about 450 miles, course 195° magnetic; from the east—Grenada, for instance—it is merely an eight-hour dead-downwind sail to Islas Los Testigos. If you're coming from the west, Panamá to Aruba . . . well, the less said about that, the better. (This subject is discussed in some detail in *Street's Transatlantic Crossing Guide*.) In a word, though, if those yachtsmen working their way from west to east use their heads, they'll explore the Venezuelan coast rather than push on through the Eastern Caribbean. They will discover some excellent cruising, despite the fact that most of it requires sailing to windward (see chapter 1, "Sailing Directions: West to East").

Close to Venezuela are the ABC islands of Aruba, Bonaire, and Curaçao. Low and windswept, they vary from the quiet, simple, and slow-moving Bonaire to the hustling, bustling, and very cosmopolitan Curaçao.

Bonaire is low, flat, and sparsely populated. Its shores rise so steeply from the sea bottom that it is almost impossible to anchor in its lee. The anchorage problem has been solved with a new marina, which has slips and a 100-ton synchro-lift dock. Adequate supplies—fresh, frozen, and canned—are available. The people are very friendly and Bonaire has some of the best diving in the world—with excellent support facilities right at hand.

If you want to connect up with the outside world from the ABC islands, go to Curaçao, with its excellent air communications and first-class hotels. Curaçao also has excellent harbors and all kinds of supplies.

Boats going westward used to skip Aruba, but it was a popular place for boats fighting their way eastward from Panamá and the San Blas Islands. However, tourism has taken hold on the island, and a new marina in Oranjestad offers all the amenities a yachtsman could want. The trip from Panamá is a long slog to windward, and in years gone by, yachts frequently stopped at Cartagena or Santa Marta or anchored behind Cabo de la Vela (all in Colombia). However, no yacht these days should even think of approaching the Colombian coast, much less anchoring off. Thus, Aruba looks like heaven after a week or so of slamming into the heavy trade winds and westerly current.

The food in the ABC islands is extremely varied. Here there is old-fashioned Dutch cooking plus a good deal of superb Indonesian cooking, and, inevitably, American food. Once you hit Venezuela, you'll find Spanish cooking, which I think is superb. The variety of fish and shellfish seems to be inexhaustible, fresh fruits and vegetables are excellent, and even the meat is good. Prices in eating places in Venezuela vary from $10 US for an expensive meal to $2 US for a cheap meal.

The climate on Venezuela's offshore islands and the ABC islands is typical trade-wind climate, with the ever-present breezes sweeping across the low islands. The coastal climate, however, is quite different. The high mountains make for the land/sea breeze routine. The trades blow during the day and either die to a flat calm at sunset or give way to an offshore breeze as the cold air comes down off the mountains at night. The land breeze frequently lasts until 1000 the next day, when the trades move in again. On the Venezuelan coast, it gets very hot in most areas during the day, but as soon as the sun goes down, the temperature drops and the cool air flows down from the mountains. In some areas, it gets positively cold at night.

For the yachtsman who loves to sail simply for the sake of sailing, the Golfo de Cariaco offers what is in my opinion the best body of water in the Western Hemisphere. Some 32 miles long and 8 miles wide, it has no current. A good, hard trade wind blows up during the day and dies out at night; there is no sea to speak of—merely a chop. Where else can one beat to windward with a no. 3 jib, genoa staysail, and reefed main with the rail down—and still have the fo'c's'le hatch open?

Shoreside life is varied. One finds small and, unfortunately, none-too-clean fishing villages, often inhabited by wives and numerous small children—the menfolk usually are at sea. There are also fairly civilized, medium-size towns, such as Cumaná; and then there is the magnificent metropolis of Caracas.

Before condemning Venezuela for the shanty-towns and shacks that surround its cities, one must realize that prior to the advent of oil and the industrialization of the country, the economy was mainly agricultural. The past twenty years has seen vast population shifts. For many of the cities, such as

Puerto La Cruz, Barcelona, and Caracas, growth has been so fast that no city planner could even hope to keep up with it. No one could possibly erect reasonable housing for all the thousands of people who are flocking in from the countryside, because the cities are not expanding—they're exploding.

One of the nicest things about cruising in this area is that the Customs procedures are not nearly as onerous as they are elsewhere. The ABC islands are about as easygoing as anywhere in the whole Caribbean. The Venezuelans like to shuffle a lot of papers, but we can hope that, under the prodding of those of us who have already cruised there and those who will go in the future, the procedures will be simplified. At the moment, one of the problems is that when sailing from one state to the next, you have to obtain a *zarpa*, which requires visiting the Port Captain's office and, in some cases, Customs and Immigration. Everyone is very friendly, but this can be a time-consuming operation. I can testify, however, that if one is accompanied by a small, blond, blue-eyed child, everything moves much faster.

Entering Venezuela for the first time can be a bit of a project, as it is necessary to visit the Guardia Nacional, Customs, Immigration, and the Port Captain, in that order. This can literally take a whole day. However, in many of the ports (e.g., Margarita, Puerto La Cruz, Puerto Cabello), local agents will take care of the paperwork for you for a reasonable fee. (See the individual port information for further details.)

Invariably, the Venezuelan officials are very conservative. Be forewarned that when going to a government office in Venezuela, you should be sure to wear shoes, a decent shirt, and trousers. If you go in wearing shorts and sandals, the officials will be inexplicably unavailable.

Regarding Customs and Immigration, it should be noted that both the yacht and all the crew members must have visas prior to entering Venezuelan waters. These visas can be obtained from any Venezuelan embassy, but it seems to be easiest to get them from the embassies in Antigua and Grenada. If crew members are flying in to join the boat, they will not need to apply for visas, as the airline will arrange for the visa as part of the ticket.

1

Sailing Directions

When sailing along the Venezuelan coast, you must have no preconceived notions of wind, weather, or tide. Nor should you believe the pilot charts put out by the US and the British Hydrographic Offices, for while they may be moderately accurate for the offshore waters, they are definitely not accurate for the coastal areas.

One of the first things the yachtsman familiar with the Eastern Caribbean notices is that the water temperature along the coast (especially along the eastern coast from the Peninsula de Paria to El Morro de Barcelona) is much colder. We regularly recorded water temperatures down to 68°F rather than the more familiar 77°F. The water along the coast is clean but murky, with visibility normally limited to about 10 feet; thus, eyeball navigation is out, and you must be sure to have a lead line, sounding pole, or fathometer.

The currents generally set to the west, but this is not universal. Along the coast there is frequently an easterly countercurrent that, of course, varies with the velocity of the wind, the state of the moon, and the topography of the area.

In the offshore islands, the weather is pretty much as it is in the Eastern Caribbean. The trade winds blow eight to nine months of the year and then are variable from mid-August to mid-October. One difference is that the Venezuelan islands are so low lying and small that they do not stop the trades; thus, the trades will blow twenty-four hours a day—only in Margarita does the wind die out at night. For those of us with wind generators, it is heaven: When *Iolaire* is in the offshore islands, she is able to run both refrigerators to our hearts' content. We could practically make ice.

Along the coast where the mountains are very high, right next to the coast at the eastern end of the Peninsula de Paria, and in the area between Cabo Codera and Puerto Cabello, the wind basically is easterly. Usually it is calm at dawn, but in

the morning the wind springs up out of the northwest, slowly working its way around to the east. Come 1600 it often is blowing at near gale velocity, but shortly thereafter it begins to die out—to the extent that, by 2000 or 2100, right along the coast, it is a mere whisper; just a breath of air that allows boats with an engine to power eastward along the coast with no trouble.

In the area of El Morro, and also the area bounded on the east by Margarita and on the west by the Islas de Píritu, the weather pattern and the numerous harbors make it pleasant and interesting to sail eastward during the day. Our experience has been flat calm until sometime around 1000 or 1100, when the wind begins to spring up from the northwest. This is when *Iolaire* takes off with our big genoa and mizzen staysail, broad-reaching on a port tack. As the day goes by, the wind veers to the north, then to the north-northeast, and finally to the northeast. As the wind builds and shifts to the east, we get rid of the genoa and mizzen staysail and switch to a double headsail rig. By 1600 it is usually blowing hard enough that beating to windward is getting to be a project rather than fun. But since it has been calm all night, the sea has not built up. At that point, between 1600 and 1700, you take a look at the chart and find an anchorage for the night. It is still blowing strong at 1800. But at 1830, the wind becomes a light breeze and by 1900 it is flat calm. My wife loves this routine, as she likes to sleep late. We are not able to set sail until 1000 or 1100, which fits in perfectly with her plans.

In the summer the wind is lighter. My Venezuelan friends say that early summer (i.e., June through early August) is the best time to explore the offshore islands, because the wind does not blow quite as hard then as it does in winter. Yachtsmen flock down to do repairs in the yards and to avoid the hurricanes, as Venezuela is south of the hurricane belt and, to the best of my knowledge, no hurricane has ever done any real damage in Venezuela. They pass to the north, sometimes close to the north, and have dumped a lot of rain on the coast, but the wind has not caused any problems. Billy Wray of *Indalo* says that in Puerto La Cruz during the summer there is little or no wind during the day and it gets very hot. By about 1300 or 1400, you are getting ready to die of the heat, but pretty regularly around 1400, the clouds suddenly open up and there is a two-hour deluge, which cools everything. The rain then disappears and the sun comes out, but he says that the rains release a great flood.

Remember that during the summer there are likely to be more south and southwest winds, which will enable you to sail eastward, rather than motor. Even an engineless boat like *Iolaire* has had relatively little trouble sailing eastward along the coast.

Finally, remember that these are merely indications, not absolutes. In 1989 we left Puerto La Cruz, heading west for Caracas, and from Américo Vespucio Marina to Cabo Codera (a distance of 85 miles), we were close-hauled with the wind first southwest, but then switching suddenly to northwest! It finally went to the northeast at Cabo Codera.

The rise and fall of the tide along the coast and offshore islands is minimal—roughly 1 foot. However, if you're foolish enough to go into the Golfo de Cardón (as it is called on the Imray-Iolaire charts), you'll discover a 2- to 3-foot tide; ditto in the Golfo de Paria, where a regular rise and fall of 2 1/2 to 3 feet rises to almost 4 feet at the springs.

When cruising the Venezuelan coast and offshore islands from November to April, always examine all anchorages with an eye to the possibility of a ground swell. This is caused not by local conditions but by storms in the North Atlantic. These can produce heavy swells that sweep the entire Caribbean, but especially the Venezuelan coast. When they arrive, they do so with unbelievable force. In 1966, a ground swell besieged the breakwater at Puerto Azul, completely demolishing it and even breaching the huge seawall at La Guaira.

For an impressive example of what the swell can do, sail along the northwest coast of Margarita and see the spectacular sand dunes, more than 100 feet high, thrown up by the effect of the ground swell. Or, if you are anchored in Los Testigos, walk over to the windward side of Testigo Grande and see the magnificent beach where the sand has been piled up in a 100-foot hill along the beach—a very powerful combination. Every time you see a white sand beach with a very steep-to foreshore and sand rising

in a bank 5 to 6 feet high, look out. This is an area subject to ground swells.

If you listen to the weather reports on Puerto Rico radio in the morning, you'll find they are not too good (see *Street's Transatlantic Crossing Guide* for details of weather reports in the Eastern Caribbean). However, they are useful in that they give reports of ground swells on the north coast of Puerto Rico. These ground swells usually reach Venezuela about twenty-four hours later.

Sailing Directions: West to East

This trip is best done during the period from June through October. Looking at these months, one thinks immediately of the hurricane season, but remember that Venezuela is south of the hurricane belt. During the winter, the offshore trades blow hard and then blow harder. During June, July, and early August, the trades blow with great consistency, but with less velocity than during the winter. From late August to early November, the trades tend to be erratic, sometimes blowing with the same velocity as during the winter, easing off at times, and dying out completely at other times.

However, close to the shore, the land/sea breeze cycle takes over, becoming more pronounced as the summer progresses; thus, even when going east, it's probably a good idea to hug the coast. The motorsailer with a big diesel should hug the coast as closely as possible, taking advantage of the countercurrent and running mostly at night. Even during the day, especially in areas of high mountains, if you're close enough to shore, there is often little or no wind, which allows you to power eastward.

An underpowered sailboat may be able to motor up the coast during the nighttime calm periods. In the morning, when the trades come in, if she's the kind that really goes to windward, she should stand off and pick up the trades about 3 or 4 miles offshore, then tack back in at night. However, if the trades are blowing right up to the coast, the best procedure is to short-tack up the beach. This is hard on the crew, but it's the fastest way to work your way eastward, as has been proved regularly when Venezuelan yachts race.

Getting from Panamá to Aruba—a distance of roughly 600 miles from the San Blas Islands—has always been difficult. It's a dead beat to windward every step of the way. In the past, you could work your way eastward to the islands west of Cartagena, a distance of roughly 150 miles, and then go on to

Cartagena, to Santa Marta, to the lee of Cabo de la Vela, and finally to Aruba. This was a long windward haul, but at least there were rest points en route. But now it is no longer advisable, as the risk of having gear stolen from your boat—or getting shot—anywhere in Colombia is too high. Today, Lloyd's and other major insurance companies will not insure your boat in Colombian waters, so beware! (For further information on sailing from Panamá to Aruba, see *Street's Transatlantic Crossing Guide.*)

While visiting the Venezuelan Hydrographic Office in March 1987, I discovered that the southern end of Los Monjes, in the entrance to the Golfo de Cardón (also known as the Golfo de Venezuela), is not a single island but rather two islands, between which one can find a passable anchorage. This provides a rest stop for the yachtsman who has been beaten to death getting around Cabo de la Vela and into the Golfo de Cardón. You can sail into the southernmost Monje, anchor between the islands (see Chart V-1), and rest in complete safety. This island has a small naval presence on it, so you are safe from the Colombian drug smugglers. Had I known this when delivering (or attempting to deliver *Skua*) east from Cartagena to Grenada— my only unsuccessful delivery—we undoubtedly would have made it, for we would have ducked in here and rested, rather than going on to Maracaibo, which was a disaster.

Once you have rested for a day or two at Los Monjes, you can then stand across the Golfo de Cardón to the eastern shore, which, even if it does not protect you from the wind, will give you protection from the sea. Then make the 30-mile jump from the lee side of the Peninsula de Paraguaná to Aruba.

By the time you reach Aruba, the worst of the trip is over, for from Aruba eastward, you can break up the trip into one- and two-day sails.

After Aruba, there is a windward slog of 60 miles to Curaçao. Here you can rest and then take off from Spanish Water to Bonaire, a 30-mile overnight slog. From Bonaire you have a choice: You can continue eastward to the offshore islands, a feasible choice for a good windward-going boat. A series of shortish, windward jumps, which can be done at night, take you to Ave de Sotavento, Ave de Barlovento, and on to Islas Los Roques. But time these overnight jumps carefully, because the lights in Venezuela are totally unreliable.

The alternative is to stand over to the Venezuelan coast and explore the coastal waters. A boat that is not too good to windward is best advised, when taking off from Spanish Water, to stand eastward on port tack and motorsail down to Chichiriviche, where you can enter Venezuela and obtain a *zarpa* (cruising permit) for proceeding eastward. When sailing from Curaçao to Chichiriviche, stay well offshore, as there is a very strong westerly current setting directly onshore. It is a low coast, hard to spot, with heavy surf and numerous wrecks shown on the

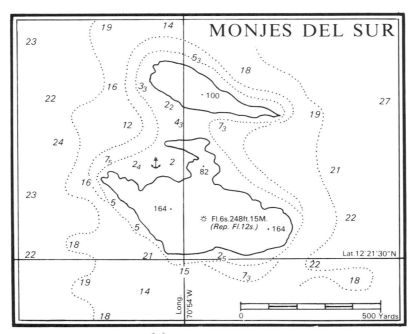

CHART V–1   Monjes del Sur

chart. The chart is marked "dangerous for navigation." Do not approach closer than 10 miles from the coast. After a stop at Chichiriviche, a short jump will take you to the national park, Morrocoy, at Tucacas.

It is an easy 25-mile jump from Tucacas to Puerto Cabello, a wonderful old Venezuelan city. Puerto Cabello has an excellent marina with a travel lift and hauling facilities up to 30 tons. Since the marina was built, about 1985, the availability of yachting supplies there has certainly improved. It's best to do the 60 miles eastward from Puerto Cabello to La Guaira by leaving in the afternoon as the wind dies down. You can power eastward as close to the coast as you dare, taking advantage of the usual easygoing countercurrent on the beach and the calm that you should find at night.

In the Caracas area, you have a choice of five harbors: Puerto Calera, Caraballeda (with the nearby Macuto Sheraton Hotel), Puerto Azul, and the most eastern one, Camurí Grande, which is strictly for shoal-draft boats.

At this point, if you want a change from coastal sailing, you can have an easy overnight reach to Los Roques, cruise the area, and then head back to the coast.

From Los Roques you should be able to lay Cabo Codera with ease. There, in Ensa de Corsarios, you will find a good anchorage. If you need to resupply, you can round Cabo Codera and enter Carenero, where there are a number of marinas suitable for sailboats, and find food, water, and ice. From Cabo Codera eastward, you have two options: either a direct 90-mile sail to El Morro de Barcelona or a jump out to Isla La Tortuga, a distance of 45 miles to the northeast.

The 90 miles east to El Morro de Barcelona is dead to windward, but if you leave in the evening when the wind is down, you can power 70 miles east to the Islas de Píritu, arriving in the morning. This will allow a stop for a swim or possibly an overnight stay. If you stop, leave at first light for El Morro de Barcelona, 18 miles to the east, and you'll get there before the wind pipes up.

The sail to La Tortuga will most likely be hard on the wind, starboard tack all the way—something many modern cruising boats don't like to do. But from the eastern end of La Tortuga to the El Morro area, you should not have too bad a sail; it should be an easy fetch on port tack.

The area from El Morro eastward to Carúpano can be covered easily in short hops. This is very good, interesting cruising, and you could end up by spending several months in the Margarita, El Morro, and Golfo de Cariaco area before going farther east.

Once you reach Carúpano, there are no two ways about it—if you stay offshore, it's a hard slog to Trinidad or Grenada. Some boats that go well to windward sail first to Islas Los Testigos—a nice, easy reach—and then, after a rest, put their heads down for the beat to Grenada. If you decide to go directly from Los Testigos to Grenada, you should stand north on starboard tack until well up behind the Grenadines, which will break the Atlantic swell. Tack back to the south, making sure you stay well north of the southern tip of Grenada, which will keep you out of the strongest of the current pouring into the Caribbean between Trinidad and Grenada.

Other people, who love to beat to windward and have boats that do it well, just stick their heads down and bull their way straight eastward from Margarita to Grenada. The often-mentioned Paul Adamthwaite, whose magnificent old 54-foot Sparkman & Stephens yawl *Stormy Weather* climbs uphill like a homesick angel, claims that doing this is not all that difficult. But you must remember that Paul is tough: He sailed *Stormy Weather* singlehanded across the Atlantic, from Bermuda to Cork in the incredible time of sixteen days, nineteen hours, and, although he likes to sail to windward, I think he is a bit of a masochist. I prefer the short hops up the coast and runs across from Uquire.

If you don't want to tackle the jump from Los Testigos to Grenada in one shot, stand south on port tack and find an anchorage along the northern side of the Peninsula de Paria. You should then work your way along the coast to the eastern end of the Peninsula de Paria. From there, stand north on starboard tack and you should lay Grenada.

The easy method of working your way east is to take off in the evening from Isla Margarita, stand over on port, tack to the coast, work your way along the coast (probably in flat calm), and continue eastward to El Morro de Puerto Santos, which has a good anchorage, a nice little town, and no rolling. (If you stop at Carúpano, you will probably roll your guts out.) Rest in El Morro de Puerto Santos. As soon as the wind dies down at dusk, motor as far east as you can get and you will reach one of the harbors on the north side of the Peninsula de Paria. (See chapter 3 and the Imray-Iolaire chart that has inserts on the harbors and coves east of Carúpano.) You will discover that they are close enough together so that you can take your time working your way eastward. It will not be a real trial but a lot of fun, and you will visit small, unspoiled coves and be able to rest, in between, on your eastward push.

If you take off from Carúpano in the evening and motorsail east, two possible stops are El Morro de Puerto Santos, which is an excellent harbor but not very far east—only about 10 miles from Carúpano—and Unare, 32 miles east of Carúpano. Unare is an adequate anchorage, but one that you should approach only during the day. The ground swell does not usually come in from the north in the summer, but when it does, this anchorage will be untenable. During the summer months, you should be able to go from Carúpano to Unare, rest, and then proceed east to a suitable cove on the Peninsula de Paria the next night. Either stop at a cove or fall off on starboard tack and sail to Grenada. It is 40 miles from Unare to the eastern end of the Peninsula de Paria, where the first anchorage is Pargo.

Universally, the advice of the experienced sailor is to work your way east to Uquire, where, as Paul Adamthwaite reports, you can buy cold beer despite the fact that you think you are in the complete backwoods. Take off in the evening or late afternoon from Uquire. The course to Point Salines, Grenada, is 355° magnetic, distance 85 miles, but of course allow for the current, which is apt to be running 1 to 1 1/2 knots to the westward. When you approach Grenada from the south on a clear night, you usually can see the lights of Morne Jaloux, the hills behind St. George's, before you see the lights of Point Salines. Remember that the Morne Jaloux lights are well to the east of the Point Salines lights, so if you keep the Morne Jaloux lights fine on the starboard bow, the Point Salines lights will eventually show up, dead ahead.

Should you decide to go to Port-of-Spain, remember that you must go all the way to the main Customs dock, another 20 miles to windward from the tip of the Peninsula de Paria. You must not anchor anywhere in Trinidad before you have officially entered.

Sailing Directions: East to West

Usually yachts leaving Trinidad or Grenada make their first stop in Venezuela in Los Testigos. You should time your arrival in Los Testigos for about 0900. When calculating your speed, remember that, on the average, there is 1 knot of current setting to the west in the channel between Grenada and Trinidad. The light on Los Testigos, when working, has a range of about 8 miles. But, like all Venezuelan lights, it is totally unreliable.

However, some yachts prefer to sail directly from Grenada to Margarita, and, if so, once again let me remind you NOT to hit La Sola, which Paul Adamthwaite says is exactly where the chart says it is—rising out of deep water. Unbuoyed and unlighted, it can trap the unwary.

Some yachtsmen who have cruised the Eastern Caribbean looking for uncrowded anchorages and a change of pace, gravitate to the small harbors on the north side of the Peninsula de Paria. If you are proceeding from Grenada, time your departure to arrive at the eastern tip of the peninsula at about 0800, and then go westward to find an anchorage.

As you sail west along the north coast of the Peninsula de Paria, remember that once past the coves on the eastern end, your next stop is Unare, an adequate anchorage in normal weather but completely untenable if the wind goes around to the north or if the ground swell comes in. The next anchorages after Unare are El Morro de Puerto Santos and Carúpano, 10 miles apart. The latter is 60 miles west of the westernmost anchorage at the eastern end of the Peninsula de Paria. Puerto Santos is an all-weather anchorage and Bahía Hernán Vásquez, one mile east of Carúpano, should be good in most weathers except when the ground swell is rolling in.

If you have gone first to Los Testigos, you have two choices: If you wish to stay in the offshore islands, you can sail from Los Testigos to Isla La Blanquilla. La Blanquilla is very low and unlit, so you must plan your arrival at Islas Los Hermanos for about midday. There are no lights in this area, but, with normal visibility, you can see Los Hermanos, a series of five 600-foot-high islands due south of La Blanquilla, from a considerable distance during the day.

Or, from Los Testigos you could head for the Isla de Margarita area. Once again, plan to arrive during daylight, since the current in this area can run as much as 2 knots to the west. From Margarita, you can zigzag back and forth to your heart's content through the area known as the Sea of El Morro, which is bounded on the west by La Tortuga, on the north by La Blanquilla, on the east by Margarita, and on the south by the Venezuelan mainland and offshore islands. There is enough cruising in this area to keep you busy for weeks, if not for months.

Westward from La Tortuga, it is an overnight sail of 90 miles to the marinas in the La Guaira area. These are good jumping-off places if you are heading for Islas Los Roques, Islas de Aves, and Bonaire. Or you can leave La Tortuga early in the morning for the 40-mile run to Cabo Codera and the anchorage at Ensa de Corsarios (see chapter 7).

From Cabo Codera, it is an easy 50 miles on 350° magnetic to Los Roques, which supposedly are lit by three lights. Since the lights are not to be trusted, be sure to make your landfall after 0900. When plotting your course, be aware that the current will be setting you well to the west (see chapter 10 for approaches to Los Roques).

The alternative is to sail 50 miles to La Guaira, an easy downwind trip. From the La Guaira area to Los Roques, it is usually an easy overnight 70-mile reach with an easterly wind. However, if the wind goes around to the north, approaching the eastern entrance of Los Roques may be a hard slog, as the course is 030° magnetic. Remember to allow for the westerly current. Usually this is a nice close reach for a good windward-going boat, but if your yacht is a bit of a barge in these conditions, better head for the western end of Los Roques (course, 010°; distance, 70 miles). You can anchor at dawn, spend the day exploring, and then work your way eastward in relatively sheltered waters.

Heading westward from Los Roques to Ave de Barlovento (meaning "windward") and Ave de Sotavento ("leeward"), you must be careful, since these islands are extremely low lying and the lights are unreliable. Both islands have graveyards of ships that sailed up on the windward side of the reefs: Ave de Barlovento is most probably the final resting place of Comte Jean d'Estrées's fleet, which foundered in 1697 (for further information, see chapter 10), while Ave de Sotavento has on its northeast corner a couple of wrecked vessels that sailed so high and dry that other yachts have mistaken them for ships underway, and have themselves sailed up on the reefs and become total losses.

It is 30 miles from Los Roques to Ave de Barlovento, and you should make your landfall at the southern end of the reef, which is marked by a small island, the ruins of a house, and a light tower. Plan a dawn departure from Los Roques in order to get to Ave de Barlovento when the sun is high and you can pick your way through the reefs.

If you continue on to Ave de Sotavento, it is a flip of the coin to decide whether to approach the island from the north or from the south. Coming from the south, you have the low land and mangroves as a landmark. From the north, there are the two wrecks visible well offshore. Keep them on the port bow and you will then pick up the light tower on the northernmost cay. Swing around the north-ern end of the reef and jibe over south to whichever anchorage you fancy. (Check chapter 10 for pilot directions in Ave de Sotavento.)

From Ave de Sotavento to Bonaire is an easy sail. Depart early in the morning for a midday arrival, remembering that the current frequently sets northwest to west by north rather than due west. You can check the bearing on Bonaire quite easily by tuning the direction finder to Trans World Radio (frequency: 800 kHz). The transmitter is located 2 miles north of Lacrepunt. (See chapter 11 for warn-ings on approaching Bonaire from the east.)

If you sail to Puerto Cabello or Chichiriviche on the mainland from Los Roques or Islas de Aves, be careful of your navigation, since if you sag to lee-ward of either harbor, it may be a tough fight back against the current. Further, the coast between Puerto Cabello and Chichiriviche is swept by breakers and is low and sandy. The coast north of Chichiriviche is particularly dangerous; do not ap-proach close to it. (See chapter 8 for further infor-mation.)

If you prefer to run down the coast from the La Guaira area, it is only 60 miles to Puerto Cabello, an ancient Spanish city with a magnificent fort that is well worth visiting. If you want to stop en route, there are a number of small coves that may be in-teresting, depending on the weather and ground swell (see chapter 8). From Puerto Cabello, you can visit Morrocoy, the national park at Tucacas, also well worth a stop.

On to Chichiriviche; but once you leave here, forget about the rest of the Venezuelan coast, as it is low, flat, and desertlike. The winds sweeping across these flat plains suck the ever-present trade winds off the Caribbean and reinforce the wind to uncomfortable proportions.

If you are heading north to the Virgin Islands, or to Puerto Rico, or through the Mona Passage back to the States through the Bahamas, you should sail from Chichiriviche to Bonaire, where you will find marinas and the possibility of resupplying before the trip back. Be sure, however, to buy plenty of water and ice in Venezuela before you leave, as both are very scarce and expensive in Bonaire.

Yachts heading westward to the Panama Canal are best advised to sail from Curaçao with full stocks of water, fuel, and ice. Check the weather before leaving, since you will risk both your boat and your life if you stop in Colombia. (For sailing directions from Bonaire to Panamá, see *Street's Transatlantic Crossing Guide.*)

The Golfo de Paria

I-1, B, D, D-1, D-11

As described in the Trinidad section of Volume III of this series, the eastern part of the Golfo de Paria is not the yachtsman's favorite area—it is shoal, muddy, and dirty with pollution from Port-of-Spain and from the various rivers that empty into the gulf. However, the pollution from Port-of-Spain does not appear to reach the Venezuelan side of the Golfo de Paria; the ebb and flow of the tide through the Boca del Dragón evidently flushes out this area extremely well. (It should be noted that in Boca Grande and the bocas to the east, the current is extremely strong: probably 1 knot on the flood and as much as 2 knots on the ebb, with numerous tide-rips and eddies that go off in various directions.) So the water on the Venezuelan side of the Golfo de Paria is clean, and as warm as the Caribbean, although I gather that in the summer it warms up so much that droves of jellyfish arrive, which makes swimming a doubtful proposition. The salinity is much less than in the Caribbean.

When we went into the Golfo de Paria in early January 1980, we were most pleased to discover little or no rain, as we had been inundated in the Eastern Caribbean for the previous month. The breeze tended to swing around to the south and die out at sunset. Then, just after sunset, the cold air came down from the high ridges to provide a light offshore northerly in the anchorage. This light breeze seemed to continue all night, followed by flat calm at dawn and an easterly breeze that arrived about 0900 or 1000.

Remember that inside the Golfo de Paria, the rise and fall of tide on springs is a full 5 feet, which comes as quite a shock to the sailor used to the average 18-inch rise and fall in the Eastern Caribbean. This rise and fall must be taken into account when anchoring.

The tides and currents had us more than a little confused, but in general, along the shore the current seems to run east and west. The Trinidad radio periodically announces high and low water in the Golfo de Paria. With that information, the chart in front of you, and a little common sense, you can do a fair job of figuring out the direction of the current. The current is strong enough to make it worthwhile to calculate the tide each day and plan your departures to sail with the tide. It is probably 1 knot in flood and 1 1/2 knots on the ebb, and considerably stronger at the points and around all headlands.

There are some attractive harbors and coves on the south side of the Peninsula de Paria that are within easy reach of Trinidad. These give the yachtsman a complete change of pace, as the climate is totally different from Trinidad and the harbors are devoid of yachts.

A word of caution, though: There seems to be a constant feud boiling between Venezuela and Trinidad over fishing rights in the gulf. Each country regularly seizes the other's trawlers and throws the fishermen in jail when they are suspected of fishing where they shouldn't. Newspapers write up the incidents, and diplomatic relations take a giant step backward, but as far as I know, yachtsmen have never gotten embroiled in these hostilities, and it seems safe to ignore the dire warnings you'll hear from the citizens of either country when you are setting off to the other's shores.

ENSA CARIAQUITA
(Chart V-2; II D-1, D-11)

Ensa Cariaquita is an extremely good harbor, completely sheltered from all winds except south-

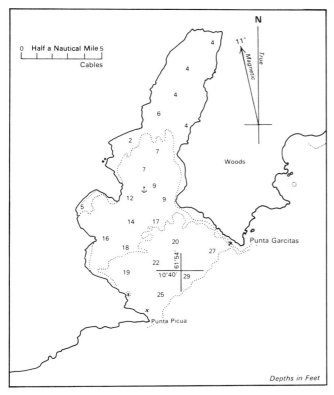

SKETCH CHART V–2   Ensa Cariaquita

the Golfo de Paria through Boca de la Sierpe (the mouth of the serpent). Immediately after anchoring, they were beset by a tidal bore in which most of the fleet lost its anchors. (Considering that a tidal bore is very seldom experienced in Boca de la Sierpe, one wonders if it was not a small earthquake, producing a small tidal wave, that caused his problem.) So, he stood northwestward across the Golfo de Paria and found anchorage under high land—which, he reported, was a good anchorage, sheltered from the sea. Morison suggests that this was near Punta Peñas. However, just south of Punta Peñas, the water is 60 or 70 fathoms deep, and even Columbus, who was used to anchoring in deep water, normally did not care to anchor in 300 or 400 feet of water. Some yachtsmen are convinced he anchored his fleet instead between Punta Garcitas and Punta Picua, where he would have found calm water shallow enough for anchoring and freshwater streams to fill his casks.

west. We stood into the harbor until Isla Patos was half obscured by Punta Garcitas and found 2 fathoms of water.

This is an interesting place. The shoal northern end is full of fish; we could see them jumping regularly, and it seemed that rod-and-reel fishermen would have a field day. The western side of the harbor has a small cove, with a big grove of coconut trees, a freshwater stream (which we did not follow, but which certainly bears exploring), and a two-story house. In front of the house, the largest pig I have ever seen in my life was lying half submerged in the water, enjoying the coolness.

Unfortunately, we were unable to buy fish— evidently they were expecting to shoot their nets the following day. Cariaquita has built-in air conditioning, as the mountain peaks, only half a mile inland, rise to more than 1,000 feet on either side of the harbor; thus, the sun does not rise until 0800 and sets at 1700, making it a very cool anchorage. There is little habitation ashore, and some nice beaches, although no long stretches of white sand.

This harbor is the subject of much historical debate. Samuel Eliot Morison's *Admiral of the Ocean Sea* identifies Columbus's first anchorage in the Americas as being just west of Punta Peñas. The explorer and his fleet had entered the southern end of

ENSA MACURO/CRISTOBAL COLON

(Chart V-3; II D-1, D-11)

This was described by our friends in Ensa Uquire as a big town. However, it did not look particularly attractive from the sea, so although we sailed into the harbor, we did not stop. When in the vicinity of Ensa Macuro (or Cristóbal Colón, whichever you want to call it), be careful of the Rocas Paticas— three separate rocks that lie southeast of the eastern point of the harbor. The easternmost one is well detached from the others and is a full mile east of the point. We saw only one of the three rocks, but it would be best to avoid the area.

Ensa Macuro is the easternmost terminus of the road that runs along the south side of the Peninsula de Paria. The old American chart shows a Customs house, but today it is no longer a port of entry. Good anchorage can be had in Ensa Aricagua, east of the broken-down dock extending from the cliff in the middle of the harbor, east of town. This would be more secluded than an anchorage west of the cliff.

ENSA YACUA

(Chart V-4; II D-1, D-11)

This is another little cove in an almost deserted area. All these coves are so close together that it is

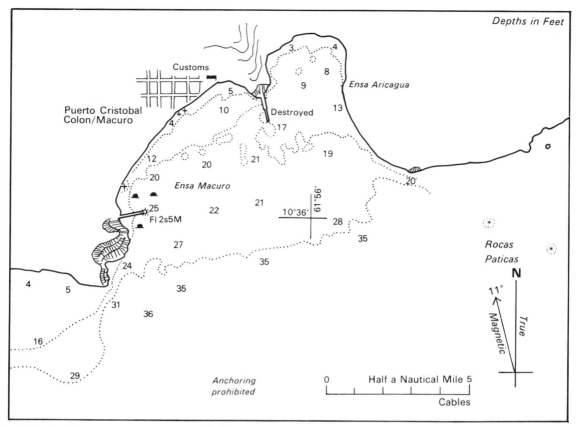

CHART V–3   Ensa Macuro/Cristóbal Colón

possible to sail along the coast, ducking in and out of them to pick one for the night.

ENSA GUINIMITA

(II D-1, D-11)

The same as Ensa Yacua.

ENSA PATAO AND ENSA UQUIRITO

(Chart V-5; II D-1, D-11)

Both harbors are attractive, but looking at them, we decided that Ensa Uquirito was the more attractive, so we anchored in 2 fathoms of water and a muddy bottom in the northeast corner.

When entering Ensa Uquirito, be careful of the shoal extending west from the southeastern point of the harbor; it appears to extend farther than the chart shows, and there is a very strong tide-rip off it.

The harbor itself is extremely attractive, with large palm groves on shore and nice-looking beaches. The point in the middle of the harbor

looks almost like a wharf. With binoculars we saw some broken-down, rusty equipment on the point, but we could not figure out what it was doing there. This definitely appears to be a harbor where one could spend a day or so exploring.

PUERTO DE HIERRO

(Chart V-7; II D-1, D-11)

This is a mining post with a large dock, a navigation light that was working, and a small village. It looked hot, dusty, and uninteresting.

ENSA CUMACA

(Chart V-7; II D-11)

This is a small, attractive cove a mile and a half east of Ensa Río Grande. A slight swell finds its way into the harbor. Keep the lead going carefully and be sure to anchor in sufficient water to allow for the 5-foot rise and fall of spring tides. The shoal shelf extends well out.

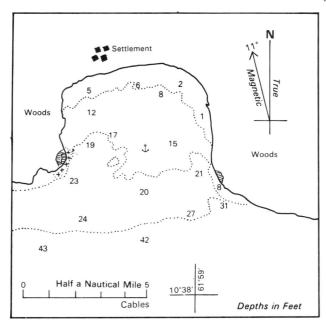

CHART V–4   Ensa Yacua

There is a small village ashore with the usual Venezuelan bar: cold beer, friendly fishermen, *contrabandista*, and ferry operators, some of whom speak a bit of English.

ENSA RIO GRANDE

(Chart V-7; II D-11)

In Ensa Río Grande we discovered an excellent anchorage in 2 fathoms of water. On entering, note that there are rocks and reefs on the western side. Also, rocks and shoals extend south from the eastern side a good 100 yards offshore. The bottom shoals rather quickly inside the 2-fathom line. Because of the spring tide, make sure that you have 2 fathoms under you when you anchor.

At the head of the cove is a river that can be followed about a quarter of a mile inland with the outboard. Moor at the head of the river and follow the rough trail for 1 to 1 1/2 miles. You will come to a small Venezuelan village populated by a combination of smugglers and workers at the mining town of Puerto de Hierro. Electricity has reached the area, and cold beer and a few basic supplies (but not many) are available There is a small church and a statue of Gutiérrez, the Venezuelan hero of the war of independence who was born in that area.

The area contains cacao trees, but they are not very well cultivated; evidently people make more money in mining or in smuggling between Venezuela and Grenada and Trinidad. One wonders if this were not a large, profitable estate in the early years of the nineteenth century.

ENSA MAPIRE

(Chart V-7; II D-11)

We did not enter Ensa Mapire, but it looked attractive, although not as interesting or as large as Ensa Río Grande to the east. But there certainly are lunchtime stops here in numerous small coves.

GUIRIA

(Charts V-6, V-7; II D-1, II D-11)

Güiria is the port of entry into Venezuela for the harbors in the Golfo de Paria. For many years it was cursed with an officious Port Captain who made life difficult for yachtsmen trying to go up the Venezuelan rivers by insisting that they take along a very expensive pilot. The same fee was charged for piloting a yacht or a 20,000-ton tanker.

Exactly what the situation is today, I don't know, as we arrived in Güiria on New Year's Eve in 1980 and went ashore at 1500 (which should have been after the Venezuelan siesta) to try to find the Immigration or Customs officer, or the Port Captain. We found the offices, but they were all locked up. We then ran across a Venezuelan who spoke perfect English and who advised us that, by law, we had to use a Customs broker, who would charge 300Bs. (about $75 US at that time) to enter during normal working hours. Since it was outside of their normal working hours (it seems New Year's Eve is a holiday), it would cost even more. We went down to talk to the Customs broker, but he spoke almost no English. He made a quick attempt to find the Immigration officer, but then he came back and said he doubted very much if we would find anyone for a couple of days.

We returned to the boat and noted that there was a Dutch salvage tug moored in the harbor, the Smith Lloyd Number 49, commanded by Captain De Graff, who said things were fairly loose around Güiria. He said that a few weeks earlier, a Swiss yacht had stopped in Güiria for a day or so, then had gone up the river, had come back to Güiria, and sailed on off. Captain De Graff was quite sure the yacht did not clear in or out.

The Smith Lloyd tug, incidentally, was about to go out and stand by an oil rig that had been estab-

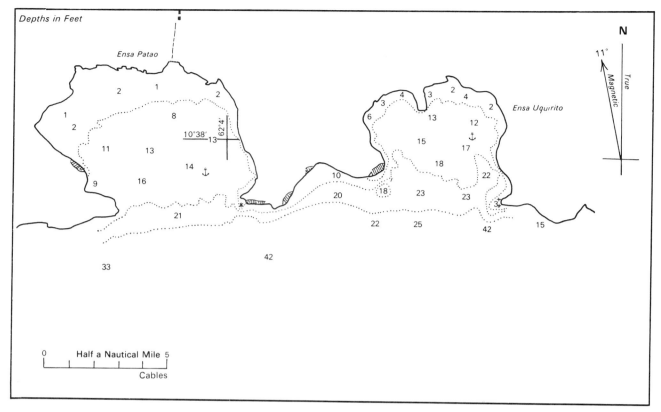

CHART V–5 Ensa Patao and Ensa Uquirito

lished off the north coast of Paria in what the skipper said was "shallow water"—only 180 feet deep!

The new artificial harbor at Güiria has plenty of dock space, but as we anchored out and as it was New Year's, we were not able to find out much about where yachts can lie. Considering the number of shrimpers that unload at the shrimp factory, I assume there must be ice, water, and diesel fuel available, as well as basic supplies.

Do not enter the harbor at night, as only one of the two harbor lights is working. Depths in the harbor are subject to some debate, but 15 feet can be carried throughout most of the harbor, so it is adequate for all normal yachts.

The Golfo de Paria gets pretty shallow west of Güiria, and the chart shows no tempting anchorages. But the little harbors just described are well worth a look if you are heading westward with plenty of time, or if you are in Port-of-Spain with a few days to spare (see Chart V-8).

They are also particularly attractive if you have been beating to windward, eastbound, along the Venezuelan coast and are thinking of heading to Grenada. Rather than continuing directly across the passage and slogging on to Grenada, you can make

a right turn through Boca Grande and spend a while exploring these harbors, resting up, and hoping for a wind shift that will let you lay Grenada on one tack. This is better than looking for a rest in Trinidad, since the only way to enter Trinidad is by sailing all the way—to windward—to the Customs dock at Port-of-Spain.

Few yachts will want to explore the rivers of Venezuela, but motorsailers or motorboats may decide that the Orinoco Delta is worth exploring. Take a spare propeller, however, in case of a bent-up wheel. This area is particularly interesting for nature lovers, as it is full of birds, fish, crocodiles, and all sorts of tropical wildlife that the average European or North American has seen only in movies. Take a shotgun and you can have duck for dinner. (Be sure to declare any firearm on board if you are questioned about firearms while clearing; for further discussion on guns in general, see *Street's Transatlantic Crossing Guide*.)

The usual way to visit the Orinoco Delta (see Chart V-9) is to pass south through the Golfo de Paria, out through Boca de la Serpiente, and fight southeastward, against the wind and current, to the mouth of the Río Orinoco. This is covered by

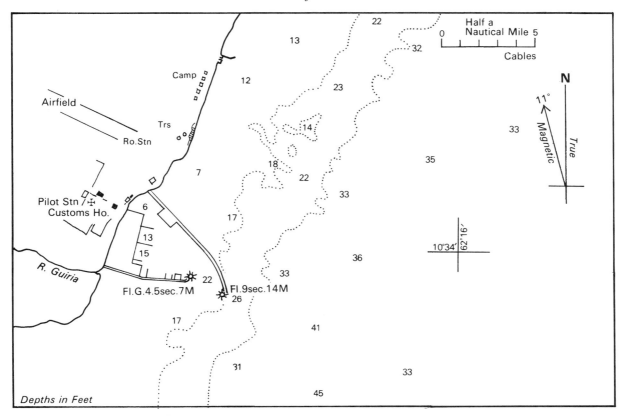

CHART V–6   Güiria

NOAA chart 24390. The chart of Puerto Grande, NOAA 24381, has more detail, and NOAA chart 24382 covers the Río Orinoco itself, up to Ciudad Guayana.

Oceangoing steamers come up this far, but exactly how much farther they go, I'm not sure. I think they continue on deepwater navigation as far as Ciudad Bolívar, which is well marked and buoyed and is the subject of new surveys by the Venezuelan Hydrographic Office.

Another possibility for exploring the Río Orinoco is to enter at Pedernales on the south coast of the Golfo de Paria and work your way from there up to the Orinoco's tributaries. Walter Cannon tried it a number of years ago. He went to the Guardia Nacional in Pedernales and was put in touch with a guide who was familiar with the river system and who spoke Spanish, English, and Guarao, the local Indian dialect. Apparently they never reached the Río Orinoco proper, having encountered a dam with no locks at Tucupita. But they had a fascinating cruise anyway, visiting Indian encampments and encountering an abundance of exotic wildlife. From Tucupita they arranged for a fine tour south around the Orinoco Delta. Sounds like a superb adventure if you have the time.

Just as we were completing the total revamping of this Venezuela guide, Alan Wilkinson and I happened to meet Poul Folkertsen in a Margarita rum shop. He recognized me and said he had information he knew would be of interest. He and his wife, Karin, had just done a trip up the Río Orinoco (1,700 kilometers, 950 nautical miles) in a 29-foot boat drawing 5 feet—with side trips in the delta and the rivers that feed into the Orinoco. They sailed and motorsailed to the head of navigation at Ayacucho. Had it been the rainy season, they would have removed their mast, relaunched, and descended Río Negro to the Amazon. There they would have had two choices—either turning to port and descending the Amazon or turning to starboard and going up the Amazon to Peru.

The previously mentioned Walter Cannon never did get up the Orinoco, as he started up the wrong river at Pedernales. If you are coming from the Eastern Caribbean, to reach the Orinoco from the Golfo de Paria, you enter the Orinoco Delta at Punta Pescadores (also called Punta El Tigre or Punta Bombeador). I quote Poul:

"After you have passed the southwest point of Trinidad, aim for the middle of Punta Pescadores. Keep going until you are about 100 yards from

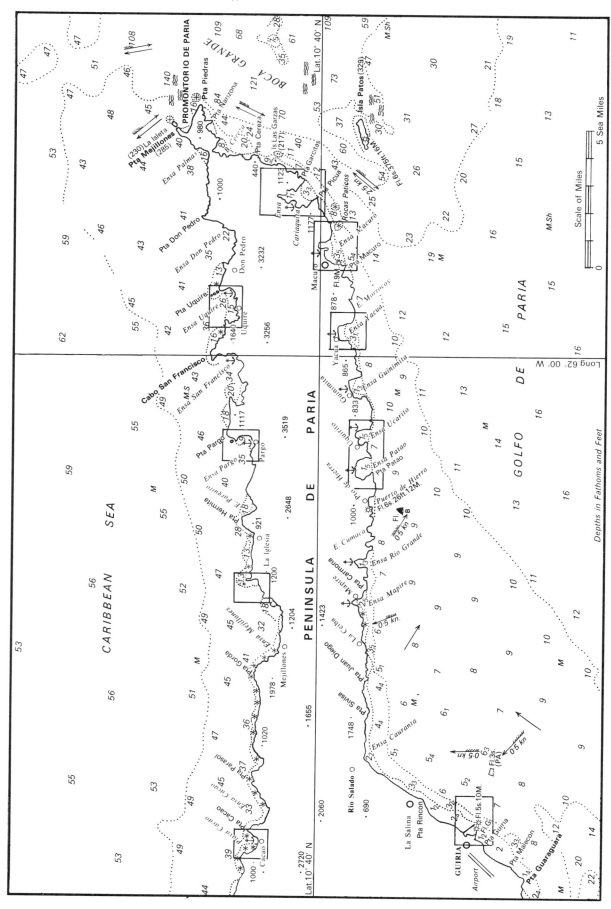

CHART V-7   Eastern End, Peninsula de Paria

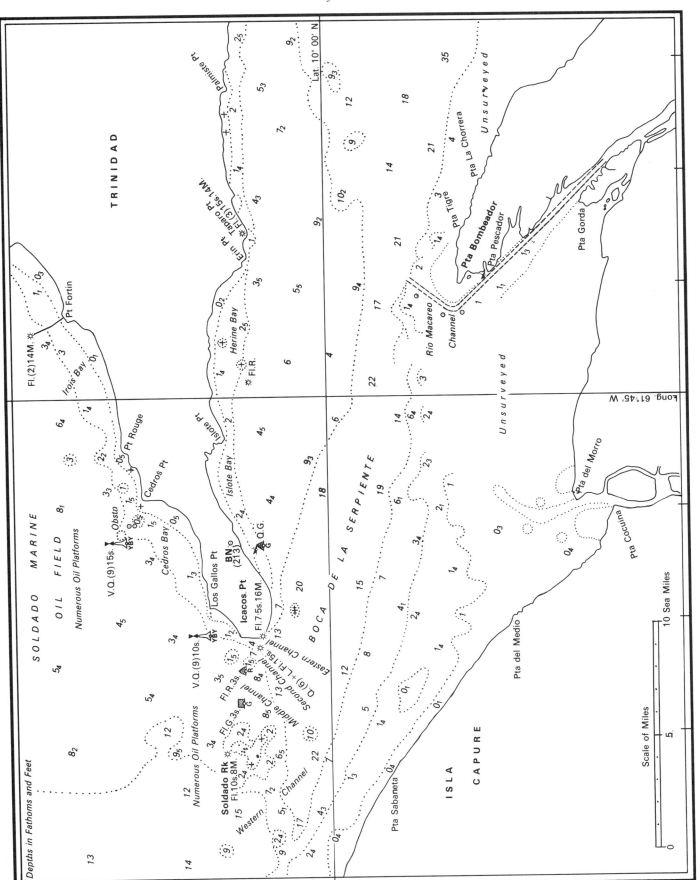

CHART V–8 Boca de la Serpiente

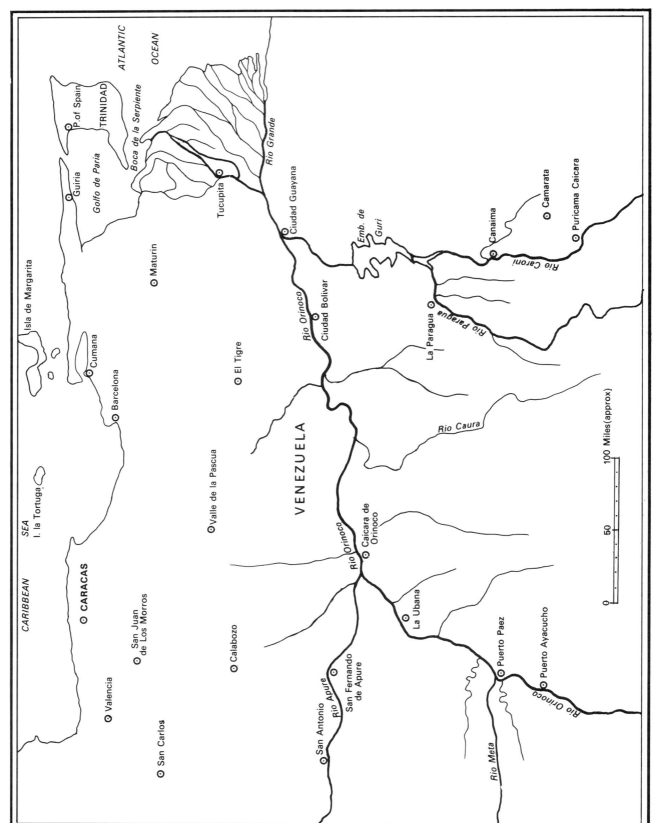

CHART V–9 Orinoco Delta and River

land. There you will find deep water. If you go farther north, it is shallow, as it is if you turn south too early. Usually there are plenty of fishing nets in this area, so don't try to go in after dark. Take the tide into consideration. You will have 8 feet or more at high water, but only 6 feet at low water. (The bottom is soft and will not damage your boat even if you should touch ground.)

"As soon as you reach the river, there is about 15 feet or more until just before Barrancas (90 miles), where there is another shallow."

Follow the river Caño Macareo up to Barrancas, where it joins the Orinoco. This is obviously the way to get to the Orinoco from a boat that is cruising the Eastern Caribbean.

However, if you have sailed across the Atlantic, from the Cape Verdes to Brazil, and are coming up the South American coast, obviously the best way to enter and explore the delta and the Orinoco is to enter Río Grande at Boca Grande o de Navios—channel depth 38 feet guaranteed to Puerto Ordaz, and the river is well buoyed. Entering the Caño Macareo via Punta Pescadores, you will have 8 feet even in the dry season, 10 or 12 feet in the wet season. The river current in the dry season is 1 to 1 1/2 knots; in the wet season, it can be as high as 2 to 2 1/2 knots. The first 30-mile stretch is tidal, so of course the current will be affected by the tide.

The area is an absolute paradise of wildlife. Eight-foot saltwater dolphins—called toninos by the locals—ascend the river, and crocodiles are plentiful. When the current is running strong, it is safe to swim, but every quiet backwater is infested with piranha. The Folkertsens always checked with the locals before they bathed. They didn't even stick a finger in the water in places where the Indians were not bathing—people have been known to have the flesh stripped from their fingers by the black piranha, the most vicious species, which is found mainly on the Río Caroní, an offshoot of the Orinoco that leads to a large lake region. The lakes are infested with black piranha. From the head of navigation on Río Caroní, you can ascend to Angel Falls via a three-day canoe trip. No, thank you. It's safer to opt for Peter Bottome's tour of Angel Falls from Margarita or Puerto La Cruz via his Aereotuy Airlines—a fantastic trip I took with my wife, Trich, and son Richard.

At Barrancas or Ciudad Bolívar (or Ciudad Guayana or Puerto Ordaz, depending on the map or chart you are using), you must clear with the Port Captain to obtain permission to ascend the river, which is buoyed the first 700 miles (1,000 kilometers) from Boca Grande to Caicara. Above the last buoy at Caicara, there is ample water in the rainy season (May through October), but reliable draft is only about 5 feet in the dry season. In this area, you have two choices: You can hire a local pilot or you can wait until one of the river barges comes along. The flat barges, which are about 200 feet long, draw 5 or 5 1/2 feet, have plenty of horsepower, and proceed at about 7 knots. They are the Venezuelan equivalent of a nineteenth-century Mississippi riverboat—no schedule. They just stop at towns, villages, and farms to pick up or drop off cargo whenever anyone signals from the bank. Swing in behind one of these barges and follow it up the river. Even if it runs aground, it will just chew its way through the mud flat and dig a channel for you. Alternatively, make a deal with the barge captain (about 1000 Bs. a day in 1990), strap your boat alongside (using plenty of fenders), and let the barge do the work. The river is unbuoyed; it is a matter of reading the water and staying on the outside of the turn to keep the deepest water.

At Puerto Páez, the Río Meta joins the Orinoco. During the wet season, you can ascend this river toward Colombia and Peru, but during the dry season, it's strictly a canoe trip.

Once you reach Ayacucho, a city of 30,000 people located 200 miles above Caicara, you have reached the head of navigation on the Orinoco. At this point, if you really want to be adventurous, contact the local Venezuelan Army post—apparently they get quite bored sitting there in the bush. They will be most happy to pull your boat out of the water, put it on a flatbed truck, and chock it up. You can truck it roughly 40 miles to the head of Río Negro. But you can only do this in the wet season. When Poul and Karin Folkertsen wanted to do it in the middle of the dry season, there was not enough water, even though they only drew 5 feet.

Getting the mast out can be a bit of a problem, as the army has no crane, but one could probably be hired locally. Poul recommends flying from Ciudad Bolívar (remember that domestic flights are incredibly cheap) to Ayacucho to check with the Port Captain, who can give you the water depths all the way to Ayacucho. From there, it is all downhill. If there is sufficient water, you can make your arrangements with the army and hire a local crane to remove your mast.

Poul is a true gypsy—by blood and by instinct. He has spent his entire life exploring backwater areas as a writer, taking still photos, films, and videos. He regards the Orinoco trip as one of his best. He said the Indians were extremely friendly and extremely helpful. They are also very curious and love coffee, cigarettes, and, of course, fishhooks. Plus, if you make this trip, don't discard any old clothes, as they are most appreciative of any old clothing. In communicating with them, Poul and Karin had to do everything by sign language, as even the local Venezuelans could not comprehend their language.

Poul suggests that even if yachtsmen don't feel adventurous enough to ascend to the Orinoco's headwaters, it's worth exploring the very interesting delta area. I myself would not undertake this trip unless I had one crew member who was fluent in Spanish—or could hire a local Venezuelan who was fluent in English.

Poul obtained his *zarpa* in Margarita, and this allowed him to get to Ciudad Bolívar, but it is a long haul to windward from Margarita to the eastern end of the Peninsula de Paria, so it is better to make your entry through Güiria, in the Golfo de Paria.

Because this trip passes through Indian territory, you'll need special permission. Thus, to work out specific details, I recommend that you write the Venezuelan Tourist Board. (Armando Duran, the present head of the Tourist Board, is a yachtsman.) The office phone in Caracas is (02) 574-2220 or 574-2124; the fax number is 35-22-13. For more information on the area, and references to published articles, contact:

Poul Folkertsen
Toldbogade 1
4000 Roskilde, Denmark

Poul made his ascent of the Orinoco with no charts—only very good Venezuelan road maps. The map book is *Gui Progreso, Mapas de Carreteras de Venezuela,* published by Seguros Progreso, S.A., and available at any good Venezuelan bookstore.

When you are arranging for permission to visit the Orinoco region, ask the Tourist Board about purchasing from them a copy of this map book, plus some books on Venezuelan birds, fish, plants, and other wildlife so you will be able to identify what you see. If you find you need to straighten out paperwork for permission, or to obtain books, I recommend you do it in Grenada, as Oscar Hernandez Bernalette in the Venezuelan consulate is a yachtsman who will understand your needs and problems. Above all, before undertaking this adventure, be sure your paperwork is in good order.

3

North Side: The Peninsula de Paria to Ensa Esmeralda

I-1, D-1, D-11, D-12

The north side of the Peninsula de Paria is relatively unexplored. It is 80 miles from Punta Mejillones to Puerto Santos, and there are no towns or roads, only fishing villages. The hills rise steeply from the water's edge, with 3,000-foot peaks a mere 2 miles inland. The valleys between the peaks drop down to 1,500 feet. The scale of the US chart is 1:250,000, and the British chart has an even worse scale! This means that little detail is shown. The charts used here (Charts V-10, V-11, V-12) have been developed from a topographical map and augmented by our dinghy exploration and help from various yachtsmen who have supplied us with their sketch charts. It must be remembered that these charts are just that—sketch charts. The names shown have been taken from the topographical map.

There are few real harbors along this coast, but there are a number of coves where you can find a shelf extending out from the eastern point, where you may be able to find bottom, drop an anchor, and obtain some shelter. Without exception, all of these harbors could be extremely uncomfortable and sometimes dangerous in periods of a northerly ground swell.

In the past, one of the problems with cruising this area has been that, although various boats have been able to find nice little anchorages in the coves here, the yachts have generally been fighting their way eastward under conditions not suitable to taking bearings and keeping track of all the rocks, hills, and points. So, when the yachtsmen have returned, or have tried to communicate the locations to other sailors, there has not been enough accurate information to make subsequent landfalls reliable. The coast along here all looks so much the same that it is practically impossible to identify any particular cove by verbal description alone. That is why, in the winter of 1978, we decided to explore the coast in *Iolaire* by sailing from Grenada and slowly charting our way westward.

When we first arrived, the geography was so confusing that we didn't even know where we were. We decided that one nice little spot, with 6 fathoms and a sand bottom, was Cabo San Francisco, but it turned out, according to local fishermen, to be a cove behind Punta Pargo. We then decided that the only way to figure things out was to get up early in the morning when it was calm and take the dinghy eastward with a lead line and a hand-bearing compass, notebook, and chart. We did that the following day, and all went well. We worked our way with the outboard to the point 8 miles east of our anchorage at Punta Pargo. This was Punta Don Pedro, the main point west of Punta Mejillones, although in fact it, like all these points, was damned hard to identify without a topographical map. At this point the outboard quit, and we had to row 8 miles back to the boat; thank God for a pair of 9-foot oars and a rigid dinghy that rowed well!

As I have already noted, the weather patterns here on the north coast of Venezuela are different from the normal trade-wind pattern. At dawn, there is usually a flat calm or perhaps a light breeze out of the west. It springs up during the course of the morning and generally works its way slowly around

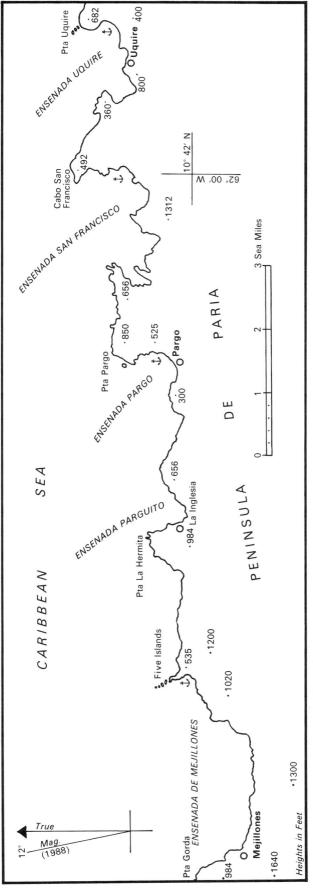

CHART V–10   North Coast, Peninsula de Paria (Uquire to Mejillones)

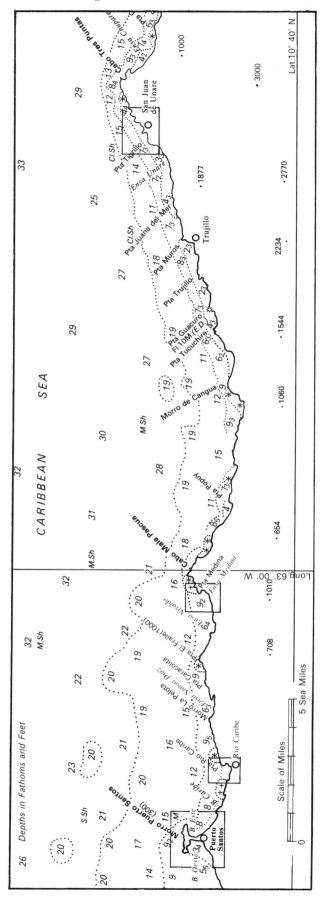

CHART V–11   North Coast, Peninsula de Paria (Ensa Unare to Puerto Santos)

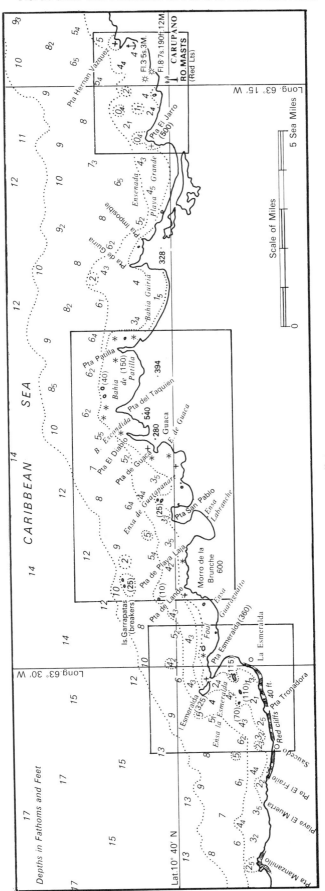

CHART V–12 North Coast, Peninsula de Paria (Carúpano to Punta Manzanillo)

to the north, and then to the northeast. It finally settles down late in the afternoon, fresh out of the east. At dusk the wind begins to die, and by 2200 it's glassy calm again.

In the winter months, when the sun's declination is less than 10° north latitude (which is about what the Venezuelan coast is), the sun goes behind the mountains to the south quite early in the evening— about 1600. Cold air drops off the mountains and makes it definitely cool on board, to the point that everyone sleeping below on *Iolaire* needed blankets, and those on deck found sleeping bags necessary. In the summer, though, when the sun's declination gets up to 23° north, it will be shining full force into all these north-facing harbors right up until sunset, heating things up and altering the temperature-control problem considerably.

Similarly, on winter mornings the sun doesn't break over the mountains in the east until 0900, with the result that the harbors don't heat up at all; in fact, on our five days along this coast, we didn't even rig the awning. This is quite a change from the usual winter routine in the Eastern Caribbean, where the awning goes up the minute the anchor goes down—and is kept up until the minute before the anchor is raised.

Another interesting aspect of this coast is the water temperature, which varies from 68°F to 70°F and is a change from the normal 77°F found in the Eastern Caribbean. The water along the coast is definitely murky, probably because it runs off the mountains and possibly from the Río Orinoco coming out of the Golfo de Paria. The water is not really dirty, but it certainly is not the crystal-clear water of the Caribbean, visibility being limited to 10 feet or so.

When anchoring along this coast, be prepared to drop plenty of line, but it need not be particularly heavy line. We noticed everywhere that the Venezuelan fishing boats always moored on incredibly light lines. (We frequently found heavy-displacement 40-foot boats anchored on a piece of 3/8-inch nylon.) During the night it is absolutely flat calm, and the anchor is needed only to prevent you from drifting ashore or out to sea. Almost everywhere it will be necessary to anchor with either bow or stern facing the swell, as the design of the boat suggests. In some areas, a Bahamian moor is advisable, as the wind will box the compass regularly and cause a simple anchor to break out.

ENSENADA UQUIRE

(Chart V-13; II D-1, D-11)

Ensenada Uquire is the easternmost anchorage on the north side of the Peninsula de Paria. It is easily identified by the three distinctive islands stretching northwestward from Punta Uquire. They are about 150 feet high and covered with trees. Note carefully that this point is unmarked on the NOAA charts; it is in the bay east of Cabo San Francisco. British chart BA 483 is also improperly marked, as Punta Uquire is shown 4 miles east of its actual position. The British chart also shows one large island northwest of the point rather than three small ones. Furthermore, the shading on the British chart would indicate a fairly large shelf south and

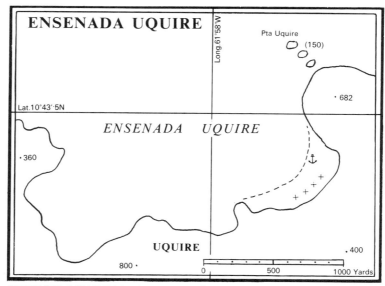

SKETCH CHART V–13   Ensenada Uquire

west of the point, but there is none. The charts show no dangers entering Ensa Uquire, and the water is extremely deep, but numerous tide-rips are so strong that they will give you heart failure, as they appear to be reefs.

To enter, round the outermost of the three islands. Give it a fair berth, as I don't trust the chart. Stand southeastward into the cove until the three islands disappear behind Punta Uquire. You will find yourself in 90 feet of water, evidently mixed sand and mud bottom. We anchored only during the day. For overnight, I recommend anchoring bow and stern, facing northwest out toward the swell. If you have plenty of line, run a line to the shore. You can probably moor bow and stern fairly close in. Sounding our way in with the lead, we found 30 feet of water closer in than I would like to anchor—considering the unpredictability of the wind and *Iolaire*'s lack of an engine. The swell breaks on the beach, but not too heavily. The best landing is on the northeast corner of the beach.

On shore, the people are friendly but speak absolutely no English. If you ask if they are fishermen, they immediately reply "*contrabandista*" and laugh. Moored bow out, stern-to the beach, are their long *piraguas*, equipped with two, three, or four 48-horsepower Yamaha outboards; evidently a two-Yamaha *piragua* is a ferry, a three-Yamaha vessel is a part-time smuggler, and a four-Yamaha boat is one of the real hotshot smugglers.

At one period this place must have been a flourishing cacao estate—you can see an old wooden gingerbread-type house, long abandoned, a very small chapel, and many cacao-drying sheds with their drying pans mounted on small railway carts. Now the village apparently exists by smuggling whiskey from Grenada and Trinidad and marijuana to those islands. Marijuana grows in patches high on the hillsides.

At the southern end of the beach, a stream flows into the harbor. Follow the stream inland to the local laundromat. Farther up the stream I found some nice pools of water about 4 feet deep and crystal-clear—a cool and wonderful place to take a good bath and wash off the salt water. The cliffs rise almost vertically behind the village, and since there is a 2-inch pipe leading up the hillside, I suspect that if you are energetic and follow the stream another half mile or so (wear sneakers to protect your feet), you will find a deepwater pool that supplies piped water to the village, and probably also a waterfall.

The cliffs on the western side of the harbor are so high and steep that the sun sinks behind the cliffs at 1645 in early January. The cliffs are also so steep

east of the anchorage that I doubt very much that the January sun comes over the rim much before 0900; thus, the area is extremely cool.

Paul Adamthwaite, owner and skipper of the famous Sparkman and Stephens 54-foot yawl *Stormy Weather*, thinks that I have undersold this anchorage. He feels it is the best along the coast. But he was able to obtain a great deal of information from the local fishermen because he speaks Spanish. Most important, he points out that there is a generator that provides cold beer, and you can purchase some basic supplies here. There are a number of places where you can find a ledge to drop anchor, but proceed with caution, with the fathometer running. Probably the best method of anchoring would be to drop your anchor and run a stern line ashore. There are three separate rivers where you can pick up water in jugs, wash clothes, swim, and (with luck) catch freshwater crayfish. The fishermen seem to prefer the bay and coves west of Cabo San Francisco to those west of Punta Pargo.

CABO SAN FRANCISCO

(Chart V-10; II D, D-1, D-11)

This extends a mile and a half out to sea, providing a deep bay for which the chart shows absolutely no bottom. However, if you sail into the southeast corner, you'll find a house and a beach, 50 yards off a 6-fathom shelf. There seems to be a light swell from the north. This is a bow-and-stern anchorage, although it appears to be quite sheltered. The house bears 120° magnetic from the anchorage.

PUNTA PARGO

(Chart V-14; II D, D-1, D-11)

See sketch chart done by Jan de Bosset (and inserted in Imray-Iolaire chart D-11), which notes rocks on the southern beach. We found a very nice anchorage in the southeast corner of the cove behind Punta Pargo. Anchor bow and stern, with one anchor in deep water and the other buried ashore in the sand.

This is a fantastic anchorage, with the mountains rising steeply from the water's edge and wild birds crying in the trees. It is absolutely calm at night and totally dark, with all lights on shore going out early in the evening. An occasional anchor light showed aboard the five Venezuelan boats that spent the night here and departed before dawn. Quite a con-

SKETCH CHART V–14   Ensenada Pargo

trast from the crowded anchorages of the Lesser Antilles.

There was a sand beach and a small village whose inhabitants spoke a Spanish dialect of which our interpreter couldn't make head or tail. But, despite the language barrier, the people were extremely friendly and helpful. The village grows some subsistence crops, such as bananas, and cacao is probably the cash crop. Paul Adamthwaite reports that the village has expanded since we were there: Fuel is now available and there is a small boatyard, with a shed roof, where local launches are built.

A stream comes down the hillside and runs

through the village. The jungle comes right down to the water's edge and looks as though it would be interesting to explore. If you intend to do this, wear an old shirt, trousers, and walking shoes, and take a sharp machete.

We sailed westward along the coast in very light airs, and, although we didn't stop, we looked carefully with binoculars and came to a few conclusions about the coves west of Punta Pargo. And, since that time, other yachtsmen have supplied us with information and sketches for these anchorages.

ENSENADA MEJILLONES

(Chart V-15; II D, D-1, D-11)

This harbor, incorrectly called Punta la Hermita in the previous edition, is easily identified by the five offlying rocks. (Be careful, however: From certain angles, there appear to be only four offlying rocks. Don't get confused.) Anchor in 3 fathoms on the southeast corner. Again, the best procedure for anchoring is with a bow line ashore and a stern anchor out in deep water to keep you from swinging. Jan de Bosset reports a small, attractive village ashore. Needless to say, these harbors are tenable only if the ground swell is not running.

PUNTA GORDA

(II D, D-1, D-11)

This is distinctive because there are a couple of houses high up on the ridge. What these people do

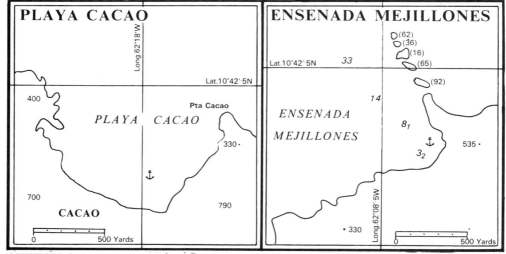

SKETCH CHART V–16   Playa Cacao   SKETCH CHART V–15   Ensenada Mejillones

for a living or how they get supplies is beyond me, as the nearest village seems to be over the top of the ridge.

PUNTA CACAO

(Chart V-16; II D, D-1, D-11)

The chart shows what appears to be a harbor behind Punta Cacao, but we found no sign of habitation. However, we talked to a fisherman who recognized the name Punta Cacao, looked at the chart, and said it was a very good harbor. I have discovered more than once, though, that sometimes the chart calls a place one thing and the locals call it another, a confusing situation that can be resolved only by going there and seeing for yourself.

After writing the above, I saw a topographical map that, although it did not have any soundings, certainly showed a deep indentation on the coast that should provide a small harbor, and a few yachtsmen have reported it as a possible anchorage.

Westward from Punta Cacao, there are no all-weather harbors until you reach Puerto Santos, 53 miles down the coast. There are, however, a couple of villages along the way that you might consider looking in on in calm weather. Tacarigua has a beach and possibly a summer lunchtime anchorage.

West of Cabo Tres Puntas comes San Juan de Unare, the eastern terminus of the road on the Peninsula de Paria.

SAN JUAN DE UNARE

(Chart V-17; II D, D-1, D-11)

Note that this sketch chart is done from an eighteenth-century Spanish chart, discontinued chart HO 2034, information gained from *Iolaire*'s 1978 cruise, a Venezuelan topographical map, and information given to me by Jan de Bosset. Use the chart with caution and send me any information you may gather.

West of Punta Tigrillo is another small cove that is easy to spot because there are rocks off the point and palm trees on the beach. West of the second point is another anchorage off the nice fishing village. This bay has a stream running into it from a freshwater lake, although I suspect the stream runs only during the wet season.

The better anchorage of the two (and even this one is not particularly good) is the easternmost of the two coves, where an anchorage—but not an all-weather anchorage—may be found southwest of a hat-shaped island. Work your way east until the outer of the two islands north of the anchorage

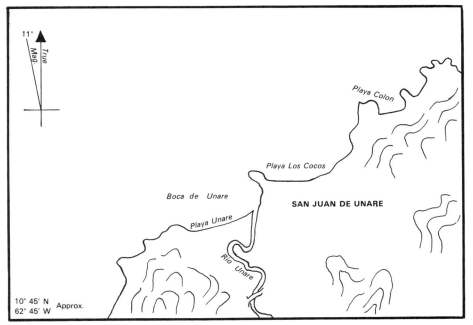

SKETCH CHART V–17   San Juan de Unare

bears 015° magnetic and a small white spot on the cliff over the western end of the small, flat beach bears 185° magnetic. Here you will find 2 1/2 fathoms with a sand bottom over mud—extremely good holding. Steep-to rocks are in the east of this anchorage, so you must anchor bow and stern, facing the northeast trade-wind swell.

A Bahamian moor would not be suitable here, for when the tide changes during the night and runs eastward, you would end up rolling uncomfortably in the beam-to swell. Be very careful to set up an anchor light, since small, fast launches sometimes come tearing through the anchorage during the early morning hours, passing between the two islands north of the anchorage and the mainland.

As long as the northerly ground swell is not rolling in, this should be a good anchorage. It has a nice beach and is within walking distance of the village. There is fair snorkeling on the rocks around the edge of the harbor. However, there is no spectacular diving, as the water is simply not clear enough.

The coast from Unare to Puerto Santos has numerous beautiful beaches, but anchoring off any of them would be pretty dubious. The coast is absolutely desertlike, with many small villages but nothing in the way of a town until Río Caribe, supposedly marked with a light at night.

ENSA MEDINA

(Chart V-18; II D-11)

Only Imray-Iolaire charts made after January 1990 will show this cove. I have been told that there is a possible anchorage at Ensenada Medina, 9 miles east of Puerto Santos. Again, feel your way in. My sketch chart has been developed from a Venezuelan topographical map and there are no soundings available.

PUNTA RIO CARIBE

(Chart V-19; II D-11)

Only charts made after January 1990 will show this harbor. Punta Río Caribe, 2 1/2 miles east of Puerto Santos, might provide an anchorage when the ground swell is not running. This is a sketch chart done from a topographical map, and no soundings are given. Feel your way in only in ideal circumstances.

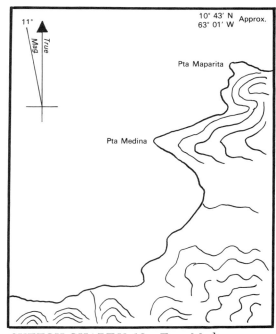

SKETCH CHART V–18   Ensa Medina

PUERTO SANTOS

(Chart V-20; II D, D-1, D-11)

This is an excellent harbor. It is an all-weather fishing port with a fish factory. Diesel fuel, water, and ice are available alongside, and 7 feet can be coaxed into the dock. It is a typical Venezuelan village—noisy, dirty, and cheerful. There is a church at the north end of the town pier, with a tower like a mosque. The harbor is packed with fishing boats, and although this is not an official port of entry for yachts, no one questioned our being there.

There are no dangers when sailing in; just keep the fathometer going, anchor in a suitable depth, and admire the beautiful Spanish-style house on the hillside at the southern end of the harbor. The muddy bottom is so soft that it's difficult to use a lead line—the lead simply disappears into the muck. A heavy anchor penetrates down through the mud to some good clay, but it was a major feat to clean off the muck when we pulled up the anchor.

The south end of the harbor appears to be deeper than the north end. I managed to find 9 feet from the south end almost right up to the fish-fuel-ice dock.

While anchored here, we found a very good-looking fishing and/or cargo-smuggling cutter, with the look of Carriacou about her. She appeared to have been constructed as a yacht, and it turned out she

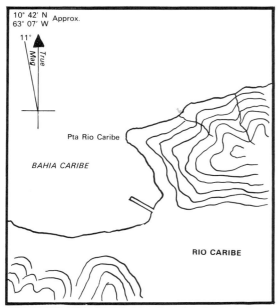

10° 42′ N
63° 07′ W Approx.

11°

True
Mag

Pta Rio Caribe

BAHIA CARIBE

RIO CARIBE

SKETCH CHART V–19   Río Caribe

was French-owned, built in Carriacou, and visiting Venezuela to pick up one of the excellently made local rowing dinghies.

This is definitely not a harbor for swimming. If you want to swim, there are beaches on the small islands to the west of El Morro de Puerto Santos with clear water and a sandy bottom.

Between the offlying islands is a shoal channel with clear water and a black sand bottom. There is a pebbly beach that would have been fine except that the fishermen evidently dry their fish there, which leaves a rather strong aroma.

While here, we met a young Swiss who was staying in town. He said he had lived in Venezuela for four or five years and that although all Venezuelans were friendly, the fishermen of Puerto Santos were the nicest people he had met in his life.

BAHIA HERNAN VASQUEZ

(Chart V-21; II D-1, D-11, D-12)

An excellent anchorage can be had in 1 1/2 fathoms of water, with good holding and a sand bottom, in the south corner of the cove southeast of Punta Hernán Vásquez. This is a beautiful harbor that would appear to be sheltered in all but the worst ground swell. It is well sheltered from winds from the north and around to southwest, and calm at night, but it would be best to use a Bahamian moor.

However, it is important to first clear in Carúpano, as the authorities do not like you to moor in Bahía Hernán Vásquez prior to clearing.

There is a big coconut-palm-lined beach with a road running parallel. The town of Carúpano is about a mile's walk or hitchhike away. Getting from the beach to the road is a project, however, since all the houses along the beach are surrounded by fences and are guarded by dogs that don't like strangers. To get to the road, walk south along the beach, find a likely looking gully, and scramble up the hill.

CARUPANO

(Chart V-21; II D-1, D-11)

Warning: It has been reported that off Carúpano a shoal bank has developed bearing about 110° magnetic from the 4-foot spot marked on the Imray-Iolaire chart and in Chart V-21. If approaching Carúpano from the west, or leaving heading west, it is recommended that you stay north of a line of bearing 290° magnetic on Punta Hernán Vásquez and continue eastward outside the above-mentioned shoal until the jail and breakwater come in line 207° magnetic. Run in on this line of bearing and all should be well. When leaving, reverse the procedure. If you enter in Carúpano, after clearing, it's wise to move to the cove on the eastern edge of Bahía Hernán Vásquez.

Carúpano is the easternmost port of entry in Venezuela, and formerly it was avoided like the plague because of the time it took to clear. Clearance procedures: Customs, Immigration, Guardia Nacional, and Port Captain. I have received various conflicting reports. A couple of boats have said it couldn't have been easier; a couple of others said they were given the run-around and had to pay people off to get their clearances. (Almost all, by the way, reported that the anchorage was rocky and rolly.)

We had our own incident a number of years ago when we anchored in the bay east of Carúpano. We had cleared into Venezuelan waters months earlier and had faithfully carried our *zarpa* with us at all times; but no one had seemed interested in looking at it. So we finally decided to go ashore without it, which turned out to be a mistake. We took the dinghy inside the breakwater and tied up west of the dock—only to discover that we had landed inside a Customs area, where we were promptly asked for our *zarpa*.

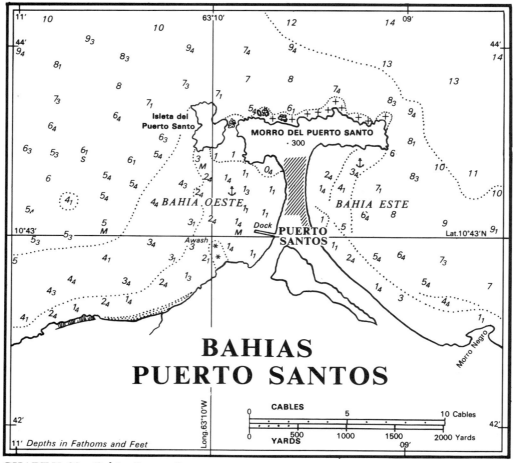

CHART V–20   Bahías Puerto Santos

We were escorted to the sergeant of the guard—actually a fifty-year-old, gray-haired corporal. He became most upset and confused, and obviously didn't know what to do. I warned my crew that we were in for a bad time. How could I tell, considering my awful Spanish? I replied that if a guy gets to this age and is still only a corporal in the Venezuelan army, then he's either an idiot or an SOB—or both.

After much discussion, we returned to *Iolaire* on one of the army's fast launches, picked up the *zarpa*, and returned to the base. But the old corporal was still not satisfied. Everyone kept telling him, "*No importante . . . ,*" but he stood his ground and insisted that we wait until his commanding officer arrived. Unfortunately, we picked the wrong day to have problems—that officer was off at some ceremony 40 miles away. He finally returned and took the corporal into his office to find out what was going on. There was a sudden explosion of Spanish, about five minutes of machine-gun-style delivery

during which, I suspect, the corporal was reduced to a private. After this royal chewing-out, the officer apologized to us and returned our papers. Some of the young soldiers escorted us down the street to a good restaurant, apologized again for the corporal, and wished us a good day. We spent the rest of the day wandering around the town, had a good lunch and a cold beer, and then went back to the boat.

The harbor of Carúpano has been expanded and dredged, allegedly to 25 feet. There are two 750-foot piers and the breakwater has been extended to reduce the awful surge that formerly found its way into the harbor. The best anchorage is stern-to the western wharf, with an anchor out to the west to hold you off. It is a high steamer dock, so make sure you moor near a ladder or it will be all but impossible to get off the boat. Fuel, water, and ice are available from the dock. If you take the dinghy, I suggest that you come in west of the piers to avoid the security guard at the head of the dock. There is

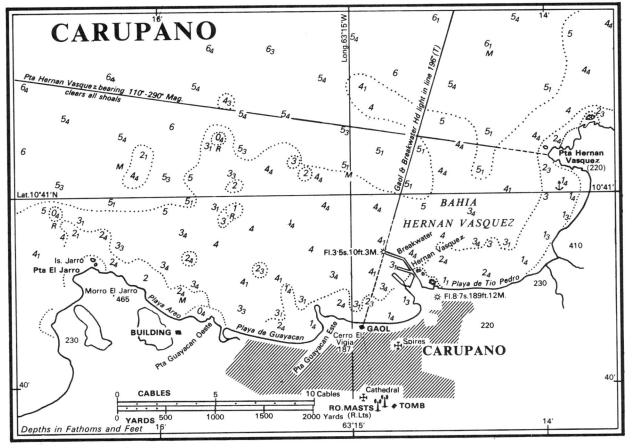

CHART V–21 Carúpano

now a 50-ton travel lift here that is used primarily to haul fishing boats, but some yachts also have used it.

CARUPANO TO ENSENADA ESMERALDA

(Chart V-12; II D-1, D-12)

This whole area on Chart V-12 has been redone on Imray-Iolaire charts printed after January 1990. Note that the US and British and the pre-1990 Imray-Iolaire charts all have the place names completely fouled up. Place names and the coastline now have been redone from topographical maps and inspection of aerial photographs of the area, plus discussions with a number of Venezuelan yachtsmen who have explored the area and have reported it as worth visiting.

However, this is strictly for the brave, as this area has not been explored in detail. There are no soundings, so proceed with caution. The Venezuelan yachtsmen with whom I spoke were all sailing boats drawing less than 6 feet. They eyeballed

their way in—or, more likely, sounded their way in, since the water is not very clear—but they did not have any notes on soundings. Any accurate soundings that yachtsmen can provide for the area would be a boon for others if it is forwarded to me for inclusion in Imray-Iolaire charts and subsequent printings or updates of this guide.

So, if you feel like exploring, proceed slowly and send a dinghy ahead with the fathometer installed. There are numerous small beaches, completely uninhabited, that would make wonderful places to anchor once you have discovered a safe channel. The stretch between Punta Patilla and Morro Taquien, for example, has a series of three beautiful beaches. This area obviously is not usable in winter when the ground swell is running, but in summer months, in calm weather, it might bear investigating.

It should be noted that if you are using the US rather than the Imray-Iolaire charts, from Puerto Santos westward you should switch from NOAA chart 24420 to NOAA chart 24431, as this has a much better scale and shows the harbors along the coast.

BAHIA ESCONDIDA

(Chart V-22; II D-1, D-12)

From aerial photographs and from accounts of Venezuelan yachtsmen, this looks like a good anchorage with a beautiful white-sand beach at the head of the bay.

ENSENADA DE GUACA

(Chart V-22; II D-1, D-12)

There is a sizable village ashore here. It must be a fairly good anchorage or a village of this size would not have grown up along the coast. The unnamed cove southwest of Ensenada de Guaca, east of Punta Guatapanare, again looks good but is unexplored.

ENSENADA LEBRANCHE

(Chart V-22; II D-12—called Ensenada Garrapata on old charts; not listed on British and US charts.)

This looks like a good harbor if the ground swell is not running, but the ground swell along the coast can cause plenty of trouble. The chart notes more than 30 feet of water inside Islas Garrapatas, yet it also notes breakers. Obviously, the sea can hump up here. There is probably also a strong east-west current. When the current is running to the eastward against a large ground swell, a dangerous situation could develop; thus, be sure to pass outside the rocks (Islas Garrapatas) north of Ensa Lebranche.

I would recommend anchoring up in the northeast corner of Ensenada Lebranche. The wind should come across the salt flats and Morro de Lebranche should protect you from the swells. The other cove to the westward looks to be too exposed to be used as an anchorage.

PUNTA ESMERALDA

(Chart V-23; II D-1)

Warning: Large mussel rafts, unlit, are anchored due south of the western end of Isla Esmeralda about midway between the white rock and Isla Esmeralda. Further, shoal water has extended southwestward of Punta Esmeralda, and the whole area south between Punta Esmeralda and Isla Casabel (the easternmost island in Ensenada Esmeralda) has shoaled. It is soft mud, so no real danger exists, but feel your way in very carefully. There are structures of some sort extending northeast of the white rock—perhaps oyster culture racks.

East of Punta Esmeralda are sheer red cliffs, with heavy surf beating on the shore. Continue westward, round Isla Esmeralda, and sail on into the bay, feeling your way with the lead line. The shoal water extends well offshore, with a bottom of soft, gooey, thick mud.

The day we anchored here, it was blowing a steady 25 knots and gusting higher. To hold, we had to let out 130 feet of line, even though we were anchored in only 10 feet of water. We ran into the usual routine: It blew the hinges off the gates of hell until after dusk, then the wind began to die, and around midnight it was glassy calm. Even in periods of ground swell, we found we were perfectly sheltered, anchored in a line between Isla Casabel and Punta Esmeralda. (See Chart V-23 from discontinued HO chart 1692.)

Exploring with the dinghy, we came to the conclusion that it would be best to anchor bow and stern facing northwest off the white-sand beach on the southwestern side of Isla Esmeralda. We found 1 fathom at a distance of 50 feet from shore, but the bottom dropped off rapidly.

Esmeralda is a large fishing village with fast, long, lean outboard *piraguas* lining the beach. There is a fish factory off to the south, and the fishermen are very friendly. I am not sure how attractive the village is now, but I have a description of it from Dr. Daniel Camejo, one of Venezuela's premier yachtsmen, who has cruised these waters for years in his yachts *Sargasso* and *Caribana* (and who has been a major source of information, guidance, and encouragement to me in my Venezuelan explorations). Dr. Camejo described Esmeralda in the late 1960s as being the most primitive place he had ever seen. The houses were all built of thatch, and whenever it rained, the whole area became flooded. He described the day he was there: It was pouring rain, and everyone was happily wandering around ankle-deep in mud and water; even the houses were ankle-deep in water. Pigs were wandering in and out of the houses, there were bits of fish everywhere, and so on. Of course, the place may have

33

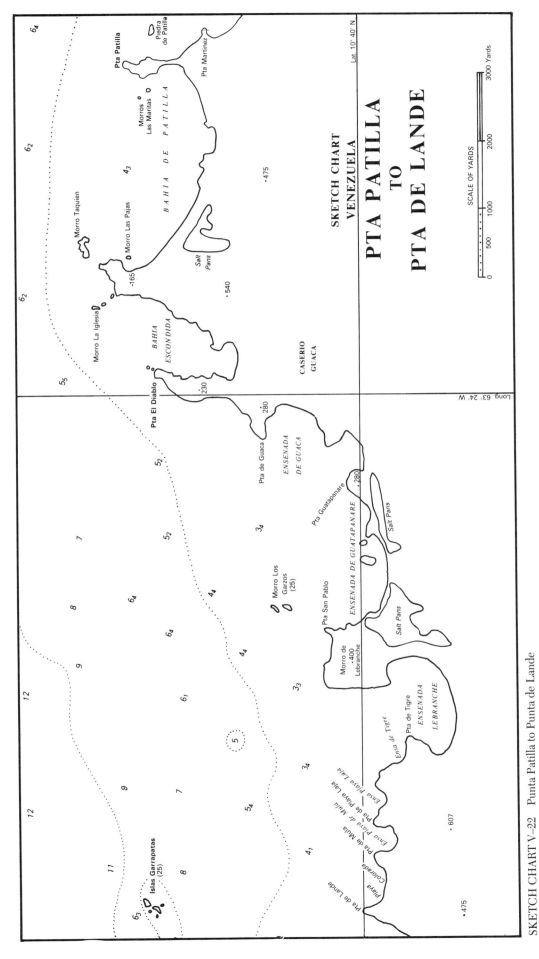

SKETCH CHART V–22   Punta Patilla to Punta de Lande

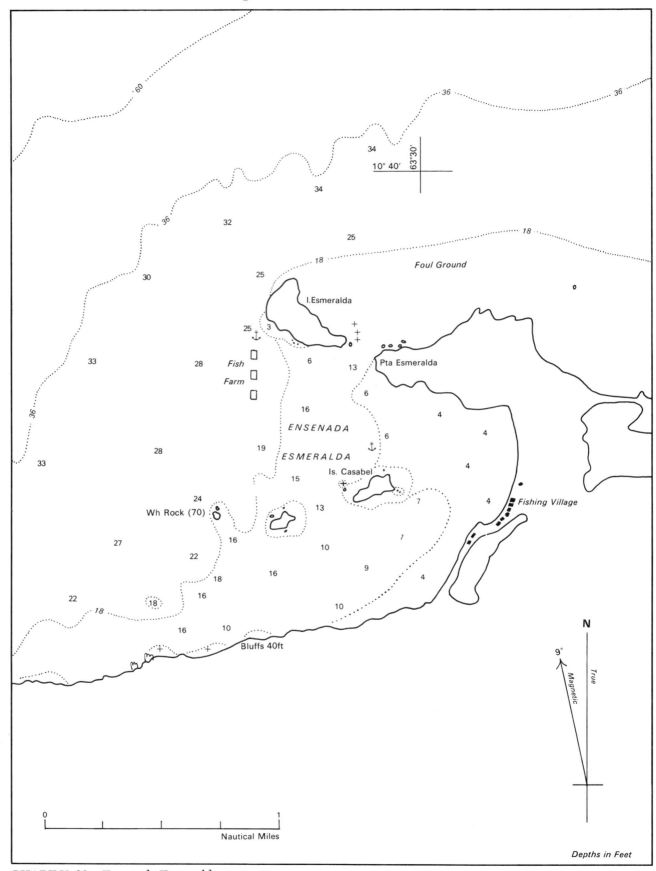

CHART V–23   Ensenada Esmeralda

changed by now, but in any case, the people are friendly and the harbor is excellent.

PUNTA ESMERALDA TO MORRO DE CHACO-PATA

Westward from Punta Esmeralda to Morro de Chacopata, there is absolutely nothing—just sand beaches between red cliffs 50 to 100 feet high. There is no possibility of anchoring anywhere along this coast, except Punta Manzanillo.

PUNTA MANZANILLO

(Chart V-12; II D-12)

Ensenada Manzanillo is a little indentation in the coast 5 miles west of Ensenada Esmeralda. Certainly not a harbor, it might provide a bolt hole to duck into at a time when there is no ground swell if the wind is blowing like crazy in the late afternoon. The sketch chart was developed from a topographical map, so no soundings are available. Only charts made after January 1990 will show this point.

NOTES

4

Isla Margarita and Adjacent Islands

II D, D-1, D-12

Isla Margarita was discovered by Columbus on one of his early voyages. Unfortunately for him, he did not tarry: Although no gold was found in the area, the island's surrounding water supported an extremely profitable pearl fishery for a couple of hundred years. To defend these, the Spanish built numerous forts that still stand in an amazing state of preservation. One of the best is at Pampatar, the port of entry.

Margarita, like the Canaries, is very much misjudged. People take a quick look at Porlamar and Pampatar and figure that they have seen the whole island. But once you get off the beaten track, there is a lot more to discover. It should be remembered that Margarita is 36 miles long; the mountains on the eastern end are 3,240 feet high and those at the western end only 300 feet lower, so the climate is quite varied.

By boat you can explore the west coast, which provides several largely unexplored anchorages. Or you can visit the wonderful area at Boca del Río. There you can take a launch through Laguna de la Restinga, which is alive with birds—especially pink flamingos—and cross to an 11-mile-long beach on the north side of the island, where you'll find good swimming and excellent seafood restaurants. You can dive in the surf and dig with your bare hands for *chipi-chipi*, Venezuela's tasty small clams.

Peter York reports that in the late 1970s, he worked his 60-foot ketch inside the lagoon by the airport. He seems to be the only sailor who has done this, but he can't remember any ranges or bearings.

It is worthwhile to tour the island in a rented car, visiting the seaside towns of Pampatar, Porlamar, and Juangriego. You can go inland to the mountain town of La Asunción and visit the various forts that were scenes of violent and incredibly cruel fighting during the Venezuelan war for independence, which began on Isla Margarita in 1811.

One excursion that *Iolaire*'s crew enjoyed immensely was the trip to the Fuentidueño pools, on the way to San Juan Bautista. The pools are not large, but they do have fresh water. And there is a barbecue grill, as well as tables and benches in an idyllic setting in the heart of the San Juan hills. Do not visit this area on a weekend, however, as you are likely to be inundated with crowds. We would definitely recommend a lunch at the Tarzan Restaurant, where the food is excellent, the atmosphere is very friendly, and the prices are amazingly low.

Most of the island is extremely dry—so dry that the principal water supply comes from a massive pipeline laid underwater from the mainland. It rains so seldom that no one is ever prepared when it does—like the time I told my crew to leave their foul-weather gear behind, only to be caught later in a deluge, the first rain in nine months.

The island of Margarita is a free port, although there is no comparison with the shopping in the US Virgin Islands or Curaçao. Interestingly, Venezuelans are restricted in the amount they are allowed to bring in each trip, but not in the number of trips per year. Thus, some people in the Puerto La Cruz-Barcelona area practically commute back and forth, carrying in the maximum allowance each trip. Unfortunately for them, the hydrofoil no longer operates—a combined result of its having run into a rock (or, according to another story, a whale) and the high cost of fuel. When the price of fuel eventually dropped, the hydrofoil was sold to another country, as Venezuela could not afford to run it.

The variety of food is much greater in Margarita than on the mainland. We made a mistake in not stocking up with cheese, sausage etc., while we were in Margarita. But sugar, which is imported, frequently is difficult to find in Venezuela, so be sure to stock up on sugar in the Caribbean islands.

Amazingly, because of the complicated exchange rate, in 1988 Scotch was cheaper in Margarita than it was in St. Barts. This occurred because if you bought what the government referred to as essential supplies, you could get 14 Bs. to the dollar, rather than the open price of approximately 30 Bs. to the dollar. By 1990 this had changed, however—the government no longer supports "essential imports."

The taxi drivers in Margarita are better than they used to be; I would no longer compare them to those of Palermo! But check the rates, as the drivers still like to make some extra money. A *por puesto* (which looks like a taxi but is really a bus) from Pampatar to Porlamar is dead easy, but even after my more recent trip, I still can't figure out where you grab the *por puesto* going in the other direction (other than by going to the main road out of town, Avenida 4 de Mayo, and trying to flag one down).

Again, as has been mentioned elsewhere in this guide, as soon as you arrive, get a map of the town; it makes everything so much easier.

Near Isla Margarita are Isla Coche and Isla Cubagua, both of which have excellent anchorages. You could easily spend two weeks visiting various anchorages on Margarita, its offlying islands, and the north side of the Peninsula de Araya (see chapter 5). Margarita also forms the entrance to the area that Dr. Daniel Camejo (the builder of the El Morro and Puerto Azul projects—see chapter 6) refers to as the Sea of El Morro, which is bounded by Margarita to the east, the Venezuelan coast to the south, Isla La Blanquilla to the north, and Isla La Tortuga to the west. This area also includes the Golfo de Cariaco and the Golfo de Santa Fé; thus, you could easily spend a month or two happily cruising this area and never visit the same anchorage twice.

PAMPATAR
(Chart V-24; II D-1, D-12)

Pampatar is one of the more popular places for entering and clearing Venezuelan waters. As with

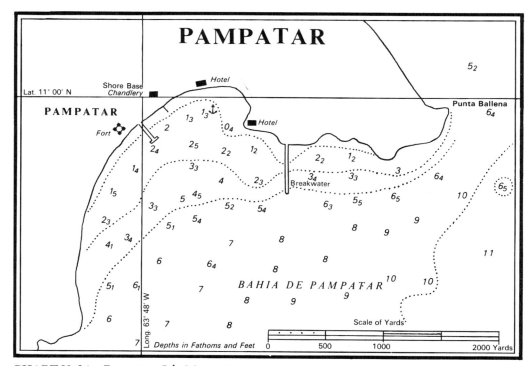

CHART V–24   Pampatar, Isla Margarita

so many other ports, however, DO NOT ENTER PAMPATAR AT NIGHT! Enter the harbor only in daylight. Sail in to the north corner of the harbor until you are in 1 1/2 fathoms and anchor either in a Bahamian moor or a Y with one anchor to the northeast and the other to the southeast. Although the wind tends to come across the land to the northeast, early in the morning it can also swing around to the east or southeast.

A breakwater has been built on the eastern side of the harbor, giving partial shelter. If the wind does go southeast and begin to blow hard (a rather common occurrence), it's time to get out and move elsewhere. Unfortunately, the "elsewhere" will be quite far away. All in all, this is not a particularly good all-weather harbor.

Pampatar's harbor is very crowded, and boats anchor in all different fashions. Some are on a single anchor to the bow, while others have a single anchor to the bow plus a spring line taken from the stern to the anchor rode so they lie beam-to the easterly wind but heading south-southeast into the swell. Others are anchored bow and stern, while still others are lying to Bahamian moors! The wind dies out in the evening, so there's often mass confusion at 2100.

The main dock was being reconstructed in January 1990, with the completion date uncertain. A marina north of town is in the planning stage, but if it gets off the ground, it will probably not be operational before 1992.

If you need water and fuel, pick them up at the water and fuel jetty in Porlamar, running in on a bearing of 153° magnetic on the end of the jetty. Eight feet can be taken stern-to—I sounded the channel in February 1989. You can also go to Boca del Río, just south of the bridge. Draft there is probably 7 feet, but you will have to check via dinghy. Gasoline is available along the beach in the various small shops that cater to the fishermen.

The onetime problems of entering Venezuela have ended. Francisco and Diana Azpurua run Shore Base Yacht Services, which takes care of just about everything, including selling copies of this guide and Imray-Iolaire charts of Venezuela. They will set up Customs clearance for a reasonable fee and can also arrange for you to obtain a *zarpa* for visiting the other harbors.

If you decide to enter yourself (which I do not advise), the present routine is to first go to Customs (located in a building east of the church) and then to the Guardia Nacional, located across the street. Then, about a mile and a half away, in the next bay to the east, you will find Immigration and the Port Captain's office. (The location is marked on the chart.) Immigration is only on duty from 0900 to 1100 or sometimes 1200, so if you call in the afternoon, you will either have to wait until the next day or go all the way to the airport. In my opinion, as long as Shore Base keeps its rates reasonable, you are wasting your time to go through all this rigmarole. Just take your papers in to Shore Base, leave them there, and let them take care of everything. The Guardia Nacional only boards if you have guns. (My advice is not to carry guns on a yacht, as they are much more trouble than they are worth!)

Shore Base's dinghy security service moors the dinghies offshore in 4 feet of water because of the ever-present surge. The man in charge of dinghy security during the day looks like and is built like "Mr. T," except that he has a Fu Manchu mustache and a smile. But I would certainly not cross him. Shore Base can arrange car rentals, point you in the right direction for money exchange, send telexes and telegrams, and arrange for provisioning, visa extensions, diesel and outboard mechanics, an electronic technician, laundry, showers, propane, gasoline, etc.—basically everything, including marine supplies.

The marine supply situation in Pampatar is in a state of flux. A foreigner chasing around trying to obtain marine supplies can forget it! Go talk to Francisco and see what he can arrange for you. Francisco is Venezuelan, educated in Burlington, Vermont; his wife, Diana, is an American from Burlington who went to the Boston Conservatory of Music. Their mailing address is: Shore Base Yacht Services, Oficina Postal Telegráfica, Pampatar, Margarita 6316, Venezuela. Phone from US: 011-58-95-78269. They stand on channel 68.

There is a wonderful old Spanish church here that is well worth a visit. The fort, too, is an absolute must. Named the Castillo de San Carlos Borromeo, it was built in 1661 and was recently restored. It is also one of the few places in Margarita where you can purchase postcards. Here, too, is the best small gift shop in the entire area, vastly superior to the gift shops in Porlamar.

In the early morning, the restaurants in Pampatar are all closed, but you can ask directions to the bakery (one block back from the waterfront and turn right), where you can obtain croissants and coffee, change money in moderate amounts, read the newspaper, and organize your day. At the head of the main commercial dock is an excellent small restaurant that serves good and inexpensive meals, and fantastic fruit-juice drinks. It has a good, clean porch overlooking the harbor—a pleasant place for lunch or a drink.

In the extreme north corner of the harbor is a small hotel that appeared to be well run. Perhaps if you rent a room there, the entire crew could have a shower at not too great an expense.

Money from Visa and American Express cards can be obtained from the Banco Italiano de Venezuela and Banco Unión de Venezuela. Only basic supplies are available in Pampatar (this includes, happily, fresh bread in the morning from the bakery), so for restocking the boat, you'll need to head toward Porlamar. Take a *por puesto* in the direction of Porlamar, but don't go all the way there. As you reach the amusement park, you will see an apartment complex on the right and a sign for C & M, an excellent supermarket and shopping complex, complete with bank, excellent Casa Azul, *ferriatería* (hardware store), pharmacy, bakery, photo shop, and so on. Do all your shopping and then take a taxi back to Pampatar. If you take a *por puesto* all the way in to Porlamar, it is extremely difficult to get back. You can pick up a bus and a *por puesto* anywhere along Avenida 4 de Mayo; a good spot is the junction of Avenida 4 de Mayo and Avenida Santiago Mariño, but sometimes the vehicles that come by are full and you have to stand around and wait until a semi-empty one comes along.

If you have rented a car, my advice is to go to the open market on the superhighway north of Por-

lamar, do as much shopping as you can there, and then return to the C & M supermarket outside of Pampatar and finish your shopping. It should also be noted that the *por puesto* to Porlamar passes a huge new amusement center that has been duly checked out by my three sons (Mark, age 9; Richard, age 20; Donald, age 21) and my secretary, all of whom went on as many of the rides as possible. The park is open only on Friday, Saturday, and Sunday nights, and they went on a Friday, which turned out to be the quietest time—with no lines. As of this writing, the cost is 100 Bs. for adults and 50 Bs. for children twelve and under. Buy a ticket at the front gate to cover all the rides. (Food is also available.) The roller coaster, which has two loops and a corkscrew, has been dubbed "Mega!!" by Mark. The ferris wheel moves slowly, with revolving seats, and it is high enough that you can get an excellent view of the park as well as most of Margarita!

PORLAMAR

(Chart V-25; II D-1, D-12)

When sailing from Pampatar to Porlamar, you'll pass Punta El Morro, where there is a dock, roughly 1,000 feet long, extending on a north-south magnetic axis, with a sheltered anchorage to the west of it. There appears to be a shipwrecking oper-

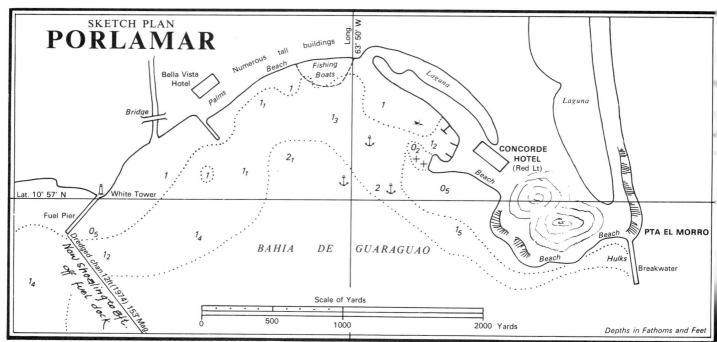

CHART V–25   Porlamar, Isla Margarita

ation—they are bringing in beat-up ships, cutting them up for scrap, and carting the scrap away—but there is little or no activity on the weekend. There is a good anchorage behind the dock breakwater, and 200 yards to the west is a small cove with a beautiful white-sand beach that is inaccessible by land—a private beach that you can enjoy just a short distance from crowded Porlamar. The only time you are likely to have company is on weekends.

In Porlamar, the best spot to anchor is west of the Hotel Concorde. In front of the Concorde are two small marinas that usually are full and have a very limited depth. I suggest you send in the dinghy to check the depth before you go, as shoaling has been reported. It is claimed, however, that you'll find 7 feet alongside at low water. Work your way in as close as your draft will permit, to get out of the roll. Water was available subject to pressure, which was very erratic when we were there in March 1989. Perhaps the problem will have been corrected by the time you read this.

Courtesy of Peter York, I discovered that the best way to approach the fuel jetty, where both fuel and water are available, is definitely not according to the range given in Chris Doyle's Venezuelan guide. Rather, the best approach is with a bearing of 153 - 333° magnetic, because back in the 1970s, a 12-foot channel was dredged to the dock to allow the hydrofoil to load and unload passengers. Peter, who supervised the dredging, reported that they dredged up sand and mud with great difficulty, as they met with a lot of rock (there was still 8 feet at low water in February 1989). If the channel has filled in since that time and you run aground, at least you will be on soft mud if you come in on that line of bearing.

The Hotel Concorde is very luxurious, but you'll find better values at the little bars along the beach south of the Concorde. I would not advise eating the oysters here, as raw sewage is discharged into the harbors in Venezuela.

If you are lying off the Concorde, the easiest way to get ice is to jump in the dinghy, take it halfway to town, and pull up on the beach where you see all the fishing boats. Right across the street is a grocery store/bar that sells bags of ice. There is also a good restaurant. For block ice, take a taxi to the western end of town and start asking for *hielo panela* or *hielo bloque*: a big ice plant. There is a dock at the ice plant where the fishing boats fill up. It is the first dock about half a mile west of the fuel dock. I would definitely not take a yacht west of the fuel dock—go down in a dinghy. Block ice is also available at the fish market.

To purchase bottled gas, go three blocks west of the cathedral, pay for the gas, get your receipt, then go out of town on the airport road for 2 miles and it's on the left-hand side. You pass the bottling plant going out and make the first possible U-turn and go back. But to save you all this trouble, Shore Base in Pampatar will do the work for you, which is much easier.

I would say that anyone visiting Margarita should rent a car for a tour of the island, and there are various car rental operations. The best deal we were able to find was Miami Car, on Avenida Santiago Mariño, on the east side of the street, behind and above the discotheque. If they do not have cars available, visit the Bella Vista Hotel, where there are five or six different car rental operations. (There is only one agency at the Concorde.) Drive out of Porlamar and head northward to the fantastic white-sand beaches on the eastern side of the island. Also worthwhile is the drive across the island to the original capital of La Asunción, a wonderful old Spanish village complete with a plaza and excellent small restaurants. It is completely bypassed by tourism, in marked contrast to the Miami-type high-rises at Porlamar. Continue on to Juangriego and stop at Santa Ana, where you can purchase hammocks and local Venezuelan artifacts. It should be noted that there may be a new marina at Punta (or Playa) Moreno, as a big land development program is underway on the southern shore there.

The only way to get a shower in Porlamar is to go to either the Bella Vista or the Concorde pool and use the open-air shower, but this should be done only to rinse off, not to lather up. (Some "yachtsmen"—better known as "water people"—have done this and have ruined things for true yachtsmen in both Trinidad and Venezuela.) But a freshwater swim and a shower will at least refresh you and remove the salt. Rooms at the Bella Vista, now completely hidden by palm trees, are inexpensive, and you might consider renting a room so the whole crew can get completely clean.

The open-air market has been moved far out of town, but it is well worthwhile visiting despite the fact that you will do more of your shopping at the CADA (on Calle Velásquez, three blocks east of the cathedral) or at the C & M shopping center halfway between Porlamar and Pampatar.

On Avenida 4 de Mayo, on the left-hand side as you are leaving Porlamar en route to Pampatar, you will find a gourmet shop that has a superb selection of cheese, sausage, and wine—at prices that Paul Adamthwaite claims beat those in St. Barts and St. Martin.

Be careful to check the opening and closing hours of the stores, as they are a little strange. We found that shops were closed from 1200 to 1400 or 1500 and then were open again until 1800 or 1900.

There is a meat market in Porlamar by Calle Igualdad, one block west of Plaza Bolívar on the southwest corner. Also, there is a butcher on Calle Narváez, on the east side of the street about two blocks south of Calle Marcano. This is supposed to bé the best butcher, but we were not overly impressed. There may be a good butcher somewhere in Margarita, but where? (I understand there may be one in Juangriego—see that section below.) I suspect that the main problem with meat in Venezuela is that unless you go to a very high-class butcher, the beef is treated like wood—cut one day and used the next.

For beer and booze, we got an excellent deal at Pepe Le Fou (Crazy Pepe) on Calle Igualdad, halfway to the Banco Italiano, on the south side of the street.

We found an excellent laundry northwest of the cathedral on Avenida Miranda, on the right-hand side of the road between Calle Rivas and Calle Oeste. There is a laundry pick-up service at the Concorde, but I suspect it is expensive. Shore Base (in Pampatar) has an excellent laundry service.

Money can be changed at the Banco Italiano Venezuela (on the corner of Calle Igualdad and Calle San Rafael—the street that leads directly out of the Bella Vista Hotel and heads due west), or on Calle Narváez (on the east side of the street, one block north of Calle Marcano), and, amazingly, by some of the stall keepers at the main market.

There are very few marine supplies in Margarita. What you will find is mainly for the local fishing boats, not yacht gear. A marine supply store is mentioned in Doyle's guide, but the only thing I could find was an excellent hardware store, Casa Azul on Calle Guevara, on the west side between Calle Maneiro and Calle La Marina. Casa Azul has two or three hardware divisions in town. The main division appears to be the one where the pedestrian shopping center is located. Another is at the C & M supermarket, and we also found another fairly good place on Calle Cedeño, on the north side of the street, two blocks from Avenida Santiago Mariño—the street with the island divider in the center. Also, there is Offshore Marine on Calle Patino, two blocks west of Avenida Santiago Mariño.

We were told that excellent marine supplies are available from Felipe Gerard (known locally as "The Frenchman") in El Valle del Espíritu Santo, a very attractive village about 10 miles from Por-

lamar. (You will have to rent a car to get there.) To find "the Frenchman" from the village's main square, walk westward, take a look at the wonderful church, then walk through it to the first street and turn right. I am told that 100 yards or so up the road, you will find a blue door. If you don't find "the Frenchman," start asking questions. (In Spanish, "the Frenchman" is *el francés*.) We visited him in 1988 and were rather disappointed in his stock, but he said he was low at the time, and a big shipment was en route. So . . . your best bet still is to give your list to Francisco at Shore Base in Pampatar.

We could never figure out where the postal service is centered and found it much easier to use the hotels when posting letters.

Augie Hollen reports that you can find English-speaking people in Porlamar at the Corporación de Turismo Venezolano, whose offices are across the street from the Ministry of Internal Affairs and about two blocks west of Plaza Bolívar, which faces the cathedral. However, despite a day of searching, I couldn't find it.

The plaza and the cathedral are well worth a visit. The airport is best avoided—there is nothing to see once you get there.

If you sail from the anchorage off the Hotel Bella Vista and head for Punta Mosquito, you are guaranteed to run aground—yet the chart shows ample water. Lay your course to wherever you are headed, go south until Punta Mosquito bears southwest, then swing around on a course to clear Punta Mosquito by at least half a mile.

BAHIA GUAMACHE

(Chart V-26; II D-1, D-12)

There used to be a very nice anchorage at Punta de Piedras. One could swing around Punta de Mangle, sail up as close as possible into the lee of the shore, and anchor in 2 fathoms of water in a beautiful and deserted anchorage. Now, Bahía Guamache is a deepwater port for Isla Margarita and, sadly, no longer an attractive yacht anchorage.

BOCA DEL RIO

(Chart V-27; II D-1, D-12)

Stand in on the starboard tack, keeping the hotel (marked on the chart and in the old edition as a hotel, but now an experimental fisheries station) bear-

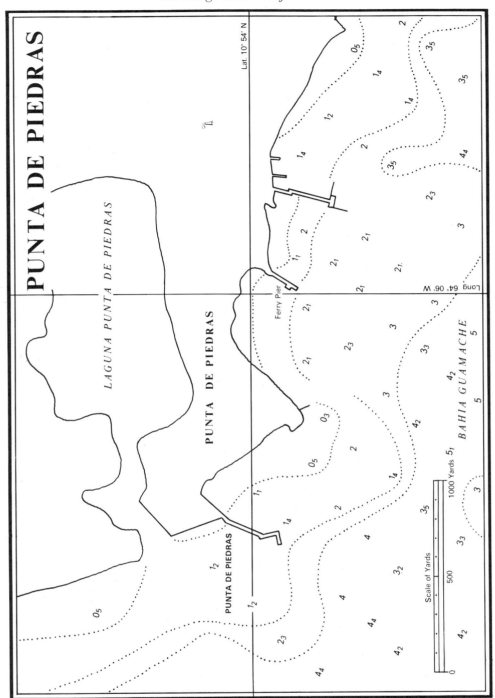

CHART V–26 Punta de Piedras (Bahía Guamache), Isla Margarita

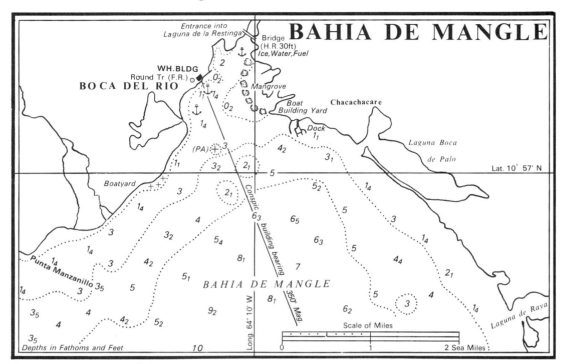

CHART V–27   Boca del Río, Isla Margarita

ing 350° magnetic. That line of bearing will lead you clear of the shoal marked on Chart V-27, keeping the shoal on the starboard hand. Hold this course until the bridge bears 035° magnetic and anchor on that point. When sailing this range, favor the western side, as there is an unmarked, invisible sunken wreck to starboard of the range. As you approach Boca del Río, there is a breaking reef on the starboard hand.

You can run in on a bearing of 035° magnetic on the bridge, but be careful of the reef on the port hand, which may or may not be marked by a small buoy. Once past this shoal, you can anchor in 15 feet of water, completely sheltered in all weather. However, people I have talked to mentioned that there were a couple of mosquitoes when the wind died down at night. In the outer anchorage, there is no problem with mosquitoes; the only problem would be a strong wind out of the south, which very seldom occurs.

We have been told that just south of the bridge at the dock, you can pick up water, fuel, and ice. I'm not sure of the draft, but I suspect 7 feet. This was noted as a worthwhile fueling stop, since no paperwork was needed and they were happy to fill your tanks at the domestic price of diesel—about 9 cents US per gallon.

Ashore in Boca del Río, we found two marine hardware stores with no yachting gear but plenty of

fishing gear, anchors, line, fenders, and the like—all at incredibly low prices. There is a fairly good supermarket and a twenty-four-hour drugstore. There are small restaurants in Boca del Río that, we are told, are good and inexpensive. Basic supplies are available.

North of the bridge you will find the *lancha* for a tour of the Laguna de la Restinga. I strongly advise against taking your own dinghy. Instead, take a *lancha*: They are very cheap, well run, and have friendly operators who will happily take you all the way back to your boat. If you insist on using your own boat, take along a guide, as there are no charts of the lagoon. You could easily be lost for days inside the mangroves, as they all look the same. It's well worth the price of a guide to see the birds, many of which are unique to this part of the world.

The guides' typical routine is to take you through the lagoon to the north side, where they secure their boats. Then, after a walk over the sand spit, you come to Ensa La Guardia, with its 10-mile-long beach. It's very commercialized in the area where the guide boat first lands, but you only have to walk east or west to find an empty beach.

In the surf off the beach, you can dive down and with bare hands come up with the little clams locally called *chipi-chipi*. Once you get the hang of the technique for opening them, it's easy: Place two clams back to back with the knuckles of the clams' shells toward each other; push hard, then twist, and they'll snap open immediately. It's much easier than prying them open with a knife. *Chipi-chipi* usually are cooked in a soup or with rice, and they are extremely tasty this way; but they also are delicious eaten raw with lime juice.

South of Boca del Río, you'll see a large warehouse and a small shipyard. Give this area a wide berth, as the shoal extends well offshore. We discovered that to our chagrin when we "parked" there in light airs early one morning. ("Parked" is when the sea is calm and the vessel is in no danger—*Iolaire* is frequently parked but seldom aground.)

It is worthwhile taking a dinghy up to the eastern side of Bahía de Mangle to see Chacachacare (see Chart V-28), as a new breakwater and harbor have been built, and this village seems to be a base for a tremendous number of Venezuelan fishing boats. These boats are mother ships for handliners fishing from small boats. The small boats sell their catch to the mother ship, which has a hold full of ice. Once the mother ship is filled with fish—or the ice runs low—she heads for home or often to Martinique, where the fish prices are higher. Most of the boats are kept in such beautiful condition that it is easy to mistake them for yachts. The shipyard at Chacachacare has a travel lift and builds wooden and steel boats, but it has no piers, so I don't know how they haul boats and move them around. If you speak Spanish, I would think that you could arrange for emergency repairs to be done here.

When leaving Boca del Río and passing westward, give Punta del Pozo a wide berth, as the shoals have extended much farther offshore than indicated on the chart.

With the trades in their normal position, there should be passable anchorages anywhere between Punta Arenas and El Morro de Robledal. Gordon Stout of *Shango* advises anchoring off Robledal. He says there usually are no other yachts, there is good shelter, and the town is small and untouristy. Shoal water extends quite far off the town, so feel your way in with a lead line and anchor in a suitable depth.

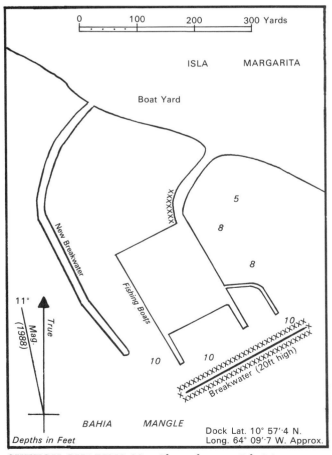

SKETCH CHART V–28 Chacachacare, Isla Margarita

ROBLEDAL

This can be a very uncomfortable anchorage when the swell is coming in from the north, as there is a chop blown off from the land. You lie facing east and the swell comes in on the port beam. About 3 miles east of Robledal, there is a shoal, not shown on the chart, about 1/4 mile offshore. There are no anchorages between El Morro de Robledal and Bahía de Juangriego. In my estimation, the whole north coast is doubtful, and it's best to stay well offshore.

JUANGRIEGO

(Chart V-29; II D-1, D-12)

You can find a good anchorage off Juangriego. It would appear to be open to the northerly swell, and obviously the swell does find its way in there at certain times, but most of the time it must be a good anchorage, since it is the major fishing port of Isla Margarita.

Anchor northwest of the pier, with the fort bearing 010° magnetic. There is 9 feet of water and the bottom is soft mud, which makes good holding but also makes getting the anchor up a messy operation. Paul Adamthwaite discovered a good anchorage south of the dock and claims he found no black mud.

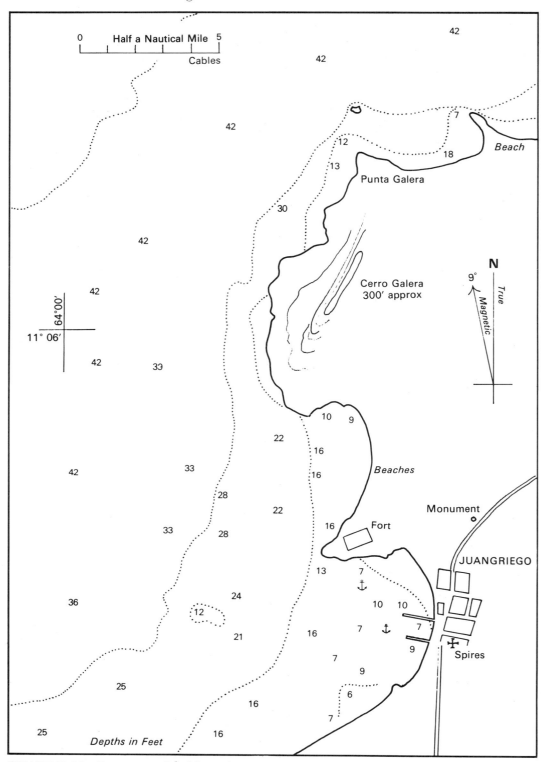

CHART V–29   Juangriego, Isla Margarita

There are two docks. The big one is farther south than the chart shows. A small stone jetty on the northeast corner of the harbor is good for tying up dinghies, but make sure you have a stern anchor to hold the boat off. The slipway and wrecks on the northeastern corner of the beach of the bay north of Juangriego no longer exist. Nor does the yacht club—it died about eight years ago.

Paul reported that he found an excellent butcher here—Señor Blatairman. Walk up to the church, take the first left after the church, then look for his shop on the right side of the street. He comes very highly recommended and will cut the meat into the portions you want, wrap it all in plastic bags, and put it in his deep freeze, so when you come back the next day, it is frozen solid. Paul said the shopping in town was not bad and that there was an excellent market with fresh fruit and vegetables.

Water is available at the dock. There is a water-skiing club and, wonder of wonders, a laundromat right on the waterfront.

The beautifully restored fort was the scene of a bloody battle on 8 August 1817, during Venezuela's war of independence, when 500 defenders were massacred after they surrendered to the Spanish troops led by General Morillo. If the weather is clear, the fort is an excellent place to visit at sunset—it's a fine vantage point from which to look for the "green flash."

There are apparently no other good anchorages on Isla Margarita. If you want to see some fantastic sandy beaches, sail along the northwest coast of Margarita between Punta Galera and Cabo Negro. These are some of the best beaches I have ever seen anywhere in the Caribbean, with sand piled in hills as high as 100 feet above the water in some places. The sand is thrown there by great northerly ground swells. In long periods of calm weather, it might be possible to anchor off the beaches for a few hours, but I definitely do not advise an overnight stop, as there is always a trade-wind swell sweeping around Cabo Negro. It's probably best to visit these beaches by car or foot.

The Adjacent Islands

LOS FRAILES

These are a group of steep-to islands 7 miles east of the northeast tip of Isla Margarita. I have never visited them, but one yachtsman reported that there

are a number of good anchorages in the lee of the islands—strictly a case of visiting when it is not blowing too hard and eyeballing your way in.

ISLA COCHE

(Chart V-30; II D-1, D-12)

This island is seldom visited, but people who have done so say it is well worth the stop. First, and most important, the buoy north of Isla Coche is about a mile west of where the DMA and BA charts show it. Proceed with extreme caution. I strongly advise that you use the Imray-Iolaire chart.

The approaches to Isla Coche are not particularly easy. When arriving from the north or west, note that the shoals off Punta La Playa, on the northwest corner near the big black sea buoy, appear to have extended much farther to the northwest. West of Isla Coche, the shoal off San Pedro extends farther out than the chart shows. The sand bank is reported to have extended westward the better part of 2 miles, with 15 feet reported on the outer edge of the shoal. People were standing neck-deep while fishing a mile offshore!

In Doyle's guide, the ferry dock at San Pedro is drawn incorrectly; it actually extends square with the shore. Directly off the dock is deep water; I suspect it was dredged for the ferry. The town of San Pedro is said to be very interesting during carnival. I am told also that there is a restaurant here, Yajaira, that is so popular that people charter planes from Margarita to fly over for the day to swim and enjoy the excellent lunches and dinners. San Pedro's dirty streets and old-style adobe houses

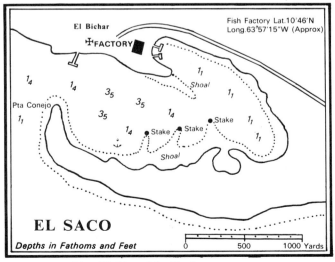

CHART V–30   El Saco, Isla Coche

with tilted roofs make it look like the setting for an old western movie about Mexico. Unfortunately, the town is developing and rapidly becoming modern, so this pleasant atmosphere is on the way out.

The head of the dock in San Pedro is the only place on Isla Coche where you can buy Polar in cans. This is important, because in the places where they sell Polar in bottles, you have to bring in a case of empties before you can buy a new case.

If you're approaching from the south, note that the shoals extend southeastward of Isla Coche for a full 2 miles. Since the bottom is shifting sand, it's possible they extend even farther than that. On the south coast of Isla Coche, take care, since I have grave doubts about the chart's accuracy. East of the main harbor are a number of small villages with no harbors whatsoever. The reef extending southward on the southeastern corner of the island is not easy to spot.

When entering the main harbor on the south coast, El Saco, give a wide berth to Punta Conejo on the starboard side, then feel your way in toward the town of El Bichar. The water will shoal around 9 feet, then stay at this depth, even close to shore. Do not go west of town, as the water shoals well offshore.

The shoal south of the sardine factory is alive with clams. The area around the harbor is low and flat, with nothing to obstruct the trades. It can blow like mad here, so it's a great place for Windsurfers, Hobie Cats, Sunfish, and the like—tons of wind and no sea. There's not much to see, but you can explore right around to the head of the harbor.

When leaving El Saco, stand southwest out of the harbor until you get into 4 or 5 fathoms, then swing northwest, but remember that the water around Isla Coche is shoal, and because the land is so featureless, it's very difficult to take bearings. So it's easy to run aground.

Probably the best course when approaching from the east is to pass El Morro de Chacopata and head from there to Isla Los Lobos. Once you have passed Isla Los Lobos, continue westward until the western tip of Isla Coche bears 320° magnetic, then jibe over and steer 230° magnetic until you approach the southern end of Isla Coche. If you are continuing on to anchor west of the island, give the western point of the island a wide berth due to offlying shoals and rocks. Carry well north, with the fathometer going, and make sure you stay in no less than 3 fathoms of water, at least until your final approach to the harbor.

If coming from the east, stay in deep water west of the buoy before coming around to head into the anchorage at Isla Coche. Stand in on port tack, aiming for the only houses on the north stretch of beach. The best anchorage is due west of what was the old salt works' manager's house. Work your way as close inshore as possible and anchor. The bottom is hard sand, with excellent holding, and there is complete shelter from the sea with the wind sweeping across the low land to the east. Anchor with a Bahamian moor in case the wind dies out during the night and comes in light from the west, swinging you onshore.

You have in front of you about 3 miles of beautiful, deserted white-sand beach. The ruins of the salt works are worth a look. Isla Coche has one of the major salt pans of Venezuela, almost as large as those at Araya (chapter 5), which allegedly are the largest in the world. You can pick up rock salt for the asking. For a very good view of the area, climb the tower next to the manager's house. North of the house are a couple of small cottages that apparently are being prepared for rental.

This spot offers clear water, plenty of *chipi-chipi* in the sand for dinner, and marvelous shelling. Hank Strauss and Gordon Stout spent three great days here and enjoyed themselves thoroughly. *Iolaire* has visited this beach on numerous occasions and always enjoys it. Early in the morning, thousands of birds gather at the reef on the end of the beach.

In 1990, when we were enjoying this lovely anchorage, Alan Wilkinson, the cartographer from Imray who draws all the Imray-Iolaire charts, pointed out that what we thought was a green weed growing on the beach was sapphire glasswort—a spiky green succulent plant found growing along the sea in England. It is also found here in Isla Coche in the northwestern anchorage, which Alan has named Nine Palms Bay.

This vegetable grows wild and is very rich in iron. To prepare it, pick the youngest and greenest shoots, tie them in small bundles, and boil them for twenty to thirty minutes—or until soft to the touch. Drain and cover liberally with butter. Using your fingers for squeezing, suck the green flesh from the woody center. The glasswort can also be eaten raw, but it is very salty. Alan also reports that it is excellent when pickled in vinegar.

Along the hillsides to the south, you will see a long series of buildings looking somewhat like a fort. This was (I'm told) a project that never quite got off the ground. The buildings were designed to hold hundreds of wayward boys from the cities of Venezuela. They hoped to rehabilitate them on Isla

Coche. There is an airport here, with a shuttle and charter service to Margarita.

In years gone by, the waters around Isla Coche were famed for their pearls. It's a pity Columbus didn't stop here, as he might have found enough pearls to silence his opponents at the Spanish court. In the late 1960s, Dr. Camejo and his crew went diving and came up with enough pearls to make his wife a necklace, which later was appraised in New York at a substantial sum! You must, however, have a license to dive for pearls. But even if you don't come up with any, you can still eat the oysters, so all is not lost.

Isla Coche is also noted for its clams. Anyone sailing in the area should get a clam rake, or perhaps several in different sizes, since the clams vary from quite small to very large. Even without a clam rake, however, you can still get enough clams to make a good old American chowder just by digging with your hands in the right places.

CHACOPATA

This is a village on the north shore of the Peninsula de Araya, south of Isla Margarita. (Chapter 5 covers the south side of the Peninsula de Araya.) We anchored in 2 fathoms with the entrance to the palm grove bearing 087° magnetic and the light on Morro de Chacopata bearing 036° magnetic. There was a slight roll and the water was clean, but not clear.

The village is southwest of the anchorage, with a long pier connected to a sardine factory. Minimal supplies are available ashore. South of Chacopata is a huge lagoon that you can enter only by zigzagging through the shoals; there is no obvious bearing. Approximately 5 feet of draft can be taken into the entrance channel, where we discovered a very strong current—probably almost 3 knots—pouring into the lagoon. A fishing boat moored was beam-to the north side of the channel, as it drops off absolutely like a wall. The crew loaded the fish cargo directly into a refrigerator truck.

A quick survey in the mouth of the lagoon showed about 5 feet, but even though we did not sound the lagoon, it looks like a great place to establish a boardsailing school—plenty of wind and no sea.

ISLA LOS LOBOS

(II D-1, D-12)

These are two small islands with a reef between them and with one small house on each island.

There is a good anchorage off the islands in 2 fathoms, but there is no beach—just rock piles.

ISLA CARIBE

(II D-1, D-12)

This tiny island is just west of the mainland locale of El Morro de Chacopata. On the north side is a beautiful white-sand beach, which could be a lunchtime anchorage in periods of calm weather but definitely is not an overnight anchorage.

On the island's southwest corner is a fishing camp, as well as a nice white-sand beach. Unfortunately, this combination is not so attractive close up—in Venezuela this usually means that the beach is littered with trash and fish guts. However, the anchorage looks good, with a white-sand bottom and good holding. Don't go south of the island, however—there is a 3/4-fathom shoal half a mile to the south. (The whole area of El Morro de Chacopata is much more shoal than shown on the chart.)

ISLA CUBAGUA

(II D-1, D-12)

This island is mainly deserted, except for temporary fishing camps on the northeast and southeast corners of the island. Because of the valuable pearl fisheries in the area, Nueva Cádiz, one of the first towns in North America, was founded about 1522 on the eastern tip of Isla Cubagua. In 1551, however, a combination of earthquake and tidal wave inundated the area and most of the town settled beneath the sea. The sunken remains are often visited by divers, and many of the ruins of Nueva Cádiz are said to be above water and accessible from shore. (If you walk from the yacht anchorages over to the ruins, be sure to take along a few bottles of water, as the long walk across the salt flats in the tropical sun can dehydrate you very quickly.)

It must have been difficult for the Spanish and the other early settlers here, because the weather side of Isla Cubagua has no harbor, so the harbor would have had to be located on the leeward side. If the ships did anchor on this side, all goods would have had to be carried a mile across the sand spit. I wonder why there are no signs of old forts, docks, or warehouses in the northeast cove, which is the obvious anchorage.

The anchorages in Isla Cubagua are in the northeast and southwest corners of the island. In the northeast corner, around the northernmost point, is a light that may not be working (although Dr. Camejo claims that the lights in Margarita usually do work, as otherwise the ferries that run between Margarita and Puerto La Cruz would be running aground continuously).

The cove on the northeastern corner of the island provides two good anchorages. Pass west of the sunken ferry, anchor close inshore, and check your anchor very carefully—we have been told that the bottom is very fouled with brush that has been dumped there. We have also been told that along the waterline of the sunken ferry, you can gather tons of big mussels—an excellent free dinner.

Sail southwest down the coast, eyeballing it in the clear water, and anchor in 2 to 3 fathoms half a mile south of the northernmost point of the fishing camp in Ensa de Charagato. There is excellent swimming and shelling in the area.

In March 1987, most of the sand spit extending from the southwest corner of the island was under about a foot of water. The BA and US charts were probably wrong, and we have tried to correct this area on the Imray-Iolaire chart, but I would definitely avoid the southwest corner of Cubagua, as the shoals extend well offshore.

Off the southwestern tip of the island is an anchorage with a large fishing fleet—usually twenty to thirty boats are anchored in shoal water. But don't be deceived: These boats have a draft of only 3 or 4 feet, and they moor with their keels only inches from the bottom. Feel your way in, as the bottom shoals considerably farther off than the chart shows. The bottom is extremely hard sand, which feels like concrete when you run aground! We know! We did it in 1978. The anchor will have difficulty penetrating this hard sand; once in, it's almost impossible to break it out. Approach this anchorage from the northwest.

We found an excellent anchorage in the first break in the cliffs north of the southwest end of the island. It shoals gradually, but there is 6 feet of water within 60 yards of the beach. To obtain some shelter from the wind, anchor behind the cliff rather than in line with the valley.

Off the north coast of Cubagua there is mostly deep water, but close to shore on the western half of the north side of the island is a shallows that extends well offshore. Paul Adamthwaite reports a good anchorage on this shelf off a distinctive valley—if it is not blowing hard.

5

The Peninsula de Araya and the Golfo de Cariaco

II D-1, D-12

From Isla Cubagua, it is a beautiful broad reach to the Peninsula de Araya. Great care must be taken to pass outside the buoy marking the northwest point of the Peninsula de Araya, as there is shoal water immediately inside, and it is *extremely* shoal. On the approach to this area, the water shoals so rapidly that a fathometer is of little use. About the time it starts registering shoal water, you'll be aground. Once you have passed outboard of the buoy, stand southeastward along the coast and head for the town of Araya.

Araya

Araya is easy to spot because of its huge white mounds that look like great mountains of snow. In fact, they are piles of salt, evaporated from the salt pans east of town. These reputedly are the largest salt pans in the world.

South of the town is the ruin of the most magnificent fort I have ever seen, built in 1622. You might wonder why such a massive fort was built in this location until you remember that in the days before refrigeration, salt was a valuable commodity: It was the only means of preserving fish and meat. Wars were fought over the salt mines of Europe, and any place suitable for the collection of salt became valuable and worth fighting for.

However, the local guide told us that this fort in Araya was destroyed not in battle but by a tremendous earthquake in 1797. Another source reports that the fort was dismantled in 1765—although how

you dismantle a fort this size is beyond me. The salt pans, it seems, were abandoned, and most of the population moved away. Those who remained became fishermen and traded their catches in Cumaná for fresh fruit and vegetables. It would certainly be easier to be a fisherman here than to try to grow anything in this area's desertlike terrain.

Looking at the enormous cracks in the walls of the fort brings home the realization that Venezuela is in an earthquake zone. It makes one wonder about all the high-rise buildings going up in Caracas and along the coast.

You can anchor at Araya anywhere along the coast from south of the church to a few hundred yards south of the fort. The problem is that you must sail very close to shore, practically running aground before dropping anchor, as the bottom drops off very steeply. The wind can come in light from the west early in the morning, so a bow-and-stern anchor is recommended. The bottom is so steep-to that a Bahamian moor won't work—your stern is still likely to swing onshore. By all means use an anchor light in this anchorage, as small, fast fishing boats and ferries shuttle in and out of Araya, heading to and from Cumaná, at all hours of the day and night. Your anchorage is right smack on their track, so hang up a bright light.

The town of Araya is interesting, and it looks like something out of the Wild West. Although little or no English is spoken here, you can still have a very good time in the evening in one of the local bars, for the locals are very friendly and always seem to be out for a good time. There is a small restaurant right under the fort. The fort is well worth a tour, but salt pans are salt pans—if you've seen one, you've seen them all. If you haven't seen one, take a look. Then pick up your hook and head south for the Golfo de Cariaco.

South of this area are too many anchorages to mention in detail, and all are backed by steep cliffs 60 feet high. There are no roads, no habitation, nothing. This is the place to get away from it all. South of Punta La Caja, especially, there are numerous white-sand beaches with shelves extending seaward: great anchorages, complete privacy, good swimming—what more could you want?

The Golfo de Cariaco

This area is a relief for yachtsmen who have spent a few months or a few years in the Caribbean, where there is the ever-present Atlantic swell—except when under the lee of a high island. The Golfo de Cariaco, 32 miles long and 8 miles wide, never builds up more than a small chop—and a good boat can easily slog its way through it. This is also an area where you can do your own exploring, since there are no detailed charts (except for one of Laguna Grande del Obispo). Gordon Stout of *Shango* says that when cruising in this area, you just find a likely spot, shove your bow up on shore, throw the anchor on the beach, and put out a stern anchor. If you look at the chart, you'll see many places where you can do this.

In the gulf, the wind usually is sucked in from the Caribbean and tends to be slightly north of east. As you beat eastward and get to the middle of the gulf, the chop builds up. All you need to do is flop over onto starboard and tack into shore. Then tack back to port as you approach the coast. As a result, you end up short-tacking along the northern shore of the gulf going east, rail down in smooth water—almost perfect sailing conditions.

As is typical of this part of the Venezuelan coast, there is little or no wind in the early morning. It begins to pick up around 1000 or 1100 as the land heats up, and it's blowing a solid 25 knots until just before sunset.

As noted above, this is a great place for yachtsmen, who not only like to sail but also like to explore. The charts, while showing the coastal contours correctly, are dead wrong in regard to water depth. The Golfo de Cariaco chart shows 20 fathoms right up to the shore for vast areas, yet in many places we discovered 9 feet of water, not 120. We checked around and came to the conclusion that

where a big gully runs down to the shore, there often will be a flat underwater plain extending offshore. All the dirt and sand that has washed down the gully forms these shelves, which provide good anchoring.

WEST OF LAGUNA CHICA
(Chart V-31; II D-1, D-12)

Here we found three anchorages to recommend, although there undoubtedly are many more waiting to be discovered. At the first, Los Cañones, we had an excellent bow-and-stern anchorage in a cove with a small fishing village and a huge graveyard at the head of a lagoon—a rather desolate and undisturbed spot. We walked south over the hill onto the road and found another anchorage, which, for lack of another name, we christened Wreck Bay. There, anchored bow-on to the beach, were some old local trawlers that apparently were being cut up for scrap.

The third cove, Puerto Réal, is a fishing village with numerous anchorages and a surprising amount of green growth around. It looks like an interesting stop for those whose Spanish is good enough to allow them to visit with the fishermen.

EAST OF LAGUNA CHICA

Along here are a number of small fishing villages, with 2- or 3-fathom shelves off the beaches. They are not too well sheltered during the day, but once sunset comes, the wind dies out. Again, use a bow-and-stern mooring.

LAGUNA CHICA
(Chart V-32; II D-1, D-12)

The US chart is completely wrong for this anchorage. We came sailing in on starboard tack about 50 yards off the western point and suddenly realized that the water was shoaling rapidly: It went from 10 to 1 1/2 fathoms, although the chart indicated no changes. We tacked and found 10 fathoms again on the other side of the harbor. Although we did not completely explore Laguna Chica, we did discover that the eastern side of the lagoon has the deepest water. There appears to be a ship repair operation at the head of the lagoon. On the southern side of the southeastern part of the harbor was

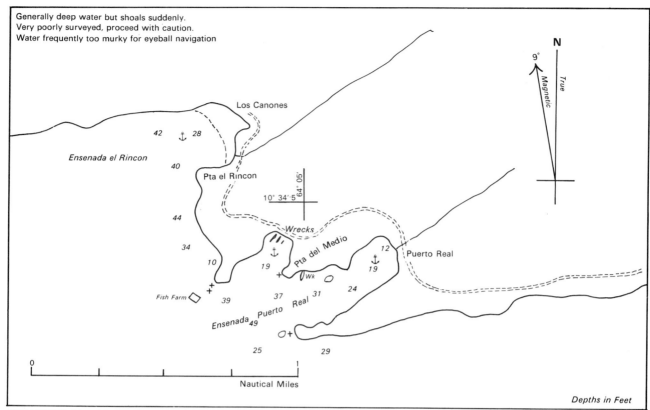

Generally deep water but shoals suddenly.
Very poorly surveyed, proceed with caution.
Water frequently too murky for eyeball navigation

CHART V–31   Ensa El Rincon and Puerto Réal

a small white-sand beach among the mangroves. Feel your way in, throw out a stern anchor, then jump ashore with a bow line and tie it to a mangrove. You'll be in your own private little world.

As you sail out of the harbor, you'll notice a house built on a small island. Its owner has no neighbors to bother him and he is king of all he surveys.

LAGUNA GRANDE DEL OBISPO

(Chart V-33; II D-1, D-12)

This is the subject of a detailed HO chart (now discontinued), although why the crew of the USS *Hannibal* took themselves up to Laguna Grande del Obispo is beyond me. Perhaps they flew over it first and the yachtsmen in the crew decided to go ashore and have some fun. Anyway, as you can see from the sketch chart, there is deep water right up to shore practically everywhere. *Iolaire* sailed into this lagoon in 1970, and we spent the better part of an hour having a wonderful time exploring, after which we anchored in the easternmost arm of the lagoon. We went ashore with the dinghy and found a small stream coming in from an almost dried-up salt

pond. After pulling the dinghy through the stream into the pond, we wandered around and found strange rocks and trees, goats running on the hillside, and an absolute desert. Half our crew thought it was fascinating; the other half wanted to get out fast, saying it seemed like another world and it gave them "the creeps." I'd have been quite happy to spend a few days there.

When entering Laguna Grande del Obispo, favor the starboard side of the channel, as there is a 1 1/2-fathom spot on the western side—undoubtedly a very hard pinnacle rock. Only maneuver in Laguna Grande del Obispo in good light, remembering that the chart was made somewhere back around 1939-40 and earthquakes have since hit the area. Note, for example, that on the northernmost arm of the harbor—the arm facing the entrance where the chart shows palm trees and sand—there is now a single palm tree, no sand, and a fisherman's shack. Also, about 100 feet off the southeastern corner of the island, on the northern side of the eastern arm, there is a 3-foot rock.

For a few miles along the north shore of the Golfo de Cariaco, between Laguna Grande del Obispo and Punta Guacaparo, there are numerous small anchorages indicated by the gullies between

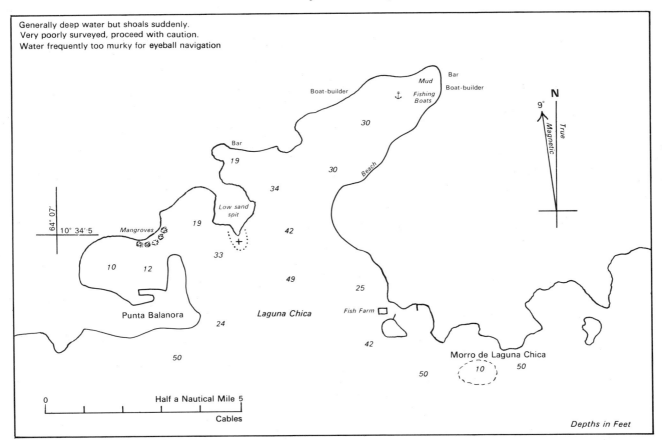

CHART V–32   Laguna Chica

the hills on shore and the bunches of green bushes on the flat plain. It's just a case of pushing your nose in, finding bottom, and anchoring bow and stern. Some of these anchorages had one or two fishing shacks, while others were completely deserted.

East of Punta Guacaparo, there is a small village. Gordon Stout found ice, beer, and a little food there—but he speaks excellent Spanish. We found a good anchorage just west of the point, close to the beach in 1 1/2 fathoms with a mud bottom. Then we had a good evening's entertainment watching the pelicans fishing while we had our sundowners.

We sailed a few miles east of the point before turning around, as the water was shoaling. My old 1832 *Sailing Directions* (written by Norie and Wilson—the great-great-grandfather of the present head of Imray) speaks of flammable gas and hot springs on shore—all of which warrants some dinghy exploring by the adventurous.

We did not have time to explore the south side of the Golfo de Cariaco. It is sparsely inhabited, and I doubt that the anchorages would be good: The hard northeast wind that sweeps the gulf would make its south coast a bad lee shore. We hope to receive reports from yachtsmen who have explored this area.

In general, you can usually count on finding anchorages wherever you see fishing camps, or where you find flat beaches spilling out from gullies and ravines.

The great thing about the Golfo de Cariaco is that it offers a smooth sea, almost no current, and an absolute absence of rain. The areas both north and south are complete deserts. This presents a new cruising ground for those who want to get away from it all.

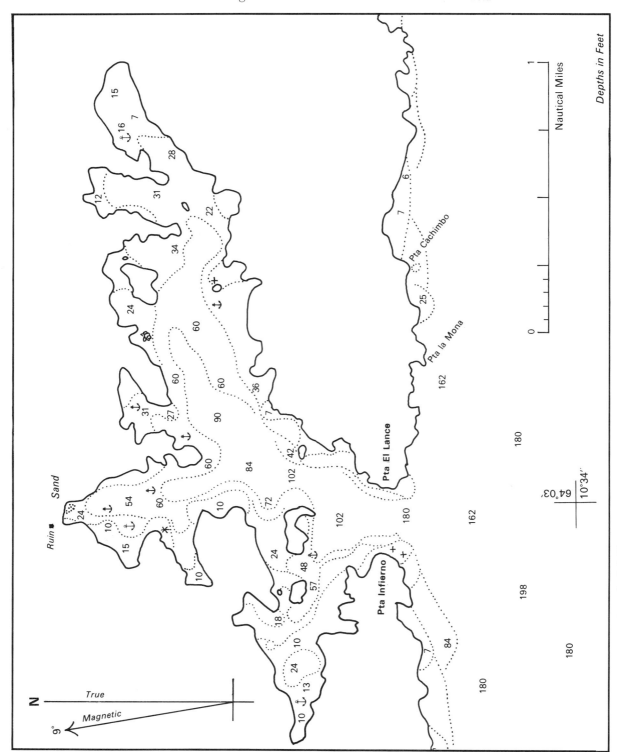

CHART V–33   Laguna Grande del Obispo

6

Cumaná to El Morro de Barcelona

II D-1, D-12, D-13, D-131

CUMANA

(Chart V-34; II D-1, D-12, D-13)

Warning: Cumaná is a rough, tough seaman's town. Females should not wander around alone, nor should they wear jewelry, especially necklaces, as even in broad daylight, Cumaná has some bold and fleet-footed snatch-and-run boys. At night, travel only via taxi; do not walk.

We found this city—located on the mainland at the entrance to the Golfo de Cariaco—to be rather attractive. The main part of town is on both sides of a river a few miles inland. There you'll find a well-shaded park, a good supermarket, a bakery, banks, shops, and an excellent market. There is also a good old-fashioned shoemaker who turns out handmade shoes. The one thing we could not find was an oven-ready chicken. All those we saw were purchased alive and squawking—so if you want a chicken dinner, you'll have to do the killing and plucking.

Why Cumaná was established where it is beggars the imagination, since the harbor is not very good. The city would seem to have been much better situated, and certainly more easily defended, had it been built farther west at Puerto Mochima, universally described in all the old guides as the finest harbor in North America. However, there are many towns in these parts built by the Spanish in incomprehensible places.

Although originally founded in 1521, the town has no really old buildings, as it is smack in the middle of the earthquake belt and it has suffered considerably. The worst earthquake was in 1766, when the entire town was flattened in a matter of minutes and the heavy tremors continued for the next fourteen months. The city was then rebuilt, but in December 1797, more than 80 percent of it was again destroyed—and again rebuilt.

Overlooking the town, the Castillo (fort) de San Antonio is well preserved and worth a visit, as it commands an excellent view of the entire area.

References to Cumaná can be a little confusing. Cumaná is the old city a mile and a half up the Río Manzanares, or one mile back eastward from the main pier. The port itself is referred to as Puerto Sucre. (This is where Customs is found, on the end of Avenida Bermúdez on the main pier.) Supposedly, in the rainy season, you can take a dinghy all the way up the river to Cumaná itself, and a century ago, there was a Customs port even farther up the river.

When approaching Puerto Sucre from the Golfo de Cariaco, stay well clear of the shoals that extend half a mile to the north of the coast. Approaching from the northwest, there are no dangers at all, but when beating to windward from the west, take care to avoid the two dangerous shoals due west of El Morro Colorado ("red cliff"), which may or may not be there when you arrive. In March 1979, they were being torn down rapidly, evidently to be used as building material or fill. If you keep northwest of a bearing of 068° magnetic between the Citadel (Castillo de San Antonio) and the twin spires of the cathedral (see Chart V-34), you'll be in deep water.

Entering Cumaná at night (something that

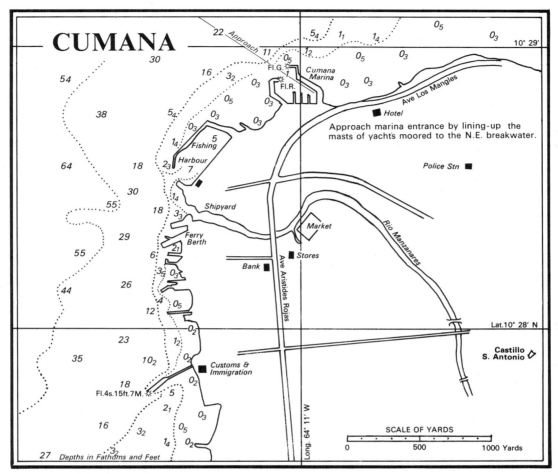

CUMANA

Approach marina entrance by lining-up the masts of yachts moored to the N.E. breakwater.

CHART V–34   Cumaná

should be avoided if at all possible), the best landmark for the anchorage off the commercial dock is a big, well-lit, white sign on a tower, reading "Segunda Segura" (*segura* means "insurance"). It bears about 080° magnetic from the anchorage on the north side of the dock. There are so many lights in the background (often from big shrimpers and tuna clippers based in Cumaná) that it is extremely difficult to see what is going on.

When approaching Cumaná yacht harbor from the north, steer 120° magnetic after you round Punta Arenas. You will spot a big, white, five-story apartment building to the left of the Citadel; aim between those two landmarks and you'll lay the marina.

The entrance to the marina was dredged to 9 feet in the summer of 1988. The axis of the channel is 320°-120° magnetic. You must stay right in the channel or you will go aground. A good range for the channel is to line up the masts of the boats that are on the northeast dock in the marina—boats facing northeast-southwest. If the masts are in line, you are in the channel; if they are not, you are not. This channel will shoal and move as time goes by, but there was still 9 feet on this range in January 1990. If you draw more than 6 feet, I recommend sending the dinghy ahead and sounding before entering. Remember that tidal springs pick up about a foot and a half of water. High water full and change (HWF&C) in Cumaná is 4 hours 40 minutes. (See *Street's Transatlantic Crossing Guide* for an explanation of HWF&C.) Also remember that the Caribbean can be 12 to 18 inches lower in June, July, and August than it is in the winter!

Avoid berthing on the west side of the harbor: In the late afternoon, when the wind picks up, such a chop builds up that you can even get seasick when tied to the dock. Plus all the oil and gas spilled from the fueling pier blows off to the west side of the harbor!

The marina is expanding, and fuel, water, electricity, and ice are available. There is also a small short-order restaurant, plus a store that carries basic supplies and a boutique. Now, if the marina would just organize a simple clearance procedure in Cumaná, as Carlos does at Zip Express in Puerto La Cruz, and Shore Base does in Margarita, then Cumaná would become a much more popular stop.

Cumaná Marina is run by Gaston, who is extremely pleasant and helpful and speaks some English (which is improving every year). Bolívar, the Mr. Fix-It for the marina, speaks no English but he has a good truck and must be very good with sign language, as he is a wonderful expediter who manages to find almost anything you need. He has contacts with machinists, welders, etc.—the works.

Reportedly, security at the marina is superb. Everyone to whom I talked felt that the Cumaná Marina was one of the best places in Venezuela to leave a boat while exploring the interior—or even while going back to the United States or Europe. The owners of one boat even left their dog on board, and they reported that when they returned, the dog had been washed and spruced up. The only problem was that he had been overfed, and they then had to put him on a diet. Not to mention the fact that the dog seemed to prefer the boatboy they had hired.

At the marina, you are a long, hot walk from town, but either a *por puesto* or a taxi (which is cheap) will get you downtown very rapidly. For shopping, only go as far as the CADA supermarket, which is at the corner of Avenida Bermúdez and Calle Aris des Rojas (due east of the main commercial dock), and grab a taxi to take food back to the boat. Via dinghy you can go up the Río Manzanares as far as the market. Or take a bus or a *por puesto* from the main road and ride into town, getting off at the main square.

Regarding the other things the yachtsman is likely to be looking for—travel agent, photocopying, banks, restaurants, etc.—these are found on Avenida Bermúdez, south of the CADA supermarket. Banking hours in Venezuela are generally 0800 to 1100 and 1500 to 1700.

The Hotel Minerva, near the marina, offers the best method for making overseas phone calls. Rooms are inexpensive, and I highly recommend that you go to the hotel for a few days to get a break from the boat. The hotel is excellent, although the restaurant without a doubt has the slowest service in the world.

There are some marine supplies available at Nauti Hagar con Marino, Avenida Perimetral Cruz, Edificio Don Adolfo.

A walk through the main plaza and the buildings around it and a visit to the cathedral are all well worthwhile.

South of the Cumaná Marina is a commercial trawler harbor with 20 feet of water in the basin. There are shipyards and an ice plant extending south to the main pier.

Cumaná is the home of a number of shipyards. The best known, and the one with the best reputation, is Varadero Caribe, C.A., founded by the late Peter Plaut and his sons John, Mark, and Mike. They are of German ancestry and arrived in Venezuela via Bolivia, Peru, and the United States. The late Mr. Plaut and his sons are all graduates of the University of Illinois, so they speak with midwestern American accents. Varadero Caribe does excellent work on yachts. They have a superb hauling and transfer system and are building up quite a reputation as rebuilders and repairers of wooden boats. They rebuilt what they claim is the oldest Baltic trader in existence (more than 100 years old) by installing a new stem and 7,000 new fastenings. (They made the fastenings themselves and had them galvanized in Caracas.)

More and more yachts are going to Varadero Caribe, but some have had difficulty obtaining hauling dates, so the rumor has gone out that the Plauts do not want the yacht business. Nothing could be further from the truth, but the Plauts point out that the yard is partially financed by the Venezuelan government, so the Venezuelan fishermen must have preference. Therefore they don't want to have more than 25 percent of their business catering to yachts. As a result, there is likely to be a three-month waiting list. Do not go to Varadero Caribe expecting instant hauling. Contact them via letter or phone and book your hauling date well ahead of time. The address is: Plaut family, Varadero Caribe, C.A., Avenida Principal El Dique, Apartado Postal 105, Cumaná, Venezuela. Tel.: 093-662564. They are presently negotiating for a site to build a marina and yacht yard in the Golfo de Cariaco.

Farther south from the trawler harbor, you will find Oriente, a facility that has a 150-foot-long graving dock and a 100-ton travel lift. A new graving dock (300 feet plus) was under construction in March 1987. The major problem with using Oriente seems to be that neither the manager nor the staff speaks a word of English. Canado, strictly a commercial operation, has two dry docks, one 45 feet long and the other 370 feet long. This, however, is not a yacht yard.

If you don't want to go to the marina in Cumaná, anchoring off can be a problem. The only possible spot is off the main commercial pier. The best anchorage is off the north side of the pier, but ashore is a private club for the Guardia Nacional. For some reason best known to themselves, the members of the Guardia Nacional do not like yachts anchored off their private club, and they insist you anchor south of the main pier. Do this with caution, however, as there are two wrecks and a couple of old ship anchors standing on end. Don't go swimming, as the main sewer outfall for Cumaná is to the east of the anchorage. As long as the wind is from the east, all is well, but if the wind comes in from the west, the smell is rather horrendous!

In the building on the south side of the main commercial pier, you will find Customs and Immigration. The Port Captain is at the trawler terminal. The Guardia Nacional seems uninterested in yachts.

Southwest of Cumaná and Puerto Sucre stretch mile after mile of wonderful sand beaches. They are great for early-morning stops, but don't spend the afternoon there, as the wind will be blowing hard out of the northeast, making the anchorages extremely uncomfortable.

PUERTO ESCONDIDO

(II D-1, D-12, D-13)

East of Puerto Escondido is a small indentation in the cliffs with a beautiful white-sand beach open to the north. This cove appears to be a fair harbor as long as the ground swell isn't running and your boat draws 7 feet or less—strictly a case of feeling your way in. Definitely favor the port side going in, as there appears to be a reef at the westernmost point, then round up behind the reef, where you should find shelter. This should be a nifty lunch stop, but I don't recommend it as an overnight anchorage.

PUERTO MOCHIMA

(Chart V-35; II D-1, D-13, D-131)

This is one of the most fantastic harbors in the area. To quote from the 1867 *Guide to the West Indies*, "take care to pass a cable and a half's length from every visible obstruction and all dangers will be avoided." (In the Royal Navy, a cable's length is 608 feet; of course, they were speaking of large ships.) It goes on: "To these advantages may be added that of free ingress and egress with the tradewind, altogether making it the best harbor in all this part of America, and indeed, one of the best in the world." As I said before, you have to wonder why the Spanish settled on Cumaná, with its poor

and hard-to-defend harbor, as the place for a major settlement when Mochima was so close by.

For the yachtsman, Puerto Mochima is absolutely fantastic, extending 4 miles inland with anchorages and coves too numerous to mention. The area is so completely sheltered that you quite literally can anchor anywhere. Many yachtsmen come back from Venezuela stating that Puerto Mochima was the high point of their cruise. It can remain so in the future only if yachtsmen behave themselves. I say this because the whole area is a national park that has been developing very rapidly. In 1987-88, you were likely to meet twenty or thirty yachts there, whereas a few years earlier, you would seldom see more than one or two. Now, however, you again see just a few yachts at a time because you are allowed to stay only twenty-four hours in the national park. (Perhaps the rules will be altered in the near future to allow stays of forty-eight or seventy-two hours.) The strict rule has been enforced because visiting "yachtsmen"—the type I refer to as "water people"—had come in to Mochima and camped out for months at a time. It was even discovered that some of the boats had been there for more than a year! This upset park officials so much that they came down with both feet and chased out everyone. Although they are very strict about the twenty-four-hour limit in Mochima, I suspect that if you are anchored in the outer harbors and don't stay for more than a few days, no one is likely to bother you.

Spearfishing, by the way, is prohibited in the park area, as is gathering oysters from the mangroves.

In the outermost harbor, on the starboard side, at Guagua, the Parks Department has set up a very attractive beach resort with a nicely maintained thatch-roofed restaurant, thatch-type beach umbrellas, and a beautiful white-sand beach that is raked and has trash barrels. A very nice operation.

If approaching from offshore, you may have difficulty locating the exact entrance, but a course that keeps the radio towers at Cerro Escondido bearing 127° magnetic will take you to the right place. Do not sail in and round the eastern projecting arm at Guagua. Here there is a protected anchorage at 2 1/2 fathoms, but a fisherman is likely to come out and tell you (with great justification) that anchoring is prohibited, because when fish come in the cove, the fishermen shoot their nets across the mouth of the cove to catch the school, and obviously they can't do it if a yacht is anchored there. South of the cove is a beautiful white-sand beach that could be a good anchorage in certain conditions, but remem-

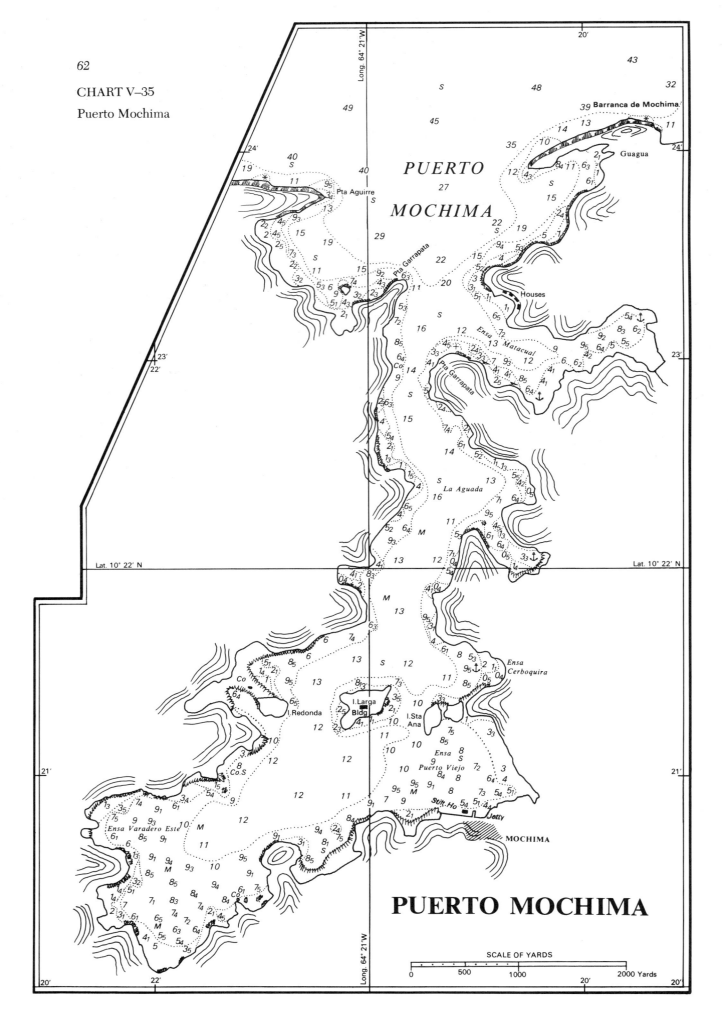

CHART V–35

Puerto Mochima

PUERTO

MOCHIMA

Barranca de Mochima

Guagua

Pta Aguirre

Pta Garrapata

Houses

Ensa Matacual

Pta Garrapata

La Aguada

Lat. 10° 22' N

Long. 64° 21'W

Ensa Cerboquira

Co

I. Redonda

I. Larga
Bldg

I.Sta Ana

*Ensa
Puerto Viejo*

Co.S

Ensa Varadero Este

Sit. Ho

Jetty

MOCHIMA

PUERTO MOCHIMA

SCALE OF YARDS

0   500   1000   2000 Yards

ber that this white-sand beach means that a ground swell comes in. Since the wind dies out at night, you would be well advised to put out a Bahamian moor, or anchor bow and stern. (You should follow this procedure along the entire Venezuelan coast.)

Maneuver in Puerto Mochima only in good light, for although we have tried to make the charts as accurate as possible, the bottom does come up to the top very suddenly and can catch the unwary with sudden vengeance. The deep indented harbor one bay north of Isla Larga is said to have excellent phosphorescence at night.

You can spend a few pleasant hours sailing in Puerto Mochima, scouting the coves, exploring the semiexposed wrecks along the edges, seeing birds nesting in the mangroves that have grown in the heads of the coves. You can also sail to the small village of Mochima, in the southeastern corner, where there are three restaurants. All are good, but at Nellie and Edgar's, the proprietors speak English.

There are no buses in Mochima, but if you walk or hitch a ride up to the main road, you can flag down a passing car for a ride into Cumaná. Taxis are also available for a reasonable price.

Water is available from a hose pipe on the dock.

The fouling conditions in Puerto Mochima are said to be extreme—you will have barnacles growing on your anchor line within a week.

There are so many anchorages in Mochima that it is impossible to enumerate them. Just sail around and find something that appeals to you and anchor—preferably not next to someone who also is looking for a solitary anchorage.

Years ago there was a canal in the western extremity of Puerto Mochima that saved small boats the 8-mile passage around the Peninsula de Manare. With tourism and yachting on the rise in Venezuela, let's hope the government will be persuaded to reopen this canal. Even if it were dug out only to dinghy depth, it would be most useful.

Many people insist that there could never have been a canal between Mochima and the Golfo de Santa Fé: At the present time, the low sand spit is not a spit but rather solid rock about 30 feet high. However, the reference to the canal dates from an 1867 guide, *Sailing Directions for the Western Hemisphere*, printed by Norie and Wilson (the people who later combined to become Imray, Laurie, Norie & Wilson, who with this author produce the Imray-Iolaire charts). There have been numerous earthquakes in the region, and obviously a volcanic upheaval changed the topography so that the canal no longer exists. I let the geologists argue the point. I'm a sailor and historian.

Mochima has been known for many years as a natural oyster bed, but recently the waters have become polluted and there have been some reported cases of *disentería*—a serious illness that causes rapid dehydration, among other symptoms. Now, however, the area is part of the national park, where it is illegal to take oysters.

BAHIA MANARE

(II D-1, D-13, D-131)

Immediately west of Puerto Mochima is an excellent anchorage tucked up in the east corner, with good holding in a white-sand bottom. The spectacular red cliffs silhouetted against the setting sun make an excellent backdrop for a sundowner—but not in periods of ground swell. The southern cove in Bahía Manare has some nice secluded beaches, but they do not offer good anchorages, as they are too steep-to and exposed to the north.

As you progress westward, Isla Venados and Caracas del Oeste open up. Turning sharply around Punta Tigrillo, you can sail back to the southeast and find a good anchorage at the head of the bay, sheltered to the east by Punta La Cruz and to the west by Isla Venados. You should be sheltered here from most of the northerly swell. If the swell finds its way even into here, you can continue south to the southeasternmost portion of Ensenada Tigrillo.

ISLA VENADOS

(II D-1, D-13, D-131)

You may find an anchorage on the western side of this island, but I haven't visited it, and I have no reports from other yachtsmen.

CARACAS DEL ESTE

(II D-1, D-13, D-131)

The American chart shows a nonexistent finger of water extending 150 yards eastward. Either this was a figment of the surveyor's imagination or it once existed but was obliterated when one of the many Venezuelan earthquakes toppled a tall slab of rock into it.

On the northwest side of Caracas del Este are a number of white-sand beaches sheltered from the east, but these are open to the ground swell and to winds from the west, which can be relatively strong at times. A better, more sheltered anchorage is found to the south between Caracas del Este and

Caracas del Oeste, in a cove at the southwestern corner of Caracas del Este. Because Caracas del Oeste lies off the west, this spot has complete 360-degree shelter.

CARACAS DEL OESTE
(II D-1, D-13, D-131)

Warning: There is one particularly dangerous spot in this area—Bajo Caracas, a completely unmarked submerged rock that undoubtedly breaks in stormy weather, but not in calm water. It is a pinnacle rock and almost impossible to spot. Its location is 1 mile north of Caracas del Oeste.

On the north side of Caracas del Oeste is a beautiful white-sand beach in a cove, but I would regard this as a daytime stop only. It's better to pass south between Caracas del Oeste and Caracas del Este to a superb little cove—just an indentation in the coast of Caracas del Oeste—completely sheltered from winds in all directions. Caracas del Este breaks the sea and the worst of the wind from the east. It also gets protection from Caracas del Sur to the south (shown on the US chart as a separate island, although it is now joined to Caracas del Oeste by a low sand spit evidently built up in past storms).

On the westernmost extremity of Caracas del Oeste is an excellent cove (with a sandy bottom) open only to the south; thus, it is completely sheltered from the northerly ground swell. When anchored here, you can go ashore in the dinghy and take a short hike over the hill to a pretty white-sand beach that is completely deserted.

ENSENADA TIGRILLO
(II D-1, D-13, D-131)

This particularly attractive area is bounded on the north by Isla Venados and the three Caracas islands, on the south by the Peninsula de Punta Gorda, and on the east by the Peninsula de Manare. The bay has more anchorages than I can possibly name. Pick one and treat yourself to a sheltered spot—dry, with clear water, clean beaches, cool breezes, and calm sea. Ideal! Further, there are numerous anchorages to be found in Posa Companario and Boca de Lord. You could spend a week in this area visiting a different anchorage every day—or staying in one anchorage and exploring the others via dinghy!

GOLFO DE SANTA FE
(II D-1, D-13, D-131)

This area is famous for its phosphorescence. One couple who sailed with me was familiar with the phosphorescent bay in Puerto Rico and reported that the Golfo de Santa Fé is better.

The greatest problem in Golfo de Santa Fé is finding water shallow enough for anchoring. In most cases, the best solution is to head in, drop a stern anchor, and tie the bow to a tree. One area with normal anchoring room, however, is in the vicinity of the village of Santa Fé. The chart shows what apparently are two rivers, but Dr. Daniel Camejo has spoken of a palm-lined beach and a flowing river with deep pools of clear, fresh water suitable for bathing and washing clothes. When we were there in March of 1979, however, we couldn't spot the river from seaward, and even when walking along the beach, we found only some rather stagnant pools.

As noted on the chart, there is a shoal suitable for anchorage west of town, but the 3/4-fathom spot east of town appears to extend farther offshore than is indicated. The sides of the shoal are almost vertical, so it is unsuitable as an anchorage.

East of the easternmost mouth of the river marked on the chart, we found a good anchorage in 1 1/2 fathoms. Taking bearings on the southwesternmost point of the Peninsula de Punta Gorda, we came to the conclusion that the shoal water extends a good 500 yards farther out than the chart indicates.

Exploring the bay east of Río de Santa Fé in the dinghy, we found, in the southeastern corner, an attractive anchorage off a sand beach, with a fisherman's cottage and palm trees. Feel your way in with a lead line and avoid the rock that bares 1 foot and is not marked on the chart; it's about 200 yards north of the anchorage.

There are numerous fishing villages in the gulf, but be sure to buy your fish in the evening when the fishermen return, since they leave early in the morning for the fish market, taking everything they didn't sell the night before.

There are so many anchorages in the Golfo de Santa Fé that it is impossible to enumerate them. Just look at the chart, sail along the shore, find a place that looks good, and drop anchor.

Peter Bottome, who knows the area quite well, says his favorite anchorage is off the palm-tree-lined beach on the northeasternmost corner of the Golfo de Santa Fé—you are likely to have the place to yourself. The bottom drops off steeply and the wind sometimes comes in light from the west, so use either a Bahamian or a bow-and-stern moor. The river that runs into the cove is like all rivers into this gulf—pretty much mudholes in the winter and streams in the rainy season.

ISLAS DE ARAPO

(II D-1, D-13, D-131)

Islas de Arapo are two interesting islands worth a visit. Disregard the US chart, as there is shoal water between the islands, not the passage shown. However, along the south shore of both islands is a shelf that makes anchoring possible. Approach these islands only in good light, as eyeball navigation is the order of the day.

The architecture on the islands is varied—a mixture of fishermen's houses and the homes of wealthy vacationers and weekenders. On the islet between the Islas de Arapo is an extremely attractive A-frame house, painted bright yellow. On the eastern end of the western Arapo is a new house whose owner is obviously an enthusiastic horticulturalist, as the land is beautifully terraced and planted right down to the water's edge. There are stone spillways crisscrossing the hillside to a large cistern that enables the owner to irrigate his terraces on this otherwise very dry land.

Augie Hollen reports that there is excellent snorkeling and fishing in the area.

This area is now part of the national park. The laws are being enforced and vacation homes are being torn down right, left, and center. Many owners are fighting the eviction and razing orders, and who knows how it will all turn out.

PUNTA COLORADA

(II D-1, D-13, D-131)

Immediately south of this point is a small, attractive cove. While not deserted (there are two fishermen's cottages and a very attractive vacation home), it's seldom crowded.

Ensa Santa Cruz, the second cove south of Punta Colorada, has a coconut-tree-lined beach and white sand with good holding, and it is well recommended by Hank Strauss. There are many fishermen's cottages, and it is connected to the main road, making it easy to get into Puerto La Cruz or Barcelona. But the noise of trucks changing gears on the hairpin turns is not conducive to a restful night.

The next cove south of Ensa Santa Cruz provides another small beach and anchorage. The bottom drops off steeply, so run an anchor ashore in the dinghy and drop a stern anchor to hold you offshore.

South of Punta Colorada is the very popular Playa Colorado, with a good beach. Again, anchor bow and stern.

BAHIA DE CONOMA

(II D-1, D-13, D-131)

On the southern side of the bay is another beach lined with coconut trees. You should moor bow and stern, with a bow line to the palm trees and a stern anchor out. During the week, you'll have it to yourself; come the weekend, it's inundated by powerboats from the Barcelona and Puerto La Cruz areas.

BAHIA DE PERTIGALETE

(II D-1, D-13, D-131)

This is easily spotted by the column of smoke rising out of the Mendoza cement factory at Vencemos—the largest in Venezuela and possibly in the world. The whole eastern area is a private club, which we stumbled across many years ago. The members took us under their wing and practically killed us with hospitality. However, this does not make the anchorage a good one, as the area is completely open to the north and the swell finds its way in under all conditions. Besides, it is too deep to lie off the club—anchoring in 100 feet of water is not my idea of carefree cruising. The only anchorage is on the shoal off the western coast of the Islas de Plata. Here there is a small marina and beach bar that does a land-office business on weekends; during the week, when we were there, it was nearly deserted.

Also on Islas de Plata is a small shipyard well run by the Robinson family, who are English. There are no side-tracking facilities, but by hauling in line, they can get four boats up at a time. Draft is limited to about 8 feet, tonnage about 20. The only way to arrange a hauling date is to go there.

BAHIA GUANTA

(II D-1, D-13, D-131)

This is the main commercial port of the Puerto La Cruz-Barcelona area. Yachtsmen should avoid it, except for going in, taking a look, and marveling at how, without the aid of tugs, the large container ships are maneuvered in and out of this tiny harbor.

Peter York is building a new yacht marina on the western side of the entrance to the harbor (see Imray-Iolaire chart D-131 for details).

BAHIA BERGANTIN

(II D-1, D-13, D-131)

This is mainly an oil-loading port formerly operated by Sinclair Oil and now run by the Venezuelan company Llanoven. This bay has been a popular stop, as it had what used to be the only marina with facilities for yachts. Club Nautico El Chaure is a small, private club run by Llanoven in the northeast corner of the harbor. In the past, Otto Castillo, the Port Captain, and friends here have been most hospitable to yachtsmen. They have a dock, water, and fuel. Club members have always been most helpful, taking yachtsmen into town for ice, laundry, and baths. There are no public showers, but sometimes the small guesthouse/motel run by the club happens to have a room available that can be rented by the day, to give the crew a chance for showers.

We should thank Otto for his part in Llanoven's antipollution campaign in Venezuela. Ballast tanks must now be pumped into settling pounds, where the oil rises to the top and is skimmed off. Besides the obvious advantage of not having the oil pumped into the ocean, this system provides a profit for the company when the skimmed oil is reclaimed.

PUERTO LA CRUZ

(II D-1, D-13, D-131)

Warning: West of the main swimming beach in Puerto La Cruz, stay well offshore. There are a number of breakwaters, not on the chart, extending a quarter of a mile out to sea to protect storm drains. They are between the western end of the town beach and the ferry pier.

Puerto La Cruz is one of Venezuela's fastest growing cities, expanding so rapidly that it is joining Barcelona. It's a major oil terminal and the focal point of the entire area. In the past, it had absolutely nothing to offer yachtsmen, as there was only the open anchorage off the town. Now this is all changed. The area is becoming a major yachting center, with the El Morro development project and the expansion of what I refer to as the Meliá Marina, now called Paseo Colón Marina.

As many as thirty or forty boats usually are anchored off the beach at Puerto La Cruz. There is an open-air public shower on the beach. You cannot leave your dinghy at Paseo Colón Marina; you must leave it on the beach. The only hope of keeping your dinghy is to chain it to a tree with a padlock and lock your outboard in place, but even that does not always work, as the thieves now carry bolt-cutters. I'm told that thirty-five dinghies disappeared from the beach in 1988. I have also been told that some boats have been burglarized while at anchor. The best policy while at Puerto La Cruz is to stay at the marina.

Paseo Colón Marina (see Chart V-36) gives excellent shelter. There is 10 feet of water at the outer end of the basin, shoaling to 7 feet at the inner end of the dock. Depending on the state of the tide, 8 (possibly 9) feet can be carried to the fuel dock. The bottom is very soft mud, so if you are a little bit deeper draft than the berth to which you are assigned, just turn on the engine and power through the mud. Security is superb. Make sure you check in at the office and have the office identify you to the guards. Otherwise, you may discover you can't get back to your boat. The staff members are very nice and could not have been more helpful.

One of the nicest things about staying at Paseo Colón Marina is that it is just a short walk to the Meliá Hotel, where you can make phone calls twenty-four hours a day. Although the rates are high, it is a great improvement over wasting hours in the telephone exchange! If you are staying in the marina, apparently you are also allowed to use the pool at the hotel.

At Puerto La Cruz, the clearance procedures were rather difficult, and they still are if you decide to do them yourself. You have to take a taxi, bus, or *por puesto* all the way east from Puerto La Cruz to Guanta, the main commercial harbor, to clear Customs and the Guardia Nacional, then go back to town to Immigration. At the junction of Avenida 5 de Julio and Calle Juncal, you will find Immigration on the third floor of the building with green tiles on the roof, next to the drugstore. Sometimes the Immigration officers will be sitting in the courtyard behind the gates, which must be opened for you before you can go upstairs. Once cleared with Immigration, you head west to the Port Captain's office, in a building at the head of the main Margarita Ferry Terminal.

Alternatively, call Zip Express, Carlos Diaz, on channel 77. For 500 Bs. (January 1990), he will take care of everything for you. If you can't raise him on the radiophone, go directly to his office on the

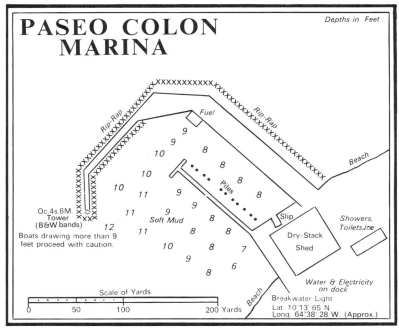

CHART V–36   Paseo Colón Marina, Puerto La Cruz

southwest side of Avenida 5 de Julio, 50 yards east of Calle Flores.

The town is loaded with good hardware (*ferretería*) stores, electrical shops, and paint stores. Plus there is a new marine supply store, MSY (usually on channel 77), located on Calle Guaraguao, between Calle Flores and Calle Carabobo—easy walking distance from Paseo Colón Marina. The owner speaks perfect English and is rapidly expanding his stock (including Imray-Iolaire charts and Street's guides). He is also a radio and electronics specialist.

If you have a lot of shopping and errands to do, or don't speak Spanish, or want to expedite matters, the man to contact is José, a wonderful Trinidadian who speaks fluent English, has a truck, and knows the area well. You can either send him to run your errands or accompany him while he answers all your questions and shows you the ropes. He will even encourage you with your Spanish and give you the phrases you "can't get along without"! He drives a white pickup truck and usually can be found around the Paseo Colón Marina.

Within walking distance of the marina is a good butcher: Walk south on Calle Carabobo for two blocks, then turn left on Calle Guaraguao. It is in the middle of the block on your left, almost next to MSY. An excellent laundromat can be found at the western side of the cathedral, and there is another laundromat within walking distance of the marina on Calle Lobo, on the street that intersects Paseo

Colón (the waterfront street right at the marina). Walk several blocks past Avenida 5 de Julio and look for the machines in the little alley to your right. A good CADA supermarket is also within walking distance. In the old part of town, near a wholesale liquor store, we saw a sign for block ice (*hielo panela*); otherwise, you can obtain block ice from an ice house just west of the harbormaster's office on the waterfront road. Or, if you have rented a car or taxi, or have hired José, drive out to Vistamar, where, on the north side of the road, there is an ice plant, plus a gas bottling plant that fills your bottles instantly and at an incredibly low price.

The open-air local market is beyond walking distance; take a cab, but be there by 0800!! It opens and closes early.

With the expansion of the marine supply store at the Américo Vespucio Marina, and the marine hardware store at the new Centro Marina de Oriente (see below), the marine supply situation in Puerto La Cruz undoubtedly is the best in all of Venezuela. In time, it should rival that of the popular harbors in the Eastern Caribbean.

It should also be noted that Puerto La Cruz has an excellent little carnival just prior to Lent.

EL MORRO DEVELOPMENT PROJECT

West of Puerto La Cruz lies a large, flat plain that formerly was a series of vast salt pans like those still in use on the Peninsula de Araya. Here, however, they have been filled in and dredged for the massive El Morro project.

It all started with the spit of land connecting El Morro de Barcelona to the mainland, midway between Puerto La Cruz and Barcelona. Over the years, small vacation houses were built along the beach at La Lechería. Then, in the late 1960s and early 1970s, Dr. Daniel Camejo secured title to the abandoned salt flats east of La Lechería, as well as title to El Morro itself. He then proceeded to dredge and fill to create a development of hundreds of building plots and 13 miles of waterways dredged to 8 feet. In the process, 15 million cubic yards of fill were removed from El Morro and other areas nearby. Eventually, the vacation complex will comprise 170 acres, 1,300 houseboat sites, 550 residential sites (each with front-door access to a waterway), and 20,000 hotel units.

Dr. Camejo is committed to preserving the ecology and avoiding pollution, whether it be noise, fumes, or sewage. As a result, the entire area has been provided with underground electric cables, and sewage lines are connected to a disposal plant. To avoid noise and gas pollution, large areas of the complex were supposed to be off-limits to internal-combustion engines, with only electric cars and bicycles allowed, but that did not come to pass.

To provide variety and color, the complex's hotels are given over to different themes: German, American, Tahitian, Scandinavian, and Italian villages provide samples of those regions' cuisines, costumes, architecture, and the like.

The ambitious project was proposed in 1970, when it was certainly the biggest development project in the Caribbean, if not the world. By 1979, $100 million had been spent, and although the development was behind schedule, all the building plots had been sold and buildings were going up.

Needless to say, with the collapse in the price of oil, the development has not taken off as fast as Dr. Camejo planned. However, when we were there in January 1990, despite the fact that vast areas still had not been built, work was progressing rapidly.

The expansion of yachting in Venezuela has been inhibited by the lack of harbors. In the Caracas area, the artificially created harbors have become so jammed that many Venezuelans have been reluctant to buy boats until they felt sure of getting a berth. This problem has been eliminated by the El Morro project, which provides spaces for literally thousands of boats.

Of particular interest to visiting yachtsmen are the two marinas built into the complex. The biggest is the large, commercial Américo Vespucio Marina at the eastern end of the complex, behind the long east-west breakwater. This facility has 18 feet of water at the entrance and an 18-foot-deep dredged basin. The smaller El Morro Marina, with 8 feet in the basin, has been developed to the west, south of El Morro peak.

AMERICO VESPUCIO MARINA

(Chart V-37; II D-1, D-13, D-131)

The entrance to this major commercial marina of the El Morro project is south of the western end of the breakwater. Deep-draft boats beware, as the channel has definitely shoaled. As of February 1988, there was a bar across the entrance to the harbor and 12 feet was the maximum draft that could be squeezed over the bar. Even then, the deepest water was found by hugging the port side of the entrance channel. Before turning south, swing to keep on the outside of the turn and then favor the port side of the channel. Vessels drawing more than 10 feet should not venture south of the main marina building and should not try to enter the inner marinas. This shoaling may change, but any boat drawing more than 8 feet should send a dinghy ahead to check the channel depths. Also, there is a small, unmarked rock with 7 feet of water over it near the entrance to the marina basin on the starboard side of the entrance channel.

Berthing can be inside the basin of the marina, where it tends to be hot and airless; the water, because of lack of circulation, is rather foul there. We felt it was better to lay along the wall stern-to the main entrance channel. You do suffer from the wash of passing powerboats, but it is still preferable to being inside the basin. An excellent painting contractor, Francisco Lopez (tel.: 69.24.20), does a fine job of painting and varnishing, and, most important, is willing to do it for a contract price. Plus he speaks perfect English.

There were a few problems as of January 1990 that we hope eventually will be cured, including a hopeless phone system with only two lines in the whole area. You might as well just forget about overseas phone calls. Showers were clean, but it was almost impossible to find the key!

On the western side of the marina is the administration building of the complex. Unfortunately, despite Dr. Camejo's best efforts, nothing has been done to shorten the paperwork routine. Do not use the shipping agent recommended by the marina

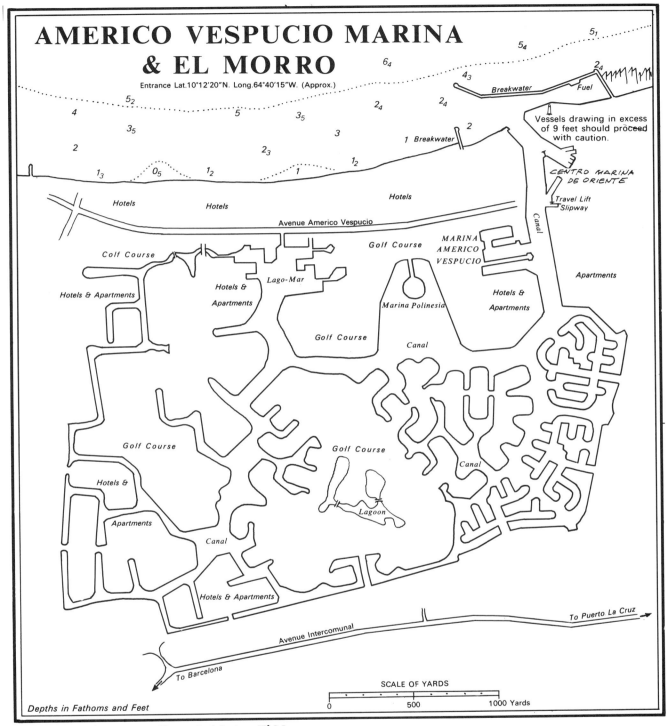

AMERICO VESPUCIO MARINA & EL MORRO

Entrance Lat.10°12'20"N. Long.64°40'15"W. (Approx.)

5_1

5_4

6_4

4_3 Breakwater Fuel 2_4

5_2 2_4 2_4

4 5 3_5 2 Vessels drawing in excess of 9 feet should proceed with caution.

3_5

3 1 Breakwater 2

2 2_3

CENTRO MARINA DE ORIENTE

1_3 0_5 1_2 1 1_2

Hotels Hotels Hotels

Travel Lift
Slipway

Avenue Americo Vespucio

Canal

Golf Course

MARINA AMERICO VESPUCIO

Colf Course

Hotels & Apartments

Lago-Mar

Hotels & Apartments

Marina Polinesia

Hotels & Apartments

Apartments

Golf Course

Canal

Golf Course

Canal

Golf Course

Golf Course

Canal

Hotels & Apartments

Lagoon

Apartments

Canal

Hotels & Apartments

To Puerto La Cruz

Avenue Intercomunal

To Barcelona

Depths in Fathoms and Feet

SCALE OF YARDS

0   500   1000 Yards

CHART V–37   Américo Vespucio Marina, El Morro

manager. The agent cost us 2500 Bs. in January 1990, after which we discovered Zip Express, channel 77, discussed above in the Puerto La Cruz section. He does it for 500 Bs.

At first glance, it appears that Américo Vespucio Marina is out in the middle of nowhere and it is impossible to get into town from there. This is not quite true, for there are a couple of different options. You can take the little ferry over to the eastern side of the harbor, walk a dusty 200 or so yards to the main road, then take a *por puesto* directly into town. Another possibility is to walk a couple of hundred yards out of the marina and pick up a *por puesto* or taxi outside of the Doral Beach Villas and head for Vistamar shopping center, where, among other things, you will find a fairly good supermarket, hardware stores, laundromat, etc.

A final option is to find Leslie—a Hungarian who arrived in Venezuela via Canada. Leslie speaks English, Spanish, and a couple of other languages and drives an old Chevrolet station wagon. You can find him by passing the word via the Américo Vespucio "telegraph" or by calling VHF channel 77, for "Clunker"—his van looks like one, but it runs, and he knows the area well. One of his specialties is running gear to Caracas to be hot-dip galvanized.

In the marina itself, there is a small, friendly, but slow short-order restaurant—as well as a good but expensive restaurant. You'll also find Horisub, C.A., a dive shop, which has a fairly good inventory and offers daily trips to various dive spots. You also can have your tanks filled and rent diving equipment. Arturo Barrios is a PADI-certified instructor and speaks English well, so if you have done your pool work, this is a great place to get your certification, as many of the dives are open and easy. Included in the price (which is very reasonable) are two dives a day, a good-size lunch (eaten at various beaches), and all the soft drinks you want. If you are particularly interested in learning about the local wildlife below, dive with Pablo Hernández, the divemaster, who seems to know what and where it all is (tel.: 8l.25.01).

The area where the marina presently is located, with the hauling facility, was sold at a very high price to a land developer in 1989. The local view is that to recoup his costs, he eventually will have to build condominiums on the site and do away with the hauling facility. But as of January 1990, everything was just as before, and the small marine hardware store (which stocks Imray-Iolaire charts and Street's guides) was figuring on tripling its size in the following few months. There was also a small grocery with ice available.

As of February 1990, the hauling facility, with its 30-ton travel lift, was still operating. Victor, head of the painting gang, speaks perfect English and can interpret. They haul only on Mondays, so figure out your hauling schedule in one-week segments. I certainly hope the yard will continue, as there is nothing better for yachtsmen than two boatyards on opposite sides of a channel competing for the same work! It keeps prices down and workmanship up.

On the east side of the entrance channel to the Américo Vespucio project, Peter Bottome and backers have built Centro Marina de Oriente, a major hauling facility (tel.: 081-69.28.19; FAX: 69.20.21). Besides running a newspaper and TV stations, Peter was instrumental in setting up the private airport south of Caracas, claimed to be the largest private airport in the world. He has not only a small commuter airline and an air charter fleet, but also a major aircraft repair and recertification facility. In addition, he restores planes—from a beautiful old DC-3 to a Catalina flying boat, to a wonderful old staggered-wing Beechcraft. Peter doesn't just fly; he has a roomful of medals for stunt piloting in a Pitt Special stunt biplane.

Because of the devaluation of the Venezuelan bolívar, it has become economically viable for Americans to fly their planes down to Peter's repair facility for major refits and recertification. Peter feels that if he can do this for aircraft, he can do the same for yachts. The hauling facility already has a 70-ton travel lift; a synchro-lift capable of hauling 240 tons is projected for 1992. It will have excellent side-tracking facilities. There is already a 400-foot-long shed where boats can be worked on in the water, while under cover, and plans include complete backup facilities—machine shop; electric, electronic, and woodworking shops; sailmaking and upholstery shops; restaurant; good showers; tight security. Peter also expects to have some rental apartments that can be reached by dinghy, so when boats are undergoing major repairs/refits, the crew can live on shore. Peter aims to catch some of the market presently dominated by yards such as Derecktor's, Merrill Stevens, Wayfarer, etc. By January 1990, the yard was already hauling boats, pilings were all in, and a prefab building was going up rapidly. By the time this book appears in print, this facility certainly will be worthwhile for yachtsmen to investigate for general hauling and painting plus major refits. It could be especially appropriate if you are planning to have work done during hurricane season, since Venezuela is beyond the hurricane belt. The yard also has a large dry-storage area, which is again no problem, since no hurricanes will come through and blow the boats out of the cradles! (This has been a major problem in the Caribbean islands.)

Peter very kindly loaned us a plane and a pilot so that we could spend time doing an aerial survey of Los Roques. During two hours in the air, we saw what would have taken a year of exploration by boat. We repeated this operation in 1989, so I feel I can truly state that our Los Roques chart is vastly superior to the DMA and BA charts of the area.

EL MORRO MARINA

(Chart V-38; II D-1, D-13, D-131)

Looking west from the breakwater in front of the Américo Vespucio Marina, you will see the 500-foot peak of El Morro de Barcelona. Tucked in under the peak is El Morro Marina, smaller than Américo Vespucio and mainly attuned to the needs of local yachtsmen. It is not connected to the main complex via the canals, so you must go out and around the peak. When approaching from the east, give the northern tip of El Morro a half-mile berth to avoid tide-rips off the point. Swing around behind El Morro and head southwest, clearing the offlying rocks that are awash at low tide. Continue west-southwest, coming slowly around to south and then to southeast as the depth of water permits. Use the lead, or keep a close eye on the depth sounder.

At El Morro Marina, the deepest water is along-side the west wall of the marina; the eastern wall has only 5 feet of water alongside. This is another full-service marina, but at the moment it caters more to powerboats than to sailboats. It has a restaurant, fuel, ice, and marine supplies, but, as in all new projects, the water supply was erratic.

El Morro is in the process of expansion. A new breakwater has been built to give more area and to try to eliminate the surge that at times has caused considerable damage to boats lying in the marina.

It is pretty much essential that you speak Spanish here. Everyone is extremely friendly and helpful, but no one on the staff speaks English. With the expansion of the marina, it may become a popular stop for yachtsmen, but its popularity is limited by the fact that there is no transportation from the marina. You must walk or take a taxi or dinghy to La Lechería, 2 miles away, where you can then pick up a *por puesto* to the shopping center at Vistamar, and there transfer to a *por puesto* to town or over to the Américo Vespucio Marina. If you need to purchase only a few odds and ends, you can row the dinghy to the beach and walk to the shops.

For serious shopping, the best place in this whole area is Puerto La Cruz.

One of the most worthwhile things to do is to borrow a car or hire a taxi just before sunset and ride to the old fort at the very top of El Morro. If it is clear, the chances of seeing the "green flash" increase rapidly with your height above water. The peak of El Morro provides the perfect setting: high, with a dead-clear vista to the western horizon.

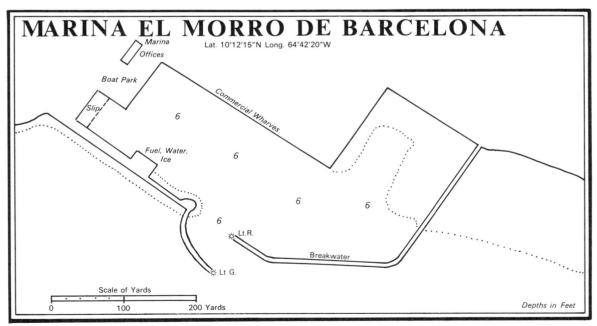

CHART V–38   Marina El Morro de Barcelona

Islands in the Puerto La Cruz— Barcelona Area

CHIMANA SEGUNDA

(II D-1, D-13, D-131)

Chimana Segunda is marked by a flashing light (10 seconds, visible at 10 miles), but as I have said many times before, don't count on seeing it at all. There is deep water all around the island, except northeast of Isla Picuda Chica, a small island off Chimana Segunda. Here, sunken rocks extend almost half a mile to the northeast. There is only one anchorage on Chimana Segunda, directly under the light on the south side of the island's western end. There are 2 fathoms of water here. Feel your way in and anchor with a Bahamian moor, as the wind undoubtedly will box the compass during the night.

CHIMANA DEL SUR

(II D-1, D-13, D-131)

This island is steep, dry, and barren, like the rest of the area. It has no real anchorages, as the bottom falls off almost vertically to about 70 or 80 feet. The only possibility is to sail on in, throw out a stern anchor, jump off the boat, and bury an anchor on the beach. There are few, if any, trees for securing a line. It seems hard to believe, but on this dry, completely barren piece of rock, there are a number of houses—probably owned by fishermen who don't like neighbors!

CHIMANA GRANDE

(II D-1, D-13, D-131)

Chimana Grande has so many anchorages that it makes up for the lack of them elsewhere in the group. The large cove at the southwestern end of the island is superb. Sail in and be careful of 180-degree wind shifts. Have a stern anchor ready and work your way up into the northeast corner. Anchor in about 2 fathoms with a Bahamian moor. Check your lines carefully, as the area is littered with coral heads. Although you may have 12 feet of water, some of the coral heads nearby will only have 5 or 6 feet of water over them.

Once you are squared away, you can enjoy watching the pelicans, as this is a nesting area. Oysters can be found in the mangroves and eaten raw or steamed lightly. Augie Hollen says that you can tell which ones are pearl oysters because their two sides form a right angle at the hinge area. Pedro Gluecksman says that pearl oysters are found completely submerged and growing on the sandy bottom, not on the mangrove stalks. He says they are even in shape, and at the opening end they have fingerlike terminals that close between each other like a praying hand. He adds that pearl oysters also can be found in the Margarita area. Good hunting! Warning: Never take oysters or spear fish until you have checked that you are outside of the national park area. And be sure to get the latest information, because the Venezuelan government is continually expanding the national park area.

Get in the dinghy and go to the head of the bay, where there is a mangrove tunnel connecting this cove to the next one east. But you'll have to sail the yacht out and around to this next cove, which has a mud bottom, 18 feet of water, and a very narrow entrance. Obviously, it's only suitable for one boat.

About a mile to the east, along the south coast, you'll find a very attractive cove with a deep valley at its head; this should funnel the wind straight into the cove, making it absolutely free of bugs. However, be forewarned: All the edges of the cove are lined with coral heads, so you'll have to anchor in the middle. Since the wind undoubtedly will whistle through all of these coves—which are too small to allow a boat to swing on one anchor—you'll have to use a Bahamian moor.

These anchorages on Chimana Grande are wonderful, as you are completely off by yourself and surrounded by birds, fish, excellent snorkeling, clear water, and a more or less deserted island to the north of you, while to the south, you can see the bright lights of Puerto La Cruz. Actually, if you have a fast dinghy, you could remain anchored in Chimana Grande and go back and forth to Puerto La Cruz, which is only 3 1/2 miles away.

The westernmost anchorage in Chimana Grande is excellent, sheltered 360 degrees in all conditions. The best anchorage is on the eastern side of the basin, between Chimana del Oeste and Chimana Grande, off the thatch-roofed building maintained by the Parks Department. The best approach to this anchorage is from the south, but be warned that in certain conditions, there is a very strong southgoing current between the westernmost tip of Chimana Grande and Punta Puinare on Chimana del Oeste. Within the anchorage, in periods of heavy weather (especially if the wind is in the north), a swell can come in the northern entrance to this basin. The shoal water and the island in the entrance break it down to a chop, so the anchorage may be a little rocky and rolly, but not unduly uncomfortable.

Enjoy this cove in the mornings and the evenings. About ten in the morning, day-trip boats come over from Américo Vespucio Marina, staying until about four in the afternoon. There is mass confusion during this period, but it is peaceful and quiet before they arrive and after they leave. Needless to say, on weekends the place is inundated with small powerboats that have made a quick run from the marina.

My diving secretary, Cheryl Tennant, reports that there is a wide range of excellent diving in the Chimana Grande area. For new or less aggressive divers, there are some very easy dives with lots of interesting plant and animal life. For more experienced divers, there are deep walls, tunnels, caves, and a wreck. Have fun!

CHIMANA DEL OESTE
(II D-1, D-13, D-131)

This island does not appear to have any anchorages.

ISLA LA BORRACHA
(II D-1, D-13, D-131)

Warning: There is a dangerous rock marked on the chart midway between Islas Los Borrachitos and Isla El Borracho. This pinnacle rock has 5 feet over it and rises abruptly out of 24 fathoms. I have tried to locate this rock three times but have not been able to do so, despite apparently clear water. It is so small in diameter that it is practically impossible to find, but I have seen an underwater photograph of this pinnacle rock, which looks for all the world like a needle standing on end. If you did run up on it, it would be a disaster. Thus, the prudent mariner will stay well clear of this area. Divers trying to find the rock should place the end of the southeastern edge of El Borracho in line with the southernmost tip of Isla Chimana del Oeste (Punta Puinare), bearing 077° magnetic. If you run along this line of bearing until the westernmost tip of El Borracho is brought to bear at 357° magnetic, you should then be exactly on top of the rock. If you find it, let me know.

Isla La Borracha (which means "drunken island" in Spanish) seems to be a most attractive island, with excellent anchorages. Punta Reina appears to extend much farther to the southeast than the US

chart shows. There is a fishing village on the point with a gray-sand beach, but be sure to use a Bahamian moor or bow-and-stern anchor in this area, since the wind frequently dies out and comes in from the west.

When anchoring for the night here, be very careful to use either a bow-and-stern or Bahamian moor, because when the wind dies out, a small swell comes into the harbor and can easily swing the boat around and put the stern up on the beach. Billy Wray of the ketch *Indalo* reports that this is an excellent overnight stop.

The entire southwest coast is one long, deserted beach extending roughly a mile and a half. Halfway down the beach, there is a dry stream bed with some stunted, scraggly trees. (I half expected to see the ghost of John Wayne galloping down the riverbed, chasing outlaws.)

At the end of the cove on the western side of Isla La Borracha is a small fishing town with an extremely interesting harbor. The harbor is surrounded by high cliffs, undercut by the sea by as much as 15 or 20 feet. The outer part of the harbor is 10 or more fathoms, shoaling at its head to 2 or 3 fathoms. The wind is extremely erratic due to the high hills—so much so, in fact, that I would strongly advise entering the harbor under power. We managed to sail in and out with *Iolaire*, but I freely admit it was rather hair-raising, as the frequent 180-degree wind shifts made it extremely difficult to maintain steerageway.

The water in the harbor is crystal clear, and this, coupled with the undercut cliffs dropping vertically into clear water, would seem to make it a diver's paradise.

Earthquakes evidently have changed the contours of the island in that the offlying rocks north and south of the western entrance to the harbor, which are shown on the chart as connected to the main island, have now broken away from it. I would not try to take a boat between the two small islands and the offlying islands that have broken away, although it would certainly be feasible to snorkel through the gap in calm weather.

ISLAS DE PIRITU
(Chart V-39; II D-1, D-13)

Islas de Píritu are two islands 15 miles west of El Morro de Barcelona that have mile after mile of beautiful sand beaches and excellent snorkeling and diving. During the week, they are uninhabited and

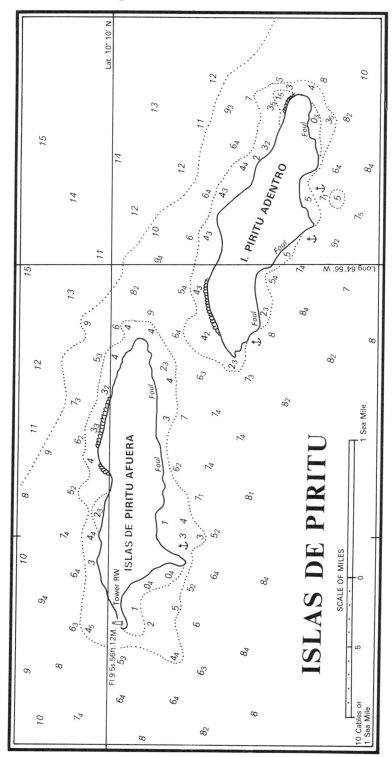

CHART V–39   Islas de Píritu

usually deserted, but over the weekend, there is likely to be a crowd of boats coming and going from the Barcelona area.

The shelter here is much better than the chart indicates. The best anchorage is where a sand spit sticks out to the southwest. In 1980, we moored *Toscana*, which draws 8 feet 10 inches, bow-on to the beach—stern anchor out and the bow line tied to a steel stake driven into the sand. This is a fantastic picture-book anchorage, one that beats the Tobago cays six ways to Sunday. If you wish to anchor off, a good anchorage can be found in 6 fathoms south of the small fishing colony on the south side of Píritu Adentro.

Anchor where shown on the sketch chart, as the areas marked foul have beautiful white-sand beaches but underwater ledges of coral that extend out 30 or 40 feet and then drop straight off into deep water.

In this area, the regular routine will be flat calm during the night, with the breeze picking up light from the west in the morning and slowly swinging around to the east and piping up to about 25 knots by 1600, then dying out shortly after sunset. Anchor accordingly.

NOTES

7

Carenero to Puerto Tucacas

II D-2, D-13, D-23

It is 95 miles from Barcelona to Puerto Carenero, but there are absolutely no anchorages along the coast. Offshore, there are anchorages at Islas Píritu (see chapter 6), but nowhere else.

CARENERO
(Chart V-40; II D-2, D-13, D-23)

Approaching Carenero from the west, especially if you are coming offshore from La Tortuga, the visibility is bad. Do not mistake the massive distinctive white apartment buildings at Boca de Paparo for the big shopping complex at Carenero. Also, when looking for the apartment complex at Carenero, you might be fooled by the white tank farm located halfway between Cabo Codera and Carenero. The actual entrance to Carenero is confusing, as the starboard-hand red buoy off Punta La Crucesita is now merely a red spar that looks more like a stake than a buoy. Inside the spar, right on the edge of the shoal, is another small buoy used by the locals as an entry mark. The port-hand buoy is missing; many people have passed between the spar and the shore and have run aground.

The best approach is to come in on a range of 315° magnetic on the big white 20-story hotel/motel/apartment house (marked by a red light at night) until you are abeam of Punta La Crucesita, then alter course to 340° magnetic. Favor the starboard side of the channel and sail on in, anchoring anywhere you like in the inner harbors. When leaving, reverse the procedure.

It should be noted that Carenero is not a port of entry. If you have a *zarpa*, you need to do nothing more, but if you come in from outside the country,

you cannot enter in Carenero. The Port Captain's office is on the port side as you enter the harbor, where the pilot launch and crew boat dock.

Only very basic supplies are available ashore. The main shopping can be done at Higuerote, which is easily accessible by *por puesto* or by dinghy (pass under the bridge east of the apartment building and head south). There are hauling facilities, as well as a mechanic/electrician who comes highly recommended, a Spaniard named Carlos Garcia. There is also a superb fiberglass man, a Korean—known locally as "*Koreano*"—who goes by the name of John. Ask anyone and the jungle telegraph will summon either or both of them in short order! There is a small marine-supply store, and a good fish restaurant (marked on the chart) where ice is also available. Showers are impossible.

Marina Carenero has a 50-ton lift, a 30-ton lift, and two 15-ton lifts and can haul 7 feet. The bottom is soft mud. They managed to haul an Ocean 60, but basically it is a case of doing it yourself. Deep-draft boats will have a problem, as there is virtually no scaffolding in the yard. The yard is set up primarily for hauling powerboats.

When in Carenero, a worthwhile trip is to take your dinghy to the bridge and go south through the mangroves, where there are all sorts of rare and beautiful birds: scarlet ibis, nesting pelicans, herons, etc. Early morning hours or dusk are the best times for birdwatching.

Astilleros de Higuerote

The first basin on the port side is not suitable for mooring, but it does have a 50-ton travel lift. Many

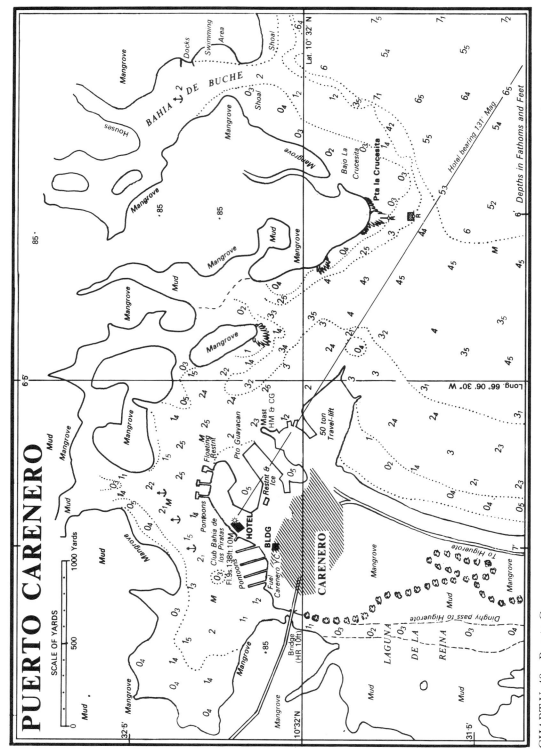

CHART V–40   Puerto Carenero

foreign-flag yachts have been hauled there. Check the depth in the hauling basin before making a commitment.

Cavafa

Located in the basin southeast of the floating restaurant, this is basically a dry stack system for ski boats, but there is a very good restaurant and they sell ice. It is a public facility where you can safely leave a dinghy.

Bahía de Los Piratas

This private club has two floating docks on the south shore, next to a floating restaurant. They have a 20-floor motel in the club, the site of which is marked in red. The building is white with a constant red light at night on the roof. It is sometimes possible to get a berth on the docks or go ashore through the club if the crew behave themselves and are respectably dressed. There's no haulout, but they do have a fuel dock.

Carenero Yacht Club

This is a private club with four floating docks. They usually allow visitors to go ashore through the club, but you are not allowed to use the club facilities. Arrangements can be made to come alongside at a modest charge. No haulout, but they do have a fuel dock.

The Port Captain's Office and Coast Guard (Guardia Nacional) in Carenero is easy to spot, since it is next to the radio mast, painted red and white.

The recommended anchorage noted on the sketch chart has good holding in mud in 12 to 15 feet of water. It is very quiet during the week, but long weekends can be a problem because of ski boats.

There is a reasonably well-stocked marine hardware store, which belongs to Señor Domingo. No English is spoken.

Carenero is a port dating from the late nineteenth and early twentieth centuries. It was once connected to Higuerote by railroad. If you want to stop and rest in this area but don't want to enter a harbor, there's an excellent anchorage behind Cabo Codera in Ensenada de Rondon (usually referred to as Ensenada or Ensa de Corsarios).

HIGUEROTE
(Chart V-41; II D-131)

There is a small, shoal-water marina for power-boats at Higuerote, about 3 miles south of Ca-

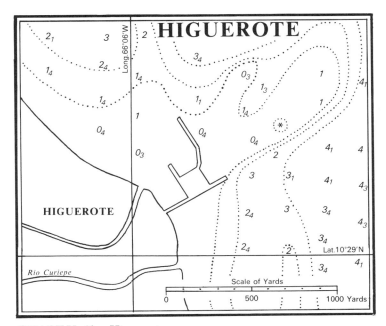

CHART V–41   Higuerote

renero. It's strictly for powerboats or very shoal-draft sailboats.

BAHIA DE BUCHE

Bahía de Buche, a half mile north of the entrance to Carenero, is an excellent, sheltered 2-fathom harbor and a popular day spot for people from Carenero. I am told it has a good swimming beach, clear water, and an excellent beach bar and restaurant. Of course, over the weekend it is likely to be extremely crowded.

Between Carenero and Cabo Codera, stay well offshore, as there is a tank-farm fueling complex halfway between the two places that has large mooring buoys twice the size of the average yacht. Knowing the Venezuelans, I suspect that these buoys are poorly lit, if they are lit at all! The Cabo Codera light is no longer flashing; it is a fixed red, visible for miles.

ENSENADA DE CORSARIOS/RONDON
(Chart V-42; II D-2, D-13, D-23)

Ensenada de Corsarios means "Bay of Pirates." It is also called *Puerto Francés* ("French Port") because in the days of the corsairs, a French pirate ship would always lie here in wait for passing vessels. This is an excellent anchorage for boats fighting their way eastward, because the mountain peaks to the east of this bay, well over 1,000 feet high, always block the wind completely. The point extending off to the northwest gives good shelter from anything except the largest ground swells. We sailed in when it was blowing a good 25 knots offshore and found a completely calm anchorage.

The beach in the eastern corner of the cove does not seem to have that "ground-swell look." Anchor west of the shed marked by two white balls about 4 feet in diameter. At the southern end of this shed, you'll notice a small white-sand beach. Work your way in and anchor in 2 fathoms of water with the conspicuous white rock off Punta el Muerto bearing 010° magnetic. We still found 3 fathoms and sand bottom with the white rock bearing 015° magnetic. I would definitely anchor in this area on a Bahamian moor with a good anchor off to the west, as the wind occasionally comes in from that direction (at least it did once when we were in the area in *Iolaire*). We were experiencing strong easterlies in La Tortuga, but Dr. Camejo in *Caribana* spent a night in Ensenada de Corsarios/Rondon facing west with a good 15- to 18-knot onshore wind. He told his skipper that he had never before experienced this in his lifetime of sailing this coast.

There is an empty beach south of the anchorage, and a quarter of a mile west of that anchorage is one with a colony of cottages, tents, and trailers. The beach looks excellent for swimming but has surf breaking on it. It has the look of a ground-swell beach, obviously not a good anchorage. A road comes down to this beach, and I would guess it leads to Carenero.

I am told that the shoreside features I described here have disappeared completely. Unfortunately, on our most recent visit, we arrived at night and departed before dawn. Even though the shoreside features are not as I described them, in the moonlight we could see a conspicuous white rock on Punta el Muerto. Using that as a reference point, we found our way in and anchored in 2 fathoms.

CARIBITO
(II D-2, D-23)

This is the only other anchorage from Ensenada de Corsarios/Rondon westward to the development surrounding the La Guaira area, and it's a lunch stop only. Located on the chart about a half mile northeast of the town of Chuspa, 15 miles west of Ensenada de Corsarios/Rondon, it is easily recognized because of its beach and, on weekends, the great number of yachts anchored there. It is not a good anchorage, as the swells come in and make things rather rolly. Here it is a must to anchor bow and stern, and make sure you anchor perpendicular to the incoming swells, which usually are fairly small.

In the La Guaira area, there are four anchorages—all private clubs—and they are described here from east to west.

PUNTA CAMURI GRANDE
(II D-2, D-23)

The Punta Camurí Grande Club is in a harbor with a reputation for having a difficult entrance that frequently shoals, making it tricky to enter and leave. I don't know how much water there is at the entrance and inside, but a local yachtsman tells me that it's not a good anchorage, as heavy swells occur.

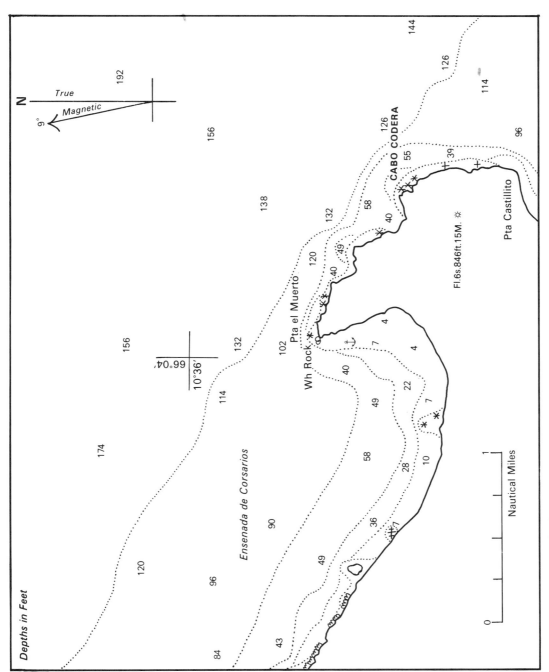

Depths in Feet

N

True

Magnetic

9°

192

156

138

156

174

120

96

84

43

90

Ensenada de Corsarios

132

114

132

120

102

Pta el Muerto

Wh Rock

40

49

58

49

36

7

49

7

22

28

10

7

4

4

7

58

40

49

40

58

132

126

CABO CODERA

55

39

96

114

126

144

Pta Castillito

Fl.6s.846ft.15M.

66°04'

10°36'

Nautical Miles

0   1

CHART V–42   Ensenada de Corsarios/Rondón

PUERTO AZUL

(Chart V-43; II D-2, D-23)

There is a large buoy off the end of the breakwater that must be left to port and a series of yellow buoys running to the shore. All boats must anchor to the shore side of the red buoys and outside the yellow buoys—in other words, outside the protective part of the harbor. When approaching Puerto Azul, do not be confused by the apartment buildings at Camurí Grande. Puerto Azul is just west of Punta Naiguatá, the second of the new developments along the coast between Carenero and Caracas.

The large, internationally famous yacht club was originally built and organized as a development by Dr. Daniel Camejo, who is now developing the El Morro de Barcelona area. It is located a quarter mile west of the point of Naiguatá and undoubtedly is one of the most spectacular yacht clubs in the Caribbean—perhaps the most spectacular north of Río de Janeiro.

As the members of this club will tell you (and can prove with photographs), the northerly ground swell here can be really massive. In 1966, the Southern Caribbean was battered by one of the worst ground swells in thirty or forty years, and it tore up the club's breakwater and docks. Although there has been no recurrence of such a swell, the club has built a breakwater 1,000 feet long, 50 feet wide, and 25 feet high. While this gives protection from the wind and sea, it tends to make the basin hot and airless.

Outside the entrance to the club is a small store with moderately good shopping, but you will find better shopping a short walk east of Naiguatá village and also farther west, at Macuto.

However, the presence of all these little shops means that no single place will have everything you need. If you discover that you have to go down to La Guaira anyway, take a bus or a *por puesto* to the Customs office, on the eastern side of the harbor, and take care of the paperwork. Then go across the street to CADA, the big supermarket, and buy everything you need. You can round up a complete two weeks' supply all in this one place. Then hire a taxi to take you back.

One problem with Puerto Azul is that unless you

CHART V–43   Puerto Azul

take your food to the boat in a taxi, there are no wheeled vehicles to transport things down to the end of the dock; this is a full mile and a half away from the stores—a long walk even without an armful of groceries.

At the head of the pier, a good white-sand beach faces directly out to the Caribbean. This often is a good spot for surfing, an active sport in Venezuela. Brian Conti, our resident surfer on board *Iolaire* in 1978, spoke Spanish and became friendly with the local surfers. It turned out, however, that they were international surfers, with knowledge of the sport in Mexico, the Caribbean, and the east and west coasts of the United States. Their verdict on the surfing at Puerto Azul was that it was "good but not great."

One aspect of Puerto Azul is similar to Martinique: A great way to relax on a Saturday afternoon is to sit on the dock or in one of the small cafés with a cold drink in your hand and watch the girls go by. The place is inundated with Venezuelan families down from Caracas for the weekend. The Martiniquais women are undoubtedly the most chic and the best dressed in the Eastern Caribbean, but the Puerto Azul girls are among the most spectacularly beautiful and most undressed in the Caribbean. Today, you'll seldom see a true Spanish-Venezuelan woman, because since World War II, there has been a great flood of immigrants from the States, Scandinavia, Germany, the Canary Islands, France, Italy—you name it. Experienced Venezuelan girl-watchers say that as the years go by, and their antecedents get progressively more mixed up, the Venezuelan women get better and better looking.

At Puerto Azul there is an elevator and transfer system capable of lifting probably 60 to 70 tons. Although it is not a full-service shipyard, the Port Captain will be able to put you in contact with carpenters, fiberglass specialists, engine repairmen, etc. Needless to say, the hauling facilities are primarily for the members of the Puerto Azul Club, although until recently they were willing to accommodate visiting yachtsmen if the schedule permitted. Now, however, because of the unacceptable behavior of visiting "water people" (note that I do not refer to them as yachtsmen), the door to the club has been closed to visiting yachtsmen. We can only hope that the situation will ease sometime in the future. Puerto Azul is a private, family-oriented club whose members are very conservative Venezuelans, many of them past retirement age. Despite this, female crews on some of the boats sunbathed *au naturel* on their boats. Others paraded topless among the families around the swimming

pool, or stripped to the skin and lathered up in the open at the pool showers. Still others decided that the drinking fountains made excellent places to bathe or wash clothes. Also, club-owned gear began to disappear, obviously stolen by visiting sailors. A final straw was the discovery that a number of the visiting sailors were trying to bribe local boatboys to steal equipment for them. Word got around that the pickings were good at Puerto Azul. At times there were as many as thirty boats freeloading off the club. As a result of all this, Puerto Azul is now—with great justification—closed up tighter than a tick.

Luckily, *Iolaire* and I have many friends who are members of the club, people who use my guides and charts. Thus, despite the closure in 1988, we were invited in 1988 and 1989 to stay as guests of the club. Exactly what the club will do in the future, I don't know. My suggestion to some members with whom I discussed the situation was that only true yachtsmen should be allowed to visit the club. They would write ahead, giving their names, name of boat, and yacht clubs with which they are affiliated. They would also supply letters of recommendation from two of the flag officers of their club. If Puerto Azul Club members followed these procedures, I think they would discover that *proper* yachtsmen who are members of proper yacht clubs are few and far between.

How can those sailors who are unwilling to join and support a proper yacht club in their home waters expect to make use of the facilities of clubs in distant ports?

PUNTA CARABALLEDA
(Chart V-44; II D-2, D-23)

Punta Caraballeda is 6 miles west of Puerto Azul, and it is easily identified by the Macuto Sheraton Hotel. It has a large breakwater and two separate anchorages. The western channel, 11 feet deep, leads to the Caraballeda Yacht Club, which is associated with the posh Caraballeda Country Club. If you can get dock space, this is a very nice place to tie up. It is a much smaller club than Puerto Azul, but it does have a restaurant, bar, and hot showers. Here you will also find good diesel mechanics and a charming, helpful secretary named Beatrice, who speaks English. More important, the country club, for which you may be able to get a guest card, is high in the hills overlooking the area. It's a marvelous old estate building that looks more like a museum than an active club. The food is excellent,

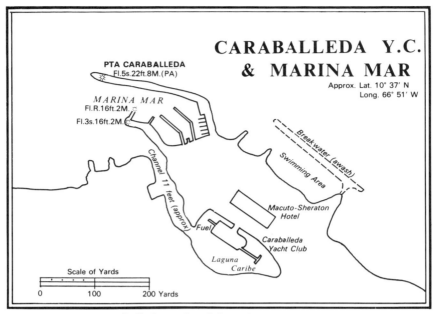

CHART V–44   Caraballeda Yacht Club and Marina Mar

the view is fantastic, and one could happily wander around the building for hours just simply admiring it. Be sure to wear a jacket and tie—not only to please the formal Venezuelans but also to keep from freezing to death. You are only a few minutes from the coast, but in the hills it gets chilly the moment the sun goes down.

There are also slips at Marina Mar, near the Macuto Sheraton. This is in general the best place for cruising people, since there usually is a berth available. Another advantage is that it's easy to get all supplies here except fuel. The marina does not have a fuel dock, but you can move to the Caraballeda Yacht Club for fuel, ice, and water. (The fuel is cheap and easy to get without too much paperwork—we hope that situation will still exist when you read this.) Shopping for food is cheaper here than at Puerto Azul, and the marina is within walking distance of the Sheraton and the Caraballeda Club.

It's easy to get to Caracas on the modern Mercedes-Benz buses that leave from just outside Marina Mar. Taxis are available, too. But make sure you obtain a pass to get back into the marina; otherwise, the taxi will be stopped at the gate and it's a long walk to the boat with no wheelbarrows to cart your gear.

Cruising yachts use this marina more than any others, so it is likely to be crowded. However, it is the only public marina in the Caracas area, and with luck, you can shoehorn your way in—the advantage of owning a narrow boat like *Iolaire* (10

feet 6 inches) versus a fat modern boat. The skipper of *Kodiak*, a 70-foot sloop owned by Lloyd Eccelstone, who stopped there, reported that everyone was cheerful, helpful, and very laid back!

John and Paula Dennis of the yacht *Chapter II*, from Canada's Prince Edward Island, report that at the Macuto Sheraton Marina, space was available for $20 US per night for a 40-foot boat, payable in US cash. Anchorage outside Marina Mar is just okay—but small and sometimes rolly. Oswald, the manager of Marina Mar, speaks perfect English and allows dinghies to tie up. For quite a few days in March, the wind was from the northwest, although light.

LA GUAIRA
(Chart V-45; II D-2, D-23)

This is 4 miles west of Caraballeda. Although it is mentioned in many guides and articles, I recommend that you avoid it. Instead, stop at one of the several marinas in the area—Puerto Azul, Marina Mar, Puerto Calera, etc.—and go by bus into La Guaira with the ship's papers, the *zarpa*, and so on. The latest information is that the Port Captain and Customs are about three blocks west of the main dock. Immigration is at the main dock, where the Guardia Nacional is located, and if you have to check in with them, sometimes the Port Captain requires that the yacht come right to La Guaira, at

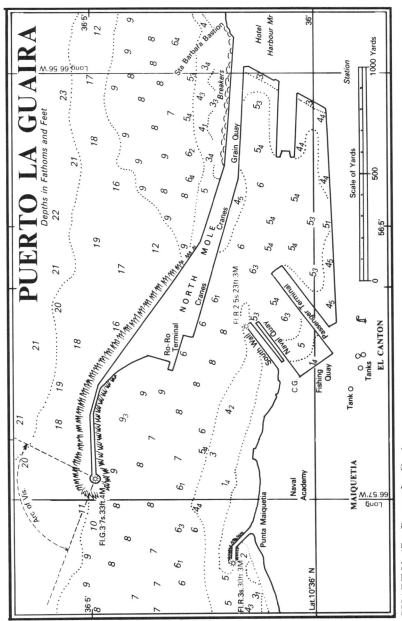

CHART V–45   Puerto La Guaira

other times he does not. They will probably want to hold your ship's papers until you leave; sometimes you can get away with a photocopy, but that is debatable. Cross your fingers and hope.

It is said that the only spot you can tie up a yacht is among the fishing boats, toward the shore on the northwest face of the west pier, near the word "Office."

The town of La Guaira provides excellent shopping just across the street from the main pier. There is a market on the main street, but we couldn't find a laundry.

PUERTO CALERA/PLAYA GRANDE YACHT CLUB
(Chart V-46; II D-2, D-23)

The marina here, called Marina Grande, is west of Maiquetía Airport. Although it is mainly for powerboat fishermen, it also welcomes "rag merchants." There is 12 feet in the entrance and the water is deep enough at the outer berths for the av-

erage yacht. There is no room to swing in this harbor, and the slips are narrow. Aboard *Boomerang*, a 67-foot yawl with 15-foot beam, we just managed to squeeze in between the pilings. In many cases, whether or not you can come in depends not on your draft or length but on your beam. Obviously, this is no place for multihulls. In fact, visiting yachtsmen generally raft up on the eastern side of the harbor alongside the wall.

John Coote says that Puerto Calera is a well-sheltered basin with a yacht club marina that can handle yachts drawing up to 10 feet in berths near the entrance. You'll find a sizable travel lift and slip, a yacht-club bar with most of the amenities (including a pool with its own bar), good security, room for yachts up to 65 feet LOA, easy access to Simón Bolívar International Airport 2 miles away, fuel and water at dockside. Recommended.

CARACAS

Caracas is not a port, but rather a city 3,500 feet up in a valley north of the coastal mountains. The

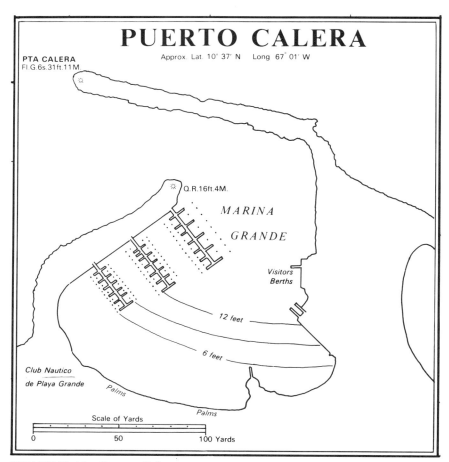

CHART V–46   Puerto Calera

mountains rise vertically out of the sea to heights of 7,000 to 9,000 feet. For years, it was such a tortuous drive from La Guaira to Caracas, even by car, that we can only wonder what it was like in colonial times, when one rode a mule or a horse. Today, it's a very quick thirty-five-minute journey (if you don't get caught in the weekend traffic) on a spectacular new highway. It climbs 5,000 feet in 7 miles, so this is not a trip for a car with a weak engine.

When driving to Caracas, be careful. It's easy to make a wrong turn and end up on the old road to Caracas, which is narrow and winds its way over hill and dale, and up and down the mountainside; it takes hours to get to Caracas that way. Someone may recommend that you take this route; it is a wonderful and scenic old road, but there are so many rock falls on the road that quite frequently it's impassable. So before starting on the old road, read the map very carefully and get local directions and information on the current road conditions.

There is a cable car from Macuto to the mountaintop and then on down, a fast and spectacular way of arriving in Caracas. The only problem is that the cable car usually is out of commission. And, despite having driven all around Macuto, I have never been able to find the cable-car terminus!

If you are in the La Guaira area, you should certainly plan on making a two- or three-day stop, as Caracas really is a fantastic city. It is spectacularly modern—with some of the most massive traffic jams I have ever seen. Many of the old buildings are worth visiting. The shops range from very cheap to very expensive, and there is a varied selection of restaurants, all of which seem to be good. In fact, I haven't yet had a bad meal in Venezuela.

The city has its Sheratons, Holiday Inns, and the like, but there are also Venezuelan-type business-men's hotels such as the Hotel Luna, where we often have stayed. It has excellent service, and even though its dining room is nothing fantastic, the hotel is within walking distance of literally dozens of restaurants. Furthermore, the price was right.

PUERTO LA CRUZ
(Chart V-47; II D-2, D-23)

Twenty-two miles west of La Guaira is Puerto La Cruz, a small indentation in the coast with a river running down to the head of the bay (not to be con-

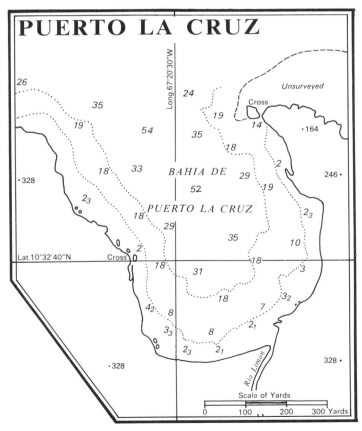

CHART V–47   Puerto La Cruz

fused with the larger Puerto La Cruz farther east). Daniel Shaw says the river can be ascended in a dinghy for half a mile. Good identifying marks are white crosses on both sides of the harbor entrance.

This is a difficult anchorage. The swells come in all the time in the winter, except on very calm days. The swell dies down in the summer months, when it can be a relatively good anchorage. The basic problem here is that it is very deep. You should allow plenty of chain or warp and always moor bow and stern with one line ashore. Rig a trip line to your anchor or you're likely to lose it.

As you enter the bay, which is lined with palm trees, head for the southeastern corner. Coming close to shore is no problem because the water is so deep, but if the wind is blowing hard, don't stay.

PUERTO MAYA
(II D-2, D-23)

This is 5 miles west of Puerto La Cruz, and it is another deep indentation in the coast with a river coming down to the head of the harbor. However, there is absolutely no protection here, and I do not advise anchoring. There appears to be a thriving fishing village at the head of the bay.

ENSENADA CATA
(II D-2, D-23)

My copy of the 1832 *Sailing Directions* for the West Indies refers to an anchorage at Ensenada (Ensa) Cata in the eastern corner of the bay behind the offlying islands. In March 1980, we sailed *Toscana* into this bay, and, using eyeball and the lead line, sailed in behind the islands in its northeast corner. You should find a calm anchorage here in 2 to 3 fathoms with a sand bottom. The water is not quite crystal clear, so we could not tell whether the dark patches we saw were coral or grass.

The main beach is attractive, almost a mile long, with white sand, palm trees, vacation cottages, and two new high-rise apartments. Landing a dinghy on the beach, though, is strictly for the brave and skillful. It would be better to land on the eastern corner of the beach and walk. There is a good restaurant on the beachfront.

PUERTO DE OCUMARE
(II D-2, D-23)

The 1832 *Sailing Directions* refers to this port as a good anchorage. On the chart it looks wide open,

but as in Ensa Cata, if you tuck up in the northeast corner, you can find a good anchorage in all normal weather. Anchored there were local fishing boats and runabouts owned by vacationers. There's a beautiful sand beach with vacation houses lining the shore.

CIENEGA OCUMARE
(II D-2, D-23)

Supposedly this is a Guardia Nacional base and anchoring is prohibited. This is a deep, sheltered harbor with excellent protection, deep water in the entrance, and a large circular reef in the center that almost breaks water. Sail into the southeast corner of the harbor and anchor in suitable depth with a Bahamian moor, as the wind will box the compass during the night. The US chart is wrong where it shows 3 1/2 fathoms; *Toscana*, drawing 8 feet 4 inches, bounced when we tacked. I am told there's good snorkeling around the reef and good fishing in the area. Mosquitoes appear at dusk but allegedly disappear during the night. The area is likely to be busy on vacation weekends.

PUERTO TURIAMO
(II D-2, D-23)

This is an excellent outer harbor, but, unfortunately, it should not be used—except possibly in an emergency—as it is a military arsenal. It is a prohibited area, and boats are not encouraged. I strongly advise you not to enter.

ISLA LARGA
(Chart V-48; II D-2, D-23)

Six miles east of Puerto Cabello, this is a low, windswept, sandy island well sheltered from the normal trade winds and sea. Light winds coming off the mainland will cause you to waltz around on your anchor, however, so a Bahamian moor is a must here. Anchor on the western side of the island, east of the sunken wreck. Anywhere is good. (Off the northwestern side of the island is the wreck of a German freighter that escaped from Puerto Cabello to avoid internment during World War II, and then either ran aground or was scuttled by the crew near Isla Larga—the stories vary.)

Approach the island only when there is good light, as there are two submerged reefs due south of

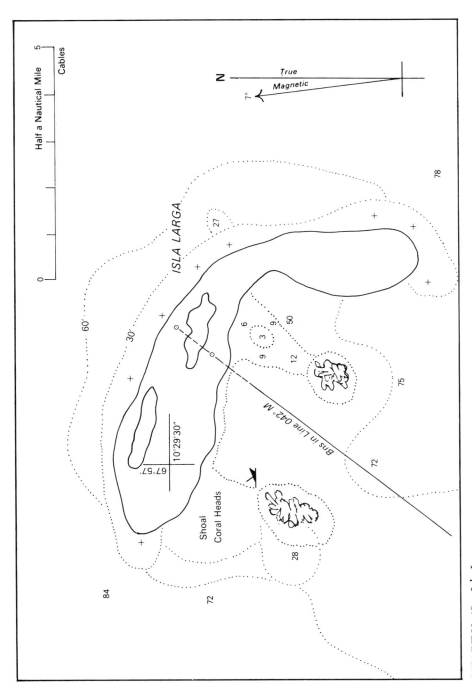

CHART V–48 Isla Larga

the north end of the island and due west of the southern arm. Both reefs are visible and easily avoidable in good light. The more visible outer reef is marked clearly on the chart. The inner reef, with only 4 feet of water over it, and unmarked, is closer to the shore in the eastern part of the bay.

Isla Larga is now a military base. After dark, boats usually are chased out. No longer is this a secluded little island. It has garbage cans on the beach and boats that bring out hundreds of day-trippers. It is still good before 0900 and after 1600, and, needless to say, weekends are more crowded than weekdays.

The deepwater anchorage is foul; make sure you rig a tripping line. If you don't like to anchor in deep water, you can anchor bow-on to the beach, thus dispensing with the dinghy. The best spot to do this is in the northeast corner of the bay if the military allows you to stay, but be sure to light mosquito coils at night, since you will be invaded by aggressive no-see-ums. There are flies and mosquitoes at dawn and dusk.

Scarlet ibis fly overhead in late August and can also be seen in Morrocoy. (Trinidad is not the only island that has scarlet ibis!) Heading northwest at sunset, they resemble bright pink geese!

It is worthwhile to stay here for a number of days, since the spearfishing is excellent and the diving on the wreck is interesting.

PUERTO CABELLO
(Chart V-49; II D-2, D-23)

At night, when approaching Puerto Cabello or the Tucacas/Morrocoy area from the north (i.e., from Aruba, Bonaire, or Curaçao), the best landmark is the huge powerplant approximately 11 miles west of Puerto Cabello. Its huge towers are topped with high-intensity strobe lights that we saw easily when anchored in Tucacas, 20 miles away. I would estimate their visibility on clear nights to be 30 miles. If approaching the Chichiriviche area from the north, note that the reef west of Cayo Borracho extends a good quarter mile west of the island. (The reef does not show on most charts.)

This is mainly a commercial and naval port, but looking at it, one can see why it has developed—it

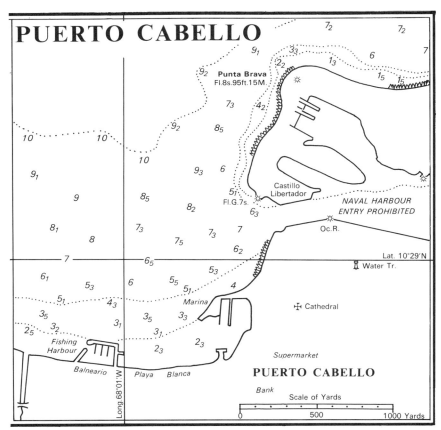

CHART V–49   Puerto Cabello

is superbly sheltered in all directions and in all winds. The naval base is on the north side, the city and commercial docks are on the south.

Puerto Cabello is Venezuela's largest port, as it is easy to see when one approaches the port and finds six or seven ships anchored waiting for dock space to unload. Being a major port, practically anything to do with mechanical repair work can be found. It must be remembered that Puerto Cabello is a seamen's town, and you should not go wandering around town after sundown unless you are with three or four young tigers. Our crew seemed to have no problems, but after 1800, I would only travel by taxi.

As is to be expected in an old port like this, there are some really marvelous old forts. Fort Solano, built in 1750, offers a splendid view of the port. Another fort is within the present navy yard. A nice little fort overlooking the harbor is well worth a visit. It was built back in the 1730s, but when you look at it, you can spot some bolts for modern gun mounts. I'm not sure if they were put in there during World War II or earlier. I've heard one story that they probably were used by the opposition (rebel) in Venezuela thirty years ago. They really got their money's worth out of the fort—built in 1730 and still being used in the 1950s.

The city of Puerto Cabello is small enough and as yet not too developed, so the old city buildings are still visible—increasingly rare these days. Many Venezuelan cities have developed so rapidly in recent years that the old sections have been swallowed up without a trace.

The marina at Puerto Cabello is not the best marina, but what it lacks in facilities, it makes up for with its staff. Port Captain José and the two secretaries in the office, Naose and Judith, both of whom speak English (the former more than the latter), could not have been more helpful. They will happily arrange your entry and onward clearance. Fuel, water, and electricity are available alongside, and there are showers and ice. The security is good but not superb, as local fishermen are moored nearby on the waterfront and kids swim out around the harbor on weekends. There is no burglary, but there are minor problems with pilfering. I would not advise anchoring out off the marina, because if you are anchored out, a 20-horsepower outboard is a magnet to light-fingered fishermen. Alongside the dock, you will always be troubled by a slight surge, but nothing horrendous.

The original concept of Puerto Cabello Marina is that it is the logical first stop in Venezuela for those coming eastward from Panamá and the last stop for those heading westward to Panamá. Considering that Puerto Cabello is a major port and has all facilities available, it would be the ideal place to have a hauling facility where yachts could haul and paint their bottoms, and where all electronic and mechanical work could be subcontracted out.

As of March 1989, it had been decided to drive the piles for the travel lift, and perhaps the lift will be installed by the time you read this guide. If so, it would certainly make a very convenient place to haul out, as the hauling facility in Morrocoy is limited to 6-foot draft and about 15 tons displacement. Further, although there is a side-tracking facility at Morrocoy, it is very primitive. Their space limits them to a maximum of about four boats. The backlog—waiting list—is usually about six weeks.

During the day you will discover that it is hot, as the dawn is absolutely airless. A breeze begins to pick up around 1000 or 1100, and by 1600 or 1700, the breeze is blowing enough to keep you cool, but there is not enough wind to keep it cool below. However, by 2200, even though the wind is very light and it might not have cooled off below, it will be cold on deck, so anyone sleeping there will want a sleeping bag or blanket.

There is a phone at the marina that can be used twenty-four hours a day, direct dialing with a phone card. There is no problem reaching anywhere in the world as long as you can buy a phone card. When we were there, we were unable to buy phone cards, even at the telephone exchange.

You can find basically all the things a yachtsman might need within walking distance of the marina. At all the other Venezuelan ports that yachtsmen visit—Porlamar, Pampatar, Puerto La Cruz, and so on—you can buy a tourist map, but there are no tourists in Puerto Cabello, so we have included here a sketch map of the city layout (Chart V-50).

For doing heavy shopping, head off to the southeast corner of town. The Banco Consolidado will change money. Right across the street from the bank there is a shop, Torni Puerto, that has an excellent supply of tools (they are a Black & Decker distributor), as well as nuts and screws, both stainless and bronze. Most important, the owner, Felix Cervellim, has been all over the world working as a welder in the oil industry. He has lived in the United States and speaks perfect English, Spanish, Italian, and French. He is most helpful at steering you in the right direction for whatever he cannot supply. Next to his shop is an electronics repair facility. Felix points out that if they can't fix it, no one can. The head of the company runs it as a side-

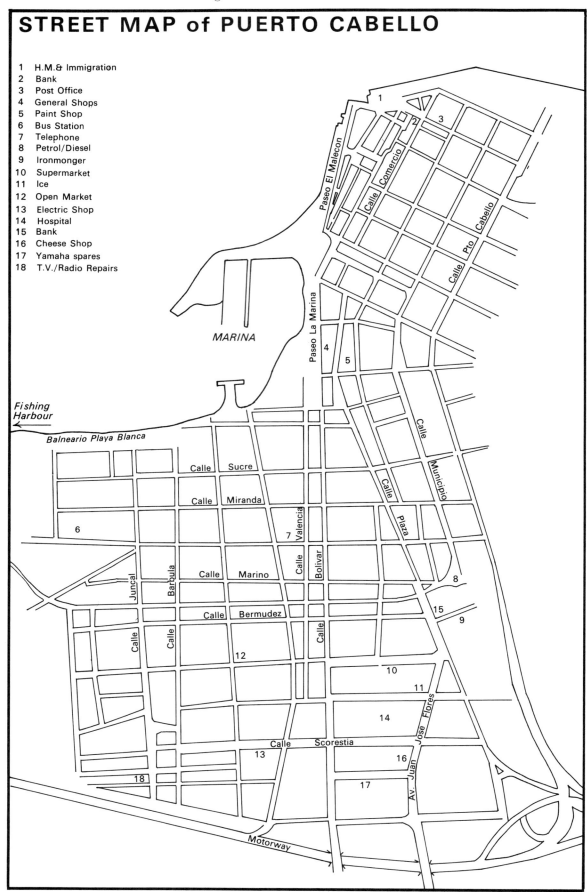

STREET MAP of PUERTO CABELLO

1   H.M.& Immigration
2   Bank
3   Post Office
4   General Shops
5   Paint Shop
6   Bus Station
7   Telephone
8   Petrol/Diesel
9   Ironmonger
10 Supermarket
11 Ice
12 Open Market
13 Electric Shop
14 Hospital
15 Bank
16 Cheese Shop
17 Yamaha spares
18 T.V./Radio Repairs

MARINA

Fishing
Harbour

Balneario Playa Blanca

Paseo El Malecon
Calle Comercio
Calle Pto Cabello
Paseo La Marina

Calle Sucre
Calle Miranda
Calle Valencia
Calle Bolivar
Calle Marino
Calle Bermudez
Calle Juncal
Calle Barbula
Calle Municipio
Calle Plaza
Calle Scorestia
Av. Juan Jose Flores

Motorway

CHART V–50   Puerto Cabello (Street Plan)

line—his main occupation is to supply the electronic equipment for the Venezuelan Army and Navy.

Also in the same complex is an extremely good *ferretería* that seems to have just about everything. Just around the corner is another nuts-and-bolts place, Sherwin Williams Paint, while nearby is the big CADA supermarket, a laundromat, and a big ice factory where you can buy block ice. You don't have to worry about getting the taxi full of water, because for 2 bolívars (about 2.5 cents US) per bag, you get heavy plastic bags. Even if you don't want the ice, it is worthwhile going to buy twenty or thirty of these bags, as they are heavy and clear—perfect for stowing clothes.

You can get a bus from the marina to CADA, but if you do, it will be wandering all over town—its route is almost as circuitous as the bus that runs from St. Thomas airport to Charlotte Amalie. I think it is easier to walk. I timed it at twelve minutes. Take a taxi back.

The market opens on Friday afternoon at 1800 and goes on late. It is also open Saturday, but Friday night is the best night. Fresh fruit and vegetables are available from small stalls everywhere you go in Puerto Cabello.

Rodolpho, an Italian, runs an excellent machine and welding shop. He can be contacted via the marina, or call 4030. He speaks Italian, Spanish, and very little English.

The best deal we made while in Puerto Cabello was to hire Marianella Roges as an expediter. She is actually a kindergarten teacher, but she sails a Sunfish, has been off on a couple of big yachts as a stewardess, understands yachtsmen's needs, knows the city perfectly, has a car, and can be hired to help solve all your problems. She can be contacted via Naose at the marina. Marianella speaks perfect English and Spanish, good French, and some Italian.

Puerto Cabello is also distinctive as the only place in Venezuela where the trains still run. The train makes five-hour runs southwestward to Barquisimeto.

There is a very nice main square in Puerto Cabello, with an interesting memorial to the Americans who landed there with General Miranda in his 1806 fight for independence; there must be interesting stories about Captain Bellorp and Lieutenants Aberug, Johnson, Kemper, Gardner, Ferris, George, and Tayerhausen.

Practically no one in town speaks English, but everyone is extremely friendly. We found an interpreter in the ship chandlery, one Nelson Ferron, who could not have been more helpful.

From Puerto Cabello westward, there are absolutely no anchorages until you reach Tucacas/Morrocoy, where there are any number of anchorages: a great exploring area, especially if you like mangroves and birds.

NOTES

8

Puerto Tucacas and Chichiriviche Westward

II D, D-2, D-23

TUCACAS

(Chart V-51; II D-2, D-23)

This is not a particularly old city, for in the days of Spanish ownership, the whole area west of Puerto Cabello was inhabited only by Indians. The Spanish never even surveyed the area accurately (this was left for the British to do when Tucacas became a fairly important copper port in the nineteenth century). By mule, copper was brought down from the mines, 60 miles away, loaded in boats, and run through the surf. (I wonder what the casualty rate was.) The barges were then sailed 10 miles north to Tucacas, where the copper was loaded onto British ships.

Later, in the 1860s, a narrow-gauge railway was built down to Tucacas. But through the years the railroad has fallen into disuse. Later on, I believe sugar was shipped out of Tucacas.

Anchorage off the town of Tucacas is not recommended, as there have been reports of muggings and robberies from boats anchored off at night. So be very cautious.

Augie Hollen points out a couple of reasons to go to Tucacas: the entire Morrocoy area is a national park and as such no beer is sold, so purchase your beer and ice in Tucacas before going there. (Ice is available in the park, but only on weekends.) A second reason to go to Tucacas, according to Augie, is that there is excellent communication via telex and/or telephone from the exchange located roughly a mile out of town. Anchor in the Morrocoy and visit Tucacas during the day via dinghy. (See below for details.)

PARQUE NACIONAL MORROCOY

(Chart V-51; II D-2, D-23)

Warning: Before this became a national park, people indiscriminately built weekend cottages on stilts. When the area was designated a park, the houses were pulled down. Some of the stilts remain, looking like channel markers, while others rotted off right at water level and are sitting there waiting to poke a hole in the boat of the unwary mariner! These could be dangerous, so look out for them. During the weekend, the area is crowded with motorboats, and their owners are friendly and usually happy to guide you to the marinas or the shipyard. If your Spanish isn't very good, Pedro Gluecksman offers a sentence in Spanish that will get you through: "*Por favor, puede usted guiarnos hasta el varadero por el canal más profundo?*" This means "Please, can you guide us to the drydock through the deepest channel?"

Created by the government, Morrocoy is immediately north of Tucacas (between Tucacas and Chichiriviche). Despite the fact that the US chart shows deep water at the entrance and no water inside, in fact there is ample water for exploring.

There are two main entrances to the park. The major one is at Boca Paiclás and the secondary one is at Boca Grande. Boca Suánchez and Boca Seca can also be used, but probably not if you draw more than 5 feet, and then only in ideal conditions.

Dr. Daniel Camejo sounded the channel from Boca Pilar to Ensenada El Placer with his 90-foot yacht and reported ample water along the route shown on the sketch chart. He noted that despite

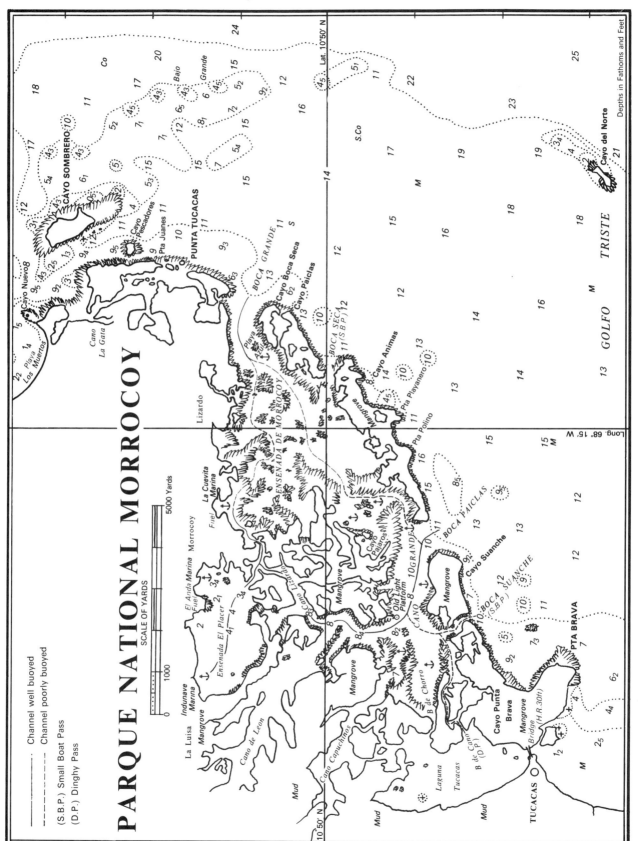

PARQUE NATIONAL MORROCOY

SCALE OF YARDS

5000 Yards

1000

0

- Channel well buoyed
- Channel poorly buoyed

(S.B.P.) Small Boat Pass
(D.P.) Dinghy Pass

Depths in Fathoms and Feet

CHART V–51 Puerto Tucacas and Morrocoy

the fact that this is a mangrove area—which, of course, is alive with birds—the water is crystal clear, just the opposite of what one would expect. He also noted that with a dinghy and outboard, you could spend weeks in this area. It's best to row quietly in the dinghy to avoid disturbing the wildlife. Besides, the area is so well sheltered that rowing would be a pleasure.

The best entrance is Boca Paiclás, which is not so easy to spot. I recommend using a back bearing of 306° magnetic on Cayo del Norte. According to Pedro Gluecksman, there is an offlying reef on the southeastern side of Boca Paiclás. Thus, you should favor the starboard side when entering. It's a case for eyeball navigation, following the route outlined on Chart V-51.

Once through the channel, swing to starboard and anchor off the white-sand beach. But be forewarned: Drop the anchor in shoal water and back off, as the bottom drops from 8 or 10 feet to 60 feet within 40 or 50 feet. If your anchor is not set in shoal water on the shelf, you will be anchoring on the backside of a slope and the anchor will never hold. This is a superb anchorage, but unfortunately, for reasons best known to themselves, the park officials did not like us anchoring there overnight and asked us to move farther east.

A popular anchorage for yachts on the weekend is inside Boca Grande, on the port hand, off the white-sand beach. You can proceed eastward from Caño Grande through Ensenada de Morrocoy, but proceed with caution, as the whole area is strewn with reefs. There are passages between the reefs, but do not trust the buoying system. The system in the Tucacas/Morrocoy area is red diamonds on the starboard side of the channel and green squares on the port side of the channel. Sometime in 1988, the entire park was buoyed, but the buoys must be viewed with suspicion. We came to the conclusion that the eastern end, in Ensenada de Morrocoy, is buoyed in such a fashion that shipwreckers and harbor pilots will never starve to death. A few of the buoys will lead you hard aground if you pass on what appears to be the correct side; and there were others that we could not quite figure out. The buoys leading west from Boca Paiclás through Caño Grande and Bahía de Chorro and on to Tucacas appear to be correct, as are the buoys for the channels leading to Ensenada El Placer and La Cuevita Marina.

As suggested above, the whole area inside the mangroves can be explored by dinghy. One area, shown in the guide maps as "Tunnel of Love," has a fairly deep channel where mangroves meet overhead. Other areas have been roped off at certain times of the year, as they are frigate-bird rookeries and the authorities don't want the birds to be disturbed. We also spotted scarlet ibis when we were there in March 1989.

You can take a dinghy from the anchorage to Tucacas, following the inside passage marked on the sketch chart. It is well buoyed, but be careful, as the local boats come flying through this passage flat out, and woe betide anyone who gets in their way.

In Tucacas, once you pass under the bridge, you will discover a new dock. Tie the dinghy up to the dock, with an anchor to hold her off. Wander into town, where you will find a very potholed road, a friendly bar and restaurant that looks quite good (on the left side as you head up the street), and a number of small, unsuper supermarkets. We are told that somewhere along the right-hand side of the street is an excellent butcher, reputedly one of the best in Venezuela. If you speak Spanish, apparently you can get him to give you all sorts of fancy cuts of meat. However, we walked up and down the street and never did find a butcher. I guess our Spanish just was not good enough.

A pay phone can be found right next to the church, across the road from the police station and next to a small shop that evidently makes a major business of supplying change for the phone.

At the top of the road, at the main road junction, you can pick up a *por puesto* headed for Puerto Cabello, a half-hour ride away. It's a scary ride, though, as all the *por puestos* and taxis try to outdo each other, letting no one pass. Thus, you are likely to be doing 70 or 80 knots down the road in a taxi that feels like it's about to lose a wheel. Scary in the extreme.

If you are in the Morrocoy park and you have a slow dinghy (like *Iolaire*'s 11-foot lapstrake dinghy with a little Seagull), it is better to tie up at the little dock on the northeastern corner of Cayo Punta Brava, hitch a ride into Tucacas, do your shopping, and hitch a ride back.

There is a hauling facility at Indunave Marina, which can accommodate 6 feet of draft and allegedly 65 feet in length. But 65 feet would only be a long-keeled powerboat—a short-keeled sailboat would probably bend the cradle. In addition, the chocking arrangement is such that it is built for hard-bilged powerboats, not deep, narrow sailboats. They do have a side-tracking facility, but it is rather primitive at best. They can probably haul no more than six boats at any one time, and even that is pushing it. The situation is complicated by the fact that there is no phone within the park, so the only way to contact the marina is to go there and talk to them. When we did that, we discovered there was a six-week waiting list. The yard has few if any marine supplies.

Basically any marine supplies you need will require taking a car, *por puesto*, or bus into Puerto Cabello, buying parts or having parts made, and carting everything back. So this is not too good a setup unless you are absolutely confident that you have everything you think you may need for the haul aboard your boat.

La Cuevita Marina has no hauling facilities, but it does have a rather derelict 30-ton travel lift—and who knows whether that will ever be resurrected.

Marina El Anda, run by Daniel Cabo, comes highly recommended. Dave and Bev Feiges of *Clover Leaf* report that "it is as secure and beautifully (and rigidly) run as anything can be." They consider it the safest place to leave a boat in Venezuela, and they found it secure from any weather and sea conditions.

CAYO SOMBRERO

(Chart V-52; II D, D-2, D-23)

Being part of the national park, Cayo Sombrero offers immaculate white-sand beaches, with trash bins that evidently are emptied regularly.

We anchored close to shore but still in about 10 fathoms of water, just south of the clearly visible reef. There's a good beach, excellent swimming, moderate snorkeling, a restaurant ashore (which was not open when we were there), and one of the inevitable wind chargers that are visible all along the Venezuelan coast. Like the one we had in our house in Grenada for fourteen years, it is a simple, rugged, cheap way of capturing the ever-present winds to make electricity.

During the week, Cayo Sombrero is basically deserted, but on weekends it is absolutely mobbed with Venezuelans who arrive in motorboats to avail themselves of the wonderful beach and excellent swimming. Augie Hollen describes the weekend at Cayo Sombrero as the best girl-watching in the entire world. Augie also reports that he dropped his stern anchor in 66 feet of water off the restaurant, ran the bow right up on the beach, and buried another anchor in the sand. He was able to jump from the bowsprit right onto the beach. Augie reports that there is also an anchorage behind Cayo Pescadores, and on weekends, as many as sixty

small boats will be anchored there, with the owners camping ashore.

CHICHIRIVICHE

(Chart V-52; II D, D-2, D-23)

This port makes an excellent stop when you're fighting eastward from the ABC islands (Aruba, Bonaire, Curaçao). Standing south along the coast, you should spot it by the mountains behind Puerto Tucacas and the offlying cays to the north of Tucacas. You can pass inside Cayo Borracho, marked by a 55-foot light flashing every eight seconds and visible 12 miles, if it is working. (Warning: The island has a long sand spit and reef that extends to the west of the island much farther than the chart indicates. Give the western side of the island a good berth.) Stand due south to pick up two buoys east of Cayo Peraza. When the city opens up to the west, head for the church on a bearing of 275° magnetic and run on in. This range is not easily seen, as the church tower is not very tall. When you're on the range, the tower is almost completely obscured by two large palm trees, and not very visible from the deck of a small boat. The channel has a dogleg to avoid the shoals south of Cayo Los Muertos. As Cayo Los Muertos comes abeam, bear left, run down to the south of town, and anchor off the main dock to do the necessary paperwork with Customs, the Port Captain, etc. Anchorage here is in 5 fathoms with a thick mud bottom. Once you have cleared, you are free to visit any number of anchorages in the area and relax.

Note also that the inner harbor is blocked by a power line only 20 feet high. The inner harbor, where Augie Hollen reports a profusion of orchids, monkeys, and falcons, can be explored via dinghy. Augie also reports that there is a dinghy passage in the head of the mangroves through to the open sea on the southern end of the coconut plantation.

While trying to solve some engine problems, we met two extremely nice Venezuelans. One, Juan Javiota, is a mechanic who has the oldest, most rusted-out Jeep I have ever seen; the frame is so rusted that it goes over bumps like a sea serpent. Its floors are wood and its fuel tank is a plastic jerry jug tied to the dashboard. The odometer shows 97,000 miles and hasn't worked in ten years. That the car runs at all proves that Juan must be a fantastic mechanic. His friend Orlando, owner of the Hotel Nautico, is extremely friendly and an enthusiastic sailor as well.

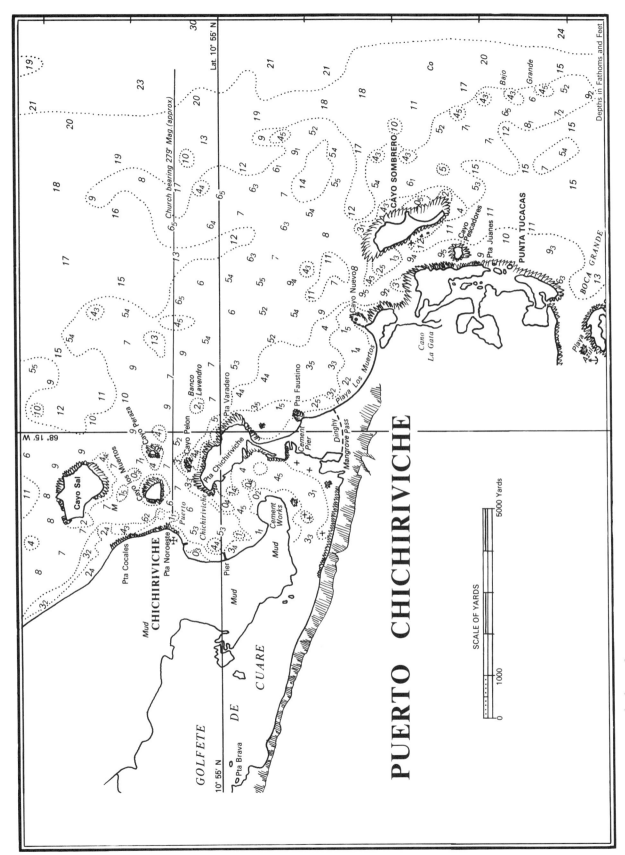

PUERTO CHICHIRIVICHE

CHART V–52   Puerto Chichiriviche

Since the 1980 edition of this guide, Chichiriviche has developed, but not in leaps and bounds. It developed mainly because literally thousands of people on holiday weekends visit Cayo Sal, Cayo Los Muertos, and Cayo Sombrero. In Chichiriviche there is now a four-story hotel that reputedly is quite good: Hotel Mario (Mario D'Orazio), Estado Falcón, tel.: 042-86114 or 86115. We found a couple of supermarkets that had basic supplies. Cube ice is available but no block ice.

Anchoring your dinghy in Chichiriviche while you do your shopping is a major project, as the wind blows directly in on the dock that all the dinghies use. A new dock is under construction. I haven't quite figured out who drew up the plans—and I wonder whether he knows anything about boats. The dock is too high to be a dinghy dock and it ends in water too shoal to be used as a commercial dock for offloading cargo—another engineering project gone wrong.

CAYO SAL

(Chart V-52; II D, D-2, D-23)

This is an excellent place to stop. Since it is part of the national park, trash baskets line the beach, so there is none of the usually inevitable Venezuelan litter. A fishing colony and three restaurants can be found ashore. They serve fresh fish and good food at reasonable prices, but no drink—so take your own beer.

The beaches are excellent, although the western ones have wall-to-wall people, but just do a little walking, and you'll find some deserted ones.

There are two separate anchorages: Off the western tip you can anchor in 2 fathoms of water, but you probably would be exposed to any northerly ground swell coming in; furthermore, the current that reverses itself between Cayo Sal and the mainland would require a Bahamian moor and would have you beam-to the swell at times.

A better anchorage is on the southwestern corner of the island, where deep water extends right up to shore; you can put a bow anchor on the beach and a stern anchor in deep water and forget about the dinghy.

The best mooring appears to be in the bight just south of the reef in the northwest part of the island. There is clean, deep water close to shore. Anchor on a Bahamian moor and prepare to be inundated with friendly Venezuelan powerboats all day Saturday and Sunday. I'm told that the island is basically deserted on weekdays—except, of course, during Holy Week.

The salt pond in the middle of the island dries out come late May and early June, when rock salt is available for the taking.

CAYO LOS MUERTOS

(Chart V-52; II D, D-2, D-23)

Cayo Los Muertos has a very nice cottage beach colony with a good anchorage off the southwestern corner and deep water close to shore. You can anchor bow and stern or use a Bahamian moor.

CAYO PERAZA AND CAYO PELON

(Chart V-52; II D, D-2, D-23)

Neither of these islands is big enough to offer a good anchorage, but both are incredibly picturesque—ideal places for the romantic to visit in a dinghy with lunch, a bottle of chilled wine, and as few clothes as possible.

HARBOR OF CHICHIRIVICHE

(Chart V-52; II D, D-2, D-23)

Within the harbor of Puerto Chichiriviche are many good anchorages, one of the best being on the mud flats southwest of Chichiriviche. The mud flats rise steeply out of 5 fathoms of water and are hard to pick out due to the murkiness of the water, so ease on in with a lead line, dropping your anchor when you get on the shelf. Because of a strong tidal current, be sure to anchor with a Bahamian moor, or bow and stern. When passing into the inner harbor, be cautious, because even though the chart shows deep water, you will notice spots that shallow down to 3/4 fathom—undoubtedly rocks rising out of 30 or 40 feet of water. The NOAA chart shows no buoys, but I have been told by Venezuelans that the harbor is buoyed. Thus, proceed slowly so that if you do come to a sudden stop, you'll get off undamaged.

GOLFO DE CUARO

(II D, D-2, D-23)

The Golfo de Cuaro is entered via the main channel, which is probably locally buoyed. Inside is the wreck of an old square rigger, the *Gaviota* (it would be interesting to know how this ship got there). Feel your way in with the dinghy, using a lead line, or else try to find out beforehand where the deep water is and isn't.

There are reputedly plenty of oysters in the mangroves, and these are excellent if steamed, not boiled: just steam them lightly until they pop open. In our college days, we found that oysters tasted much better if steamed in beer instead of water.

CAYO BORRACHO

Warning: Most charts do not show the reef extending to the west of the island—give it a wide berth when proceeding northward.

In settled weather, a daytime anchorage could be found south of Cayo Borracho. There are beautiful white-sand beaches, but the reef extends a good quarter mile to the west of the island.

The Coast West of Chichiriviche

The coastal area west of Chichiriviche (II D-2, D-23) is not really worth visiting, since it offers mere open roadsteads that give little shelter. They would be completely untenable if a ground swell started to come in, and even if you were able to anchor off, you would be unable to get ashore in the dinghy.

The area from Punta San Juan to Punta Zamuro is marked as dangerous for navigation. In particular, note that northeast and northwest of Punta Agüide are two 1 1/2-fathom spots well offshore. These are completely unbuoyed, and the coast is low, with no ranges. In other words, do not approach this coast.

Be aware also, if you are working your way along this coast, that there are land and sea breezes. Basically, the sea breezes come from the north to the southeast and the land breezes come from the south to the west-southwest. This happens frequently, but not invariably. Generally, the sea breeze starts at 1000 and lasts until sunset and the land breeze blows from 2200 until 0800.

The westerly current in the Golfo de Tucacas tends to follow the coastline. It sets northward from Puerto Cabello to Puerto San Juan, then curves around, following the coast and turning again northward from La Vela de Coro, passing northward off the east coast of the Peninsula de Paraguaná, then funneling with high velocity between Aruba and the mainland.

Because of the lack of harbors in this area, boats passing eastward are advised to fight their way from Aruba to Curaçao, then Curaçao to Bonaire, and then stand southeast from Bonaire. Except in an emergency, no landfalls should be made west of the Tucacas area.

However, if you are driven down onto the coast and want to stop and rest, below are a few excuses for anchorages.

CAYO SAN JUAN

(II D-2, D-23)

An anchorage can be found under Cayo San Juan at 1 1/2 fathoms, or farther offshore if your draft is greater. The bottom is mixed sand and mud. A swell hooks up around both ends of these islands, so probably the best way to moor is bow and stern, lining up the boat so that the swell is taken on the bow or the stern.

PUERTO CUMAREBO

(II D-2, D-23)

This is an open roadstead sheltered from the prevailing wind and current by the new dock. Remember, however, that it is wide open to the northerly swell. Hart and Stone, in their *Cruising Guide to the Caribbean*, speak highly of this port and of the good resorts nearby: Santa Rosa, Bella Vista, and the small Balneario Hotel for meals. They also praise the local dish, *talkary*, made of goat meat—evidently not quite as tough as the goats we found on Isla La Blanquilla. They arrived on a Sunday when everybody was in a holiday mood, so they had a good time. However, I am very dubious of the wisdom of breaking your trip at this port.

LA VELA DE CORO

(II D-2, D-23)

This is another open roadstead and is basically the port for the city of Coro, 7 miles away. About the only reason to make this stop is to visit Coro, which is reputed to have some first-class examples of Spanish colonial architecture. The city dates back to 1527 and its cathedral to 1583. It has a good museum with much history of Nueva Andalusia, and it also is the place where General Francisco de Miranda landed in 1806 and hoisted the national liberation flag for the first time.

West of La Vela de Coro and all the way into the Golfo de Cardón (or Golfo de Venezuela), there are no anchorages. Since the gulf is shallow and there are deserts on either side, my advice is to forget it. To the east lies the Peninsula de Paraguaná, to the west the Peninsula de Guajira. Both peninsulas have deserts, but the Peninsula de Paraguaná also has mountains rising to 2,800 feet, with a low, flat desert between them. As a result, the land heats up and sucks the trade winds off the sea, thus increasing their velocity.

It blows so hard in the Golfo de Cardón in the winter months that down in Maracaibo (which is much more sheltered), all the local yachtsmen pack up sailing from late November and don't start again until April.

Our one adventure in the gulf is better forgotten about. We picked up a boat in Cartagena (Colombia) for delivery to Grenada and fought our way from Cartagena to Cabo de la Vela, then around the Peninsula de Guajira. We got as far as Los Monjes and then discovered that the boat not only did not want to go to windward under sail or power but also was exhibiting a great desire to go to the bottom; thus, we eased sheets and ran off down the Golfo de Cardón to Maracaibo, hoping to ship the boat back to the States. This course of action nearly turned out to be a complete disaster.

First of all, upon arrival in Maracaibo, we broke so many regulations—coming up the channel at night, not taking a pilot on board, not having the correct papers, etc.—that the authorities were ready to throw us in jail (evidently we were the first yacht to clear into Maracaibo in years). Luckily, we were able to contact Dr. Camejo on the phone; I don't know what he did, but the next day they were ready to give us the keys to the city rather than throw us in jail. The final insult, however, was that we never were paid for the delivery. (Delivery skippers should be paid in advance!)

The one good point of this misadventure was that while stranded in Maracaibo, we took the opportunity to talk to many yachtsmen, tug skippers, and pilots. They pointed out that not only does it blow hard in the Golfo de Cardón, but because of the shoal bottom, the seas can hump up so badly that if the wind goes around to the north, even the big tankers sometimes cannot leave Maracaibo. If *they* must wait for the weather to moderate, then it's clear that yachts should never go any farther in these conditions than absolutely necessary. If you're driven into the Golfo de Cardón and want to rest

for a few hours, you can probably anchor behind Punta Gallinas. After a day or so, put your head down again and resume your fight eastward. If you want to stay longer, enter at Las Piedras.

LAS PIEDRAS

(II D-2, D-23)

This is the port of entry for the west coast of the Peninsula de Paraguaná. It is of interest only to the yachtsman fighting his way east from Panamá who is looking for a place to enter Venezuelan waters and resupply, or who finds the beat to Aruba impossible. The next Venezuelan anchorage to the east is Chichiriviche (about 210 miles).

The Customs pier is in Ensenada Caleta Guarano, south of Bahía Boca de las Piedras, where all formalities may be completed. Inquire here about the best place to anchor. I would suggest going over to Club Nautico Shell, where you'll probably find someone who speaks English and knows the area. As I've said before, yacht club members in Venezuela are very helpful to visiting yachtsmen. There are huge oil refineries in the area, a big shrimp industry, and tons of wind—35 to 40 knots during the day is not at all uncommon. But if you're tucked up under the eastern shore, at least no sea can build up against you, and you can get some rest.

LOS MONJES

(Chart V-1)

These are three different groups of islands poking up out of the ocean floor of the Golfo de Cardón (or Golfo de Venezuela). Most yachtsmen, including ourselves, thought they were nothing but mountain peaks with no possibility of anchoring to leeward of them. However, as Chart V-1 indicates, in Monjes del Sur there is an anchorage of sorts between these two islands. This is certainly a perfect spot to stop and rest when working your way eastward from Panamá. There is a Venezuelan military base on the island, so when anchoring there, you will be safe from drug smugglers and a good distance from Colombia. Exactly how good the anchorage is, I'm not sure. Once you have rested and girded your loins for battle, then you can decide whether to head for Aruba or to go down to Las Piedras. Rest there and then try for Aruba.

If heading for Aruba nonstop, cross the Golfo de Cardón on port tack, try to obtain some shelter from the land to windward, then make the tack to Aruba. But remember when tacking out to Aruba that the current between Aruba and Venezuela can run as high as 4 knots, and certainly at all times it is running at least 2 knots westward.

MARACAIBO

(II D-2, D-23)

There isn't much to recommend Maracaibo to yachtsmen, and, as I mentioned above, if you run into bad weather there, you may be stuck for days. If for some reason you have to go in there, however, remember that there is a strong current in the mouth of the channel. If it's blowing really hard, the wind against the sea could build up to the point that it would be dangerous for a small yacht to enter the channel. In general, enter on the flood tide and leave on the ebb; but if it's blowing hard out in the Golfo de Cardón, wait until slack water to make your exit. It is required that you take a pilot on board, but exactly how you get a pilot on or off the boat with the sea conditions that prevail off the mouth of the channel, I don't know.

When and if you get into Maracaibo, there are absolutely no suitable anchorages for yachts! If you draw under 5 feet, you may be able to squeeze into the anchorages of Club Nautico de Maracaibo or the Caribbean Yacht Club of Maracaibo. Both basins are very shoal, but the clubs are extremely friendly.

Club Nautico de Maracaibo is a big, modern, typically Venezuelan social club. The Caribbean Yacht Club was founded by Shell employees, and its home is a double-decker ferry boat. It's very informal and has an active small-boat racing fleet, including a number of Stars. Racing Stars in the conditions one encounters in this area is simply a form of madness. It must be contagious, however, because even the *Norteamericanos* contract the disease and participate with enthusiasm.

Lago de Maracaibo, south of the city, is shallow and full of oil-drilling rigs. Its bottom is crisscrossed with oil pipes and its shore is flat and unattractive— no place for yachtsmen.

NOTES

9

Eastern Offshore Islands: Los Testigos, La Blanquilla, La Tortuga, La Orchila

II D, D-1, D-11, D-14

Having described the full length of the Venezuelan coast, we now jump back 500 miles to the east to look at the area's offshore islands—a complete change of pace. These islands, described here and in the following two chapters, stretch in an east-west direction in more or less of a line parallel to the coast, an average of 60 miles off. They are surrounded by crystal-clear water and are in the easterly trade-wind belt. They are largely uninhabited, and, with the exception of El Gran Roque, have no supplies for the yachtsman.

These islands are like the Virgins and the Grenadines of twenty years ago. The waters have not been fished out and the anchorages are seldom crowded. The fishermen are universally friendly and helpful. There are miles of deserted beaches; smooth, bug-free anchorages cooled by the trades; and no sign of developers—in short, what everyone dreams of as tropical islands. Enjoy it while it lasts!

Islas Los Testigos

Los Testigos (Chart V-53; II D-1, D-11, D-14), a group of small islands 90 miles southwest of Grenada, provide a convenient landfall for yachts going to Venezuela. These islands are dry, and they formerly were inhabited by fishermen who camped ashore for a few months at a time. Now, however, there is a permanent settlement of fishermen who sell their catch daily to a "buy boat" that then heads for Martinique, where the fish bring the highest prices.

When approaching Islas Los Testigos, don't forget what I have stressed a number of times about Venezuelan lights. There is a light at the top of Testigo Grande, which officially flashes once every twelve seconds and on a clear night should be visible about 15 miles. But it usually is not working; probably no one wants to climb to the top of this 800-foot mountain with a battery on his back; or, if someone manages to do it, it's highly likely that a fisherman will climb up afterward and put the battery to other uses.

Sail in from the south, because once you round the southern point of Testigo Grande, you'll be running downwind and downcurrent. (From the fishermen we ascertained that the current always runs northwest between Testigo Grande and Iguana; it never reverses.) If you enter from the north, you'll be beating to windward against both wind and current and probably will have to use your engine. Thus, I'll describe the anchorages going from south to north.

Los Testigos has many anchorages, and it is impossible to say which is the best, for what may be a good anchorage one day will be impossible the next. Sail around for a while, survey the wind and swell conditions, and check where the local fishermen are anchored. (Many people claim the anchorage

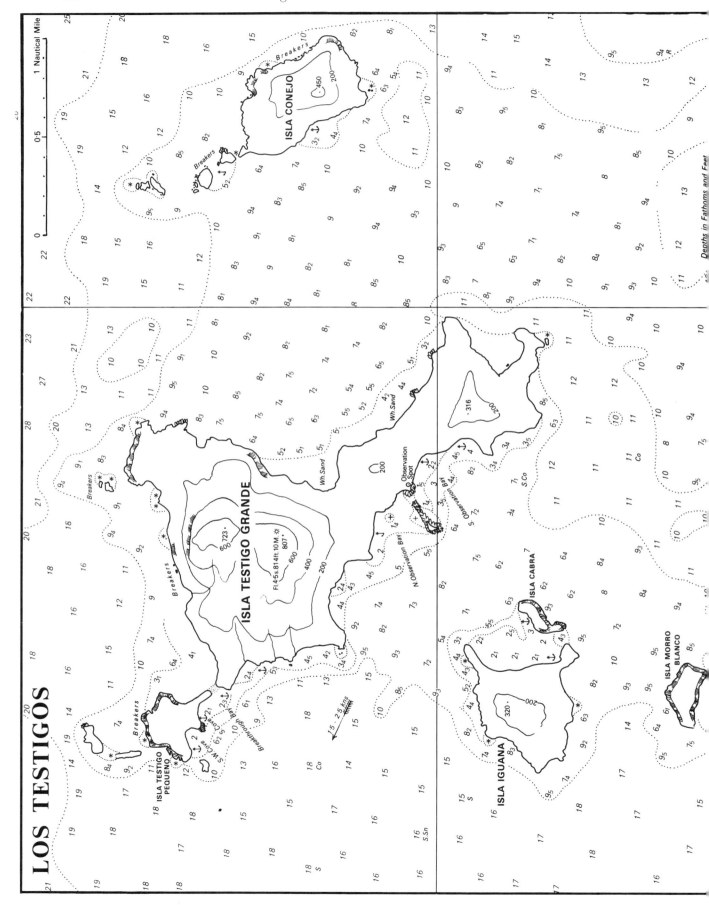

LOS TESTIGOS

ISLA CONEJO

ISLA TESTIGO GRANDE

Fl.45s.814ft.10M.
807

ISLA TESTIGO
PEQUEÑO

Breakers

Breakthrough Bay

ISLA CABRA

ISLA IGUANA

ISLA MORRO
BLANCO

Observation
Spot

N Observation Bay

S Observation Bay

Wh.Sand

Depths in Fathoms and Feet

1 Nautical Mile

north of Isla Cabra is not so good, yet when we were there, probably because of weather conditions, all the fishing boats were anchored over by Isla Cabra. Other yachtsmen have reported that they have come to Testigos and found no one anchored north of Isla Cabra.)

After spending three days in Los Testigos in February 1988, examining all the anchorages via dinghy and discussing the situation with fishermen, we came to the conclusion that the best anchorages are northwest of Testigo Grande—either off the south beach on Testigo Pequeño or in the southwest cove. Both were excellent, with good sand beaches, not too much swell, and plenty of wind blowing across the low land—in our estimation, just about perfect.

ISLA TESTIGO GRANDE

(Chart V-53; II D-1, D-11, D-14)

Approaching from the south, the first extremely good anchorage we found is due west of the 300-foot peak of Testigo Grande. Sail on in, drop a bow anchor, and then put an anchor or line ashore on a rock, bush, or tree. Moor facing west; there is no swinging room, as the fishing boats arrive around midday and stay until about 0400, when they leave for the fishing grounds. They anchor with amazingly light lines and small anchors, indicating that this anchorage must be sheltered in all conditions.

North of the above anchorage and south of the "observation spot" marked on the chart is Sand Gully Bay, a deep gully between two high hills with sand right down to the water's edge. Anchor bow and stern. Why the fishermen don't use this one, I don't know.

There is a soft sand beach, and if you follow the gully through the hills, there's another beach on the other side. This is roughly half a mile long and a quarter of a mile deep, with soft sand that spreads 100 feet up the hill. It is completely deserted and ideal for joggers and surfers. The sand, blown by the ever-present trades, has been banked up to a height of around 100 feet. It's one of the most magnificent expanses of white sand I've seen anywhere in the Caribbean.

On the water's edge are numerous wells typical of Testigo made from fifty-five-gallon drums sunk into holes dug in the sand. Evidently brackish water can be accumulated in this way, and although it's obviously not the world's best drinking water, it is potable—at least for goats and tough Venezuelans.

North Observation Bay is easily identified by the two new houses erected on the beach. There is a tolerable anchorage off the beach, and one or two yachtsmen have said it is excellent, although both days we were there, a slight chop made it a little rolly. Again, you can walk across to the windward side to find another white-sand beach. The British and American charts are wrong: There is a dinghy passage with 1/2 fathom of water between the observation spot marked on the chart and the island and reef to the west of the observation spot.

ISLA TESTIGO PEQUENO

(Chart V-53; II D-1, D-11, D-14)

The sea has broken through between the northwesternmost part of Testigo Grande and the main island to create this separate little island. However, this is not how it looks on the British and American charts—which are both wrong. There are two anchorages:

Southwest Cove: Where the British and American charts show no soundings, there is a full 2 fathoms in the middle of the cove and 1 1/2 fathoms around the edge. It is imperative to tuck yourself right up inside the cove and anchor either with a Bahamian moor or bow and stern, as the current between Testigo Pequeño and the small island to the south of it can be extremely strong. Hank Strauss reckons that the current gets up to 4 knots. The cove is large enough for just one boat. For birdwatchers, it's heaven on earth: There are brown-booby nests in the area, the sea-grape trees serve as a nesting area for huge flocks of birds, and we saw, by actual count, forty frigate birds wheeling overhead.

South Cove: There are 2 1/2 fathoms at 150 yards off, gradually shoaling as you get closer to yet another beautiful white-sand beach. The wind whistles across the low sand spit and the shoal channel where the sea has broken through, guaranteeing a bug-free anchorage. Again, with the reversing current and wind dying out at night, a Bahamian moor or bow-and-stern mooring is needed. The beach on the south side of Testigo Pequeño is calm and excellent for children. If you want good surf, just walk over to the windward side.

ISLA IGUANA

(Chart V-53; II D-1, D-11, D-14)

Iguana Island is the site of the main village of Los Testigos, which formerly was nothing more than a bunch of corrugated iron shacks built on stilts. The fishermen used to camp out with their families for long periods. Recently, the government has financed the purchase of prefabricated houses, making the island much more comfortable for the fishermen. There is one teacher plus a small schoolhouse. The Guardia Nacional is housed in a futuristic modular building that looks rather like an orange igloo. Electricity for the module is provided by a wind charger—the same kind that we had at our house in Grenada. With the aid of this and a good radio, the office is in communication with Caracas every day.

The officer in charge must have been chosen for his tact and cheerfulness, as every yacht he has boarded reports that he has mentioned to them that although they had stopped illegally (they should have first cleared in Carúpano), he felt that they were doing no harm at all, being just a cruising yacht. "Sit back," he says, "and enjoy yourself, despite the fact that your being here is illegal." He does, however, check everyone's passport, and then sends the name of the boat with crew list to Caracas. This suffices for preliminary entry, and once you reach Carúpano or Porlamar, you will need to make your official entry.

Anchorage off the town is not too good (even the fishermen pull their boats up onto the sand). It's interesting to see the small children with their tin boats; I was reminded of my early days in the Caribbean when small boys in St. Croix, St. Thomas, and many other islands would build themselves 6-foot tin boats by pinching a length of corrugated iron from a building site. They would get two pieces of wood, half the width of the corrugated iron, and bend the corrugated iron in half lengthwise, then nail the pieces of wood between the bent-up ends of the iron to form a bow and stern, bedded in with plenty of tar to make it watertight. Another piece of wood was jammed in to keep the middle apart—and, voilà! a canoe, built in less than a day and lasting almost forever. A small boy could make one of these boats go like the wind, using hands or paddles. A few of the more adventurous kids made double paddles to increase their speed. These simple canoes trained excellent small-boat sailors, for if they were capsized, the boats sank like a stone. The boys would then dive down, stand the boat on its end, and give it a good, hard shove. The boat would pop up about half full of water, and, after bailing it out, off they'd go again. These boats have more or less disappeared from the Caribbean, but there they were in Los Testigos. We saw maybe twenty or so here and on other Venezuelan islands.

They were particularly interesting in that they had transom sterns, unlike their Eastern Caribbean counterparts, which were all double-enders.

ISLA CABRA
(Chart V-53; II D-1, D-11, D-14)

Just east of Isla Iguana, this is an anchorage for fishermen who wish to be near the town. Anchor bow and stern northwest of the island in order to be completely sheltered from sea and wind, which normally hooks around the south end of Testigo Grande and is well south of east. Even if the wind swings around to due north, the anchorage is still sheltered, as the 800-foot-high hill on Testigo Grande breaks up the worst of the wind. The sea has no more than a mile of fetch, so only a small lop can build up.

It is perfectly possible to pass between Isla Cabra and Isla Iguana. There is a known depth of 12 feet, but at certain stages of the tide, there's a very strong current running from south to north.

ISLA CONEJO
(Chart V-53; II D-1, D-11, D-14)

This is the easternmost island of the Testigos group, and I have no reports of it, but looking to windward off Testigo Grande, we noticed that there were two fishing boats anchored on the shelf due west of the hill on Isla Conejo and another anchored at the two offlying islands directly north of Isla Conejo. Since this was late in the afternoon, I'm sure they were there for the night, as the boats come back in the late afternoon to anchor and start out again before dawn.

The fishermen usually have plenty of fish and lobsters, which they are more than willing to trade for bottles of Scotch. Other yachtsmen have reported that medical supplies are even more welcome, especially among the children. A steady diet of fish does not lead to overall health, and minor cuts and bruises tend to infect and fester; thus, Band-Aids, adhesive tape, cotton, gauze bandages, and, most important, large quantities of antibiotic ointment are all appreciated. More than one yachtsman has doctored up all the cuts and bruises he could find and then been inundated with gifts of fresh fish and lobster.

Augie Hollen, who loves to live off the land, points out that if you have a rifle, you may want to try the wild goats that abound on the island. However, having tasted goat meat on La Blanquilla, I think I'll leave them alone. He also points out that there is very little vegetation on the island except cactus, so if you load up with fresh fruit and vegetables in Grenada, you can also trade these for fish and lobster.

The fishermen's children love to act as guides to visiting yachtsmen, and communication is not that difficult as long as you have a Spanish phrase book handy.

ISLA LA BLANQUILLA
(Chart V-54; II D-1, D-14)

La Blanquilla lies 50 miles northwest of Isla Margarita, 65 miles northeast of Isla La Tortuga, and 95 miles north of El Morro de Barcelona. It is likely to be a hard beat from Tortuga. From the Puerto La Cruz area, allow a full twenty-four hours, as the current may set to the west at anywhere from 1 to 2 knots, making it a tough fetch on starboard tack. It is, of course, just an easy overnight sail from Margarita.

If the wind is well in the north and you cannot lay your course to the island—about 025° magnetic, allowing for the current—I'd be inclined to forget the whole operation unless your boat goes well to windward.

If you cannot lay the island from the Puerto La Cruz area but still want to visit Isla La Blanquilla, it is best to tack eastward in the smooth water near the Peninsula de Araya and Isla Margarita, working close up under Punta Arenas. From there to Isla La Blanquilla, the course is roughly north, which usually can be laid fairly easily.

Isla La Blanquilla is low and flat, but it's easy to find, as to the east lie Islas Los Hermanos, a group of six steep-to islands that rise out of deep water to a height of 600 feet, making them visible at a great distance.

Isla La Blanquilla is a wonderful cruising spot with numerous good anchorages. There are practically no people on the island, since it is far enough away from the mainland that tourists and yachtsmen seldom visit. Many of those who used to visit arrived by small aircraft on holiday weekends, but the private airstrip is now closed. The only airstrip now open is at the small naval base established to make sure drug smugglers do not make use of the island.

The local fishermen are most friendly and helpful. There is another more or less permanent group of residents who live on the eastern end of the is-

land. They catch and butcher goats, then dry the meat. When we were there, we were presented with a live goat, but when they realized we would be hopeless at butchering it, they took it away and brought it back already butchered. Sadly, though, my most excellent cook, Alston, tried cooking it three different ways and each time it still tasted like very tough shoe leather.

All along the western coast of the island, you'll find one beautiful sand beach after another. They are not completely deserted, being inhabited by Venezuelan fishermen who take their catch ashore to dry and salt it for shipment to the mainland or to Martinique.

A major reason for visiting Isla La Blanquilla is the spectacular cove on the western side of the island, north of Punta de la Aguada. With cliffs on both sides, the cove is less than 200 yards wide and only about 300 yards deep.

There is a white-sand bottom, and you could anchor bow and stern, facing out into the swell; a visit ashore reveals one of the most fantastic settings I have ever seen. Despite the cove's great beauty, however, the anchorage is likely to be rolly, so I would advise anchoring in the cove south of Punta de la Aguada (see Chart V-54; then take the dinghy ashore and walk a mile across the land or take the dinghy around to the other cove.

The head of the cove is a beautiful white-sand beach with an overhanging cliff that extends out to form a wide cave with a white-sand floor. On the hottest, most blazing day, you can sit in the shade under the cliff and be cool; those who want the sun can lie out on the beach. The cliff extends over the beach enough so that the back edge of the cave is shady until midafternoon.

One wonders what a night ashore would be like, with a blazing fire in front of the cave, the moon overhead, crystal-clear water washing onto the beach—even a middle-aged couple in the twilight of their love life might find new romance!

South of Punta de la Aguada are two good anchorages (see Chart V-54) where you usually can find a couple of the typical small Venezuelan fishing boats anchored, buying fish from the even smaller boats that fish off the beaches north of Punta de la Aguada. The best anchorage is north of the 6-foot-high island with the scarecrow mounted on it. Work your way inshore, anchor bow and stern, and keep a careful eye on the weather, as such steep-to sand beaches are only produced by the ground swell. If the ground swell begins to build up, get out.

Anchorage is good either north or south of the

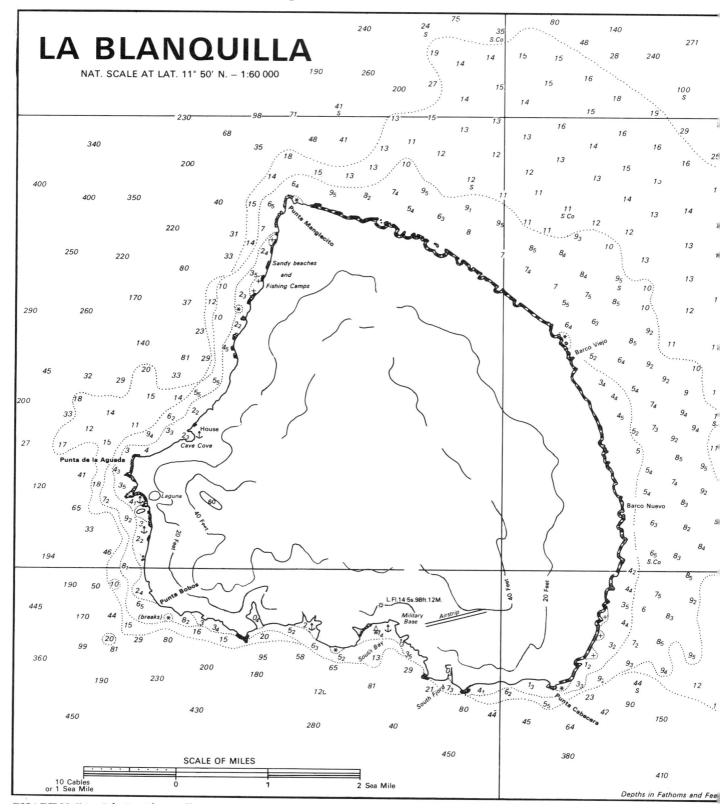

LA BLANQUILLA

NAT. SCALE AT LAT. 11° 50′ N. – 1:60 000

Punta Manglecito

Sandy beaches
and
Fishing Camps

Barco Viejo

House
Cave Cove

Punta de la Aguada

Laguna

40 Feet

20 Feet

Barco Nuevo

S.Co

Punta Bobos

(breaks)

South Bay

L.Fl.14·5s.98ft.12M.

Military
Base

Airstrip

40 Feet

20 Feet

South Fjord

Punta Cabecera

SCALE OF MILES

10 Cables
or 1 Sea Mile

0   1   2 Sea Mile

Depths in Fathoms and Feet

CHART V–54   Isla La Blanquilla

reef in the big bay south of Punta de la Aguada, but we preferred the northernmost anchorage. We anchored in 3 fathoms of crystal-clear water with excellent snorkeling close by.

There are a number of graves on the island with interesting markings, and someday I hope to ascertain the background of each. One of them is unusually well tended, with a little garden full of well-watered flowers—on a (practically) desert island! We were told that this is the grave of the "patron saint" of the island—a young girl who came across the Atlantic in a sailing vessel in the last century, on her way to marry the man she loved. The skipper of the ship took a liking to her but she resisted his advances, and he killed her in a fit of rage. It seems strange, however, that the captain should have stopped at Isla La Blanquilla to bury her, and the local people don't explain the whole story. Anyway, she is buried on the hillside. The fishermen adopted her grave and have kept it beautifully tended for well over a hundred years, believing that as long as the flowers bloom on her grave, the fishing will be good.

The south coast of La Blanquilla (see Chart V-54) has numerous good anchorages. The only danger is the rock off Punta Bobas, which just breaks in the swell. It can be spotted easily and probably provides excellent fishing and snorkeling.

Southwest Cove (marked in yellow on the old Imray-Iolaire charts but now an insert sketch) does have 9 feet of water inside the cove. However, the entrance is extremely difficult, and only experienced sailors should attempt it—and then only in perfect light and ideal conditions. The entrance is from the southwest, behind the reef, and then turns roughly due north.

As mentioned above, Isla La Blanquilla now has a small naval base on the south coast. The staff is said to be extremely helpful to yachtsmen in distress. The new airstrip is right next to the base.

SOUTH BAY

(Chart V-54; II D-1, D-14)

South Bay lies east of Punta Bobas. It is fairly large and has a number of anchorages. The western cove of South Bay has probably only 4 feet of water, but it has a beautiful white-sand bottom. The middle of South Bay has ample water for a boat of any size; just ease on in until you find a suitable depth, and then anchor. I recommend a Bahamian moor.

For those who really want to anchor by themselves, the easternmost cove of South Bay is an excellent spot; obviously, bow-and-stern mooring is indicated, as there is no swinging room. There are cliffs all around, and a good white-sand bottom; once you get in, there is simply no possibility of anyone else's getting in—although it should be noted that the naval base and its airstrip are located on the cliffs above you.

SOUTH FJORD

(Chart V-54; II D-1, D-14)

This is totally misrepresented on the US chart, which shows white all the way in, meaning 6 or more fathoms of water. Yet the cove actually appears so shallow that nothing more than a dinghy could get in. Once in, of course, it is perfectly sheltered. Here is a chance for an explorer to sound the cove very carefully and report what size boat could be squeezed in.

When wandering on terra firma on La Blanquilla, be very careful to wear some good, heavy shoes, because even though there are trails from one end of the island to the other, the ground is covered with all sorts of low bushes and prickly vines. This is definitely not an island to explore barefoot or in sandals.

La Blanquilla is actually the only island on the Venezuelan coast (except Margarita) that had natural groundwater, streams, and so on. But now only deep groundwater can be found. On the southeastern point of the island, near the palm beach, local fishermen get their water supply from wells, but I would strongly discourage you from trying this water unless you are really in need.

ISLA LA TORTUGA

(Chart V-55; II D-1, D-13, D-14)

Isla La Tortuga is 50 miles west of Isla Margarita, 52 miles from El Morro de Barcelona, and 65 miles from Isla La Blanquilla; thus, it is an overnight sail from practically anywhere. It is a low island (120 feet high) and not easy to spot. It supposedly has lights marking Cayo Heradura on its northwestern side and at Punta Oriental on the southeastern corner.

The island is semi-inhabited; some yachtsmen report an abandoned fishing village, while others report that there is a thriving fishing village on the

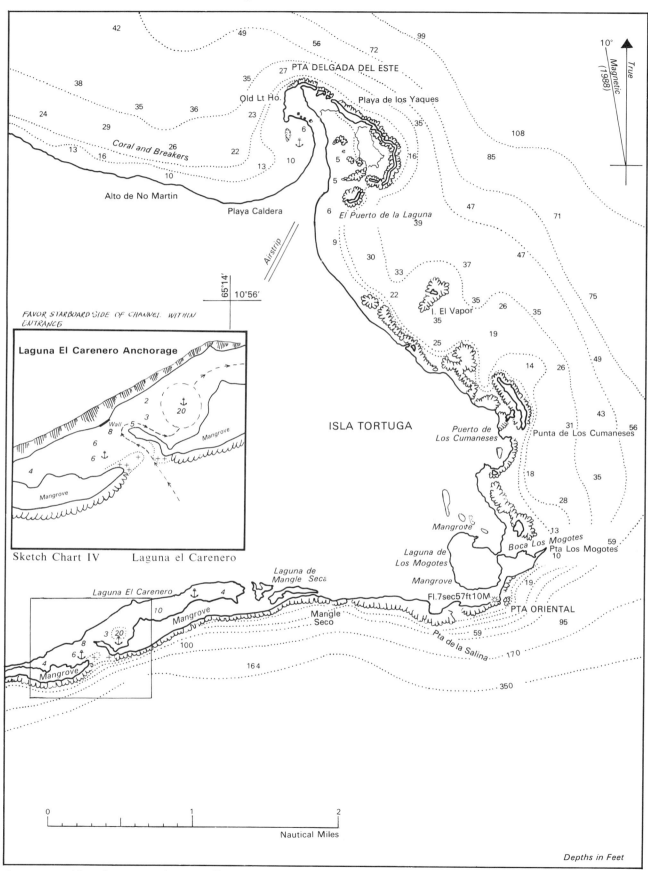

CHART V–55   Isla Tortuga (East End)

same spot. So I conclude that it is inhabited only some of the time.

There are numerous anchorages on Isla La Tortuga, and mile after mile of white-sand beaches. If you don't like neighbors, you only have to walk down the beach to find solitude. The reefs and lagoon east of Punta Delgada del Este form a shoal wading pool with fine snorkeling and shelling.

PUNTA DELGADA DEL ESTE

(Chart V-55; II D-1, D-13, D-14)

Give the northwestern tip of Punta Delgada del Este a wide berth; be guided by the color of the water and check the fathometer or lead line. Work your way into the northeast corner, where there is the least swell. Anchor in about 1 1/2 fathoms, about 200 yards out; 5 feet can be carried practically up to the beach. Powerboats moor bow and stern here. In periods of ground swell, of course, this anchorage would be untenable.

The beach extends south and curves westward. Along the beach to the west of the anchorages are offlying coral heads alive with fish but exposed to the ocean swell. A short walk across the sand spit brings you to the sometimes-occupied fishing village. Here we found fishermen emptying lobster traps and putting the lobsters into burlap bags for a quick run to the mainland, 55 miles away. The high speed of the Venezuelan launches has to be seen to be believed.

We also discovered that the US chart for the area east of Punta Delgada del Este is completely wrong. Where the chart shows solid reef, there is a big basin perfectly protected by the offlying reef.

EAST COAST OF LA TORTUGA

Warning: This area is best visited only in settled conditions by boats drawing 4 feet or less.

Inside the offlying reef, half a dozen Venezuelan fishing boats anchor. Probably 5 feet can be squeezed behind the reef, possibly 6 feet, but that would be the maximum. The entrance is either southwest or northeast of the southwesternmost part of the reef. If using the channel northeast of the westernmost part of the reef, you would enter heading approximately due west until the inner reef is cleared, then round up and anchor in a suitable

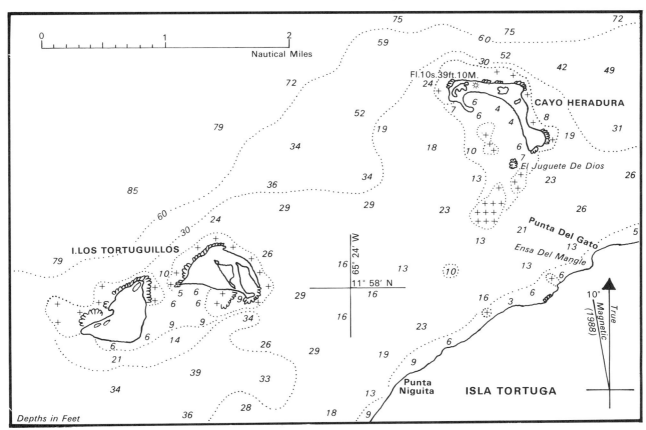

CHART V–56   Islas Los Tortuguillos and Cayo Heradura, Tortuga

depth. If entering from the southwest of the southern reef, as soon as the reef comes abeam, head approximately north by east and work your way north as depth permits.

At the north end of the lagoon, it shoals. A dinghy can be taken out to the offlying reef and islands due east of Punta Delgada del Este. You can also reach this point by walking out along Delgada to its outer edge and then wading along in sneakers. The shelling should be fantastic here.

NORTH COAST OF LA TORTUGA

One can sail westward down the coast of Isla La Tortuga. A couple of yachtsmen have told me that they had an excellent anchorage to the south of Punta Ranchos o del Medio with a beautiful white-sand beach and no roll, but they all said it was during a period of quiet weather with the wind south of east. In the winter months, with the ground swell rolling in, I am sure this anchorage would be completely untenable. West of Punta Ranchos is a good anchorage in the lee of Cayo Heradura.

I have been told by boats that visited here that the anchorage at Isla Los Palenquines on the north side of La Tortuga is not worthwhile, as the whole area is nothing but dead coral. It is almost impossible to get your anchor to hold, and there are no fish.

CAYO HERADURA

(Chart V-56; II D-1, D-13, D-14)

Cayo Heradura is another island with miles of white-sand beach. The anchorage is shoal and the best entrance is around the north end of the island; head south and work your way back up to the anchorage. The southern end of the island has extended much farther south than the US chart shows, and it practically joins the offlying reef. The bottom shoals gradually and is mixed grass and sand, but since the spots of sand are a full 2 feet below the grass, it is very easy to get false readings from the lead line or the depth finder. We were getting 9 feet on the lead and then suddenly ran aground, but there was no problem, as the wind blew us back off and we anchored.

However, when anchoring, be sure to get your anchor down in one of the sand holes, for there is no hope of its holding in the grass. Four feet of water can be carried to the beach, so powerboats can

sneak right up on shore. Anchorage behind Cayo Heradura is strictly eyeball navigation. The whole operation should only be undertaken by experienced reef pilots, as there is a lot of debate as to the depth of the water and the location of the coral heads.

There is less swell in the middle of the beach. If the shack in the middle of the beach is brought to bear at approximately 035° magnetic, you will, apparently, be in the right spot.

Cayo Heradura is a national park, so there are trash cans on the beach. Spearfishing is not permitted. Palm trees have also been planted, and when exploring the shore, you'll discover a monument to Baron von Humboldt, the nineteenth-century explorer and geographer. It has been reported that there is excellent snorkeling off the southeastern tip of the island.

ISLAS LOS TORTUGUILLOS

(Chart V-56; II D-1, D-13, D-14)

Two and a half miles southwest of Cayo Heradura lie the Islas Los Tortuguillos, the "Little Turtles." Both have lagoons inside the reef that are crystal-clear and so shallow that they are warmed by the sun almost to bath temperature. There is good shelling and snorkeling around the edges of the reefs surrounding both islands on the seaward side. According to the US chart, which does not agree with the Venezuelan chart, the sheltered sides of both islands have shoal water extending well offshore, making an approach difficult in all but the smallest dinghy. On the western end of the southern corner of Los Tortuguillos, however, you can anchor within 200 yards of the shore. (Bruce Cameron, a most experienced sailor, reported that in settled conditions he found a good anchorage off the western end of the south coast.) Drop a stern anchor and run a bow line onto the beach. The normal trade winds usually will keep you lying to your bow anchor despite the current, which in Los Tortuguillos probably reverses at springs. However, if conditions leave you in any doubt, use a Bahamian moor.

An anchorage can be had between these two islands; there appears to be more water than the old Imray-Iolaire chart shows. This has now been corrected with the help of a new Venezuelan Hydrographic Office survey, which shows a 6-foot pass between the two islands. But I would not try using this pass until I had first investigated it by swimming through or by passing through in a dinghy and sounding carefully.

It has been reported that there can be a fair amount of ground swell in the area between the two islands. This evidently comes and goes. Proceed with caution in the area between the two islands, as shoaling has been reported.

SOUTH COAST OF LA TORTUGA (FROM WEST TO EAST)

The south coast of Isla La Tortuga is steep-to, with a number of small coves and anchorages; the best known of these is El Carenero.

BOCA DE CANGREJO

(Chart V-57)

The sketch chart was developed from a Venezuelan government chart and exploration by *Iolaire*'s dinghy. The entrance range is 025° on the middle of the mangroves (see profile sketch). There is 12 feet, shoaling to 7 feet, then to 6 and 5 feet. Anchor immediately after passing the coral head. The bottom is mostly clean white sand. Fishermen have a small camp by the cliffs, but it obviously is a

temporary shelter, without a semipermanent tin roof.

BOCA DE PALO

(Chart V-57)

The sketch chart has been prepared from a Venezuelan chart and the soundings from *Iolaire*'s dinghy in February 1988. The eastern entrance is completely reef-blocked. You can eyeball in the western entrance, range 025° on the center of the mangroves that have small white-sand beaches at either end. Dodge coral heads when entering. There is 12 feet in the outer channel, but it shoals gradually to 4 feet. Anchor inside the shelter of the reef with 6 feet of water (4-foot-draft boats can anchor anywhere in the lagoon). This is another great place to explore in a dinghy.

PUNTA DE LOS NEGROS

The older charts are wrong about this; the shelf extends much farther out. Feel your way in, work as close to the reef as possible, and anchor in sand. But be warned: The holding is not good. The bot-

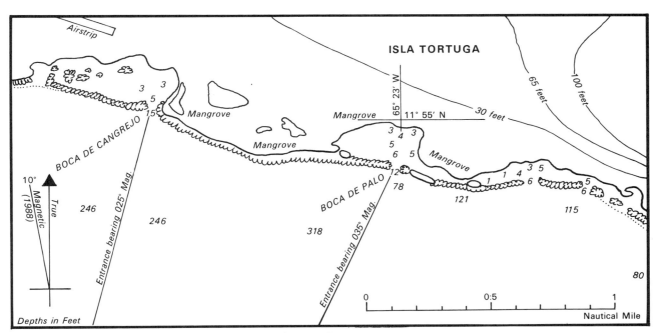

SKETCH CHART V–57   Boca de Cangrejo and Boca Palo, Tortuga

tom is sand and dead coral. You are anchoring on the back side of a slope, so squeeze as close to the reef as you can, get one anchor down, back off, then run out another anchor in a dinghy. Next put on a face mask and snorkel to check that you are held securely. We encountered a strong easterly current that swung us almost beam-to the wind, despite having the mizzen up and a wind of about 30 knots. Therefore, you have to be sure to have a stern anchor out. As long as the wind is east of north, this is a superb anchorage.

There are gaps in the reef that enable a dinghy to get through. You will find a vast area, about half a mile long, of beautiful white sand. There's good snorkeling here, but there aren't too many fish.

PUNTA PIEDRAS

In good conditions, when the wind is north of east, one can anchor on the shelf; we saw a fishing boat anchored there. We also saw some nice small beaches in the area. It looked as though there probably would be good diving.

LAGUNA EL CARENERO

(Chart V-55; II D-1, D-13, D-14)

Numerous boats have found themselves in difficulties while trying to enter Carenero, and one, in fact, sank. In all cases, as far as I have been able to ascertain, the boats were trying to enter a channel that is littered with coral heads (axis of the channel is approximately 280° magnetic) under impossible light conditions. In three cases I know about, the boats were entering the channel between 1700 and 1800 with the sun in their eyes, so they could see absolutely nothing. *Iolaire* has never entered the channel, as the only time we arrived there, it was blowing about 35 to 45 knots—obviously not the moment to experiment with a reef-strewn channel. However, information from some experienced sailors (and from my observations during two trips in a low-flying plane) is that the channel leads approximately 280° to 290° magnetic. Favor the windward (starboard) side of the channel—one should always do that, since if you run aground on the windward side of the channel, you blow off into deeper water, whereas if you go aground on the leeward side of the channel, the wind and sea are always pushing you harder aground and you have no hope of getting off. In the center of the channel, I am told,

there is a big coral head with only about 4 feet of water over it, which one must avoid. I have been assured that between the coral heads at low water, there is 6 feet; at high water springs in the winter, there evidently is 7 1/2 to 8 feet. Hug the windward side of the channel so closely that you are only a boat length from the beach.

Once you are inside the lagoon, I am told, there is plenty of water, but the bar seems to be about 6 feet deep just inside the entrance. Anchor according to your depth but be prepared for mosquitoes at night. The lagoon is a great place for boardsailing and exploring in a dinghy and there is excellent birdwatching at dawn and dusk. Some boats have reported excellent anchoring bow-on to the beach, stern anchor out in the entrance to Carenero Harbor.

As can be seen, Isla La Tortuga is an island with tons of possibility. If the wind is north of east, there are four good anchorages on the south coast alone, plus more on the west coast and a good anchorage on the northeast corner if the ground swell is not coming in.

Isla La Orchila

The Venezuelan government forbids yachtsmen from stopping at Isla La Orchila (covered by NOAA chart 24443 and II D-2), since there is a military base here. However, it is comforting to know that the island can be used dependably as a night landmark, since the 15-mile light apparently is almost always on, and the loom from the lights of government buildings is visible 20 miles away. Regulations require that you pass at least 5 miles from the coast of La Orchila.

This island is described by almost all Venezuelan yachtsmen (and those Americans lucky enough to have been there) as one of the nicest islands off the Venezuelan coast—and I agree. However, it is now an unfriendly place: You might happen to anchor there and get away with it for a few hours, but when the army arrives, you will be chased out unceremoniously, sometimes at gunpoint, and irrespective of the prevailing weather conditions.

Thus, no one but a damned fool would stop off at La Orchila unless he had obtained a pass to do so from the Guardia Nacional. Even if you have secured such a pass, make sure there are lots of stamps on it; then, as soon as you arrive at La Orchila, present yourself to the military base on the eastern side of the south cove.

NOTES

10

Western Offshore Islands: Los Roques, Las Aves

II D, D-2, D-22

Los Roques

Islas Los Roques is an area that comprises about sixty cays forming a 25-by-20-mile bank roughly 70 miles north of Caracas. Only about twenty-five of the cays are named, and except for El Gran Roque, which rises to a height of 180 feet, none is more than 10 or 15 feet high. Some have palm trees, others mangroves, and a few are mere sand hills.

Being only an overnight run from Caracas, these islands might be expected to be full of Venezuelan yachts, but except for the big holiday weekends, this is not the case. Of the 355 square miles of Los Roques, an area of approximately 8 miles north to south and 15 miles east to west is listed on the American chart as being an unsurveyed wasteland of coral heads. Here is an area where the brave can sail and explore to their hearts' content.

Being low and flat and offshore, Islas Los Roques are smack in the trade-wind belt, where the major variation is from "blowing hard" to "blowing harder." The passage out can be quite bumpy, and the seas, as one approaches the eastern end of Los Roques, can vary from large to massive.

However, once you get inside Los Roques, the reefs break the Atlantic swell. And even though you could have trouble on the north side with the ground swell during the winter, once you get securely anchored in the shallow water behind the cays, it would be almost impossible to be disturbed.

In Los Roques, as anywhere else, yachtsmen seem to exhibit the lemming instinct, one boat following another to certain anchorages. However,

those who are a little more adventuresome can find their own stopping places off the beaten track.

For many years, much of Los Roques has been a national park. In the late 1980s, the Parks Department began exercising its authority, banning spearfishing, garbage dumping, and other harmful activities in many areas. Now, in 1990, the Perez government is making a strong effort throughout Venezuela to preserve the national park areas. In Los Roques, there is both a new Parks Department director and a new Port Captain, and both are enforcing the rules. When arriving in Los Roques, you must present your *zarpa* to the Port Captain on El Gran Roque and pick up a copy of the latest Parks Department regulations. This is important, as anchoring is absolutely forbidden in some areas.

When approaching Los Roques from the Caracas area, you have two choices. The first course is to sail close-reaching or hard on the wind and pass east and north of Los Roques, then enter via passage 3 or 4 (see chart II D-22 or Chart V-58). If it is between 1000 and 1400 and you know what the heck you are doing, you can enter at passage 2.

The advantage of arriving by this route is that once in Los Roques, you can do all your exploration and sailing dead downwind. The disadvantage of this route is that while heading over from Caracas, you will be close-reaching under normal conditions. When the wind is blowing right out of the east, it will be very lumpy; if northeast, it is likely to be a hard beat. I am not sure about the currents, because the first time we went to Los Roques from Caracas, we experienced virtually no set to the

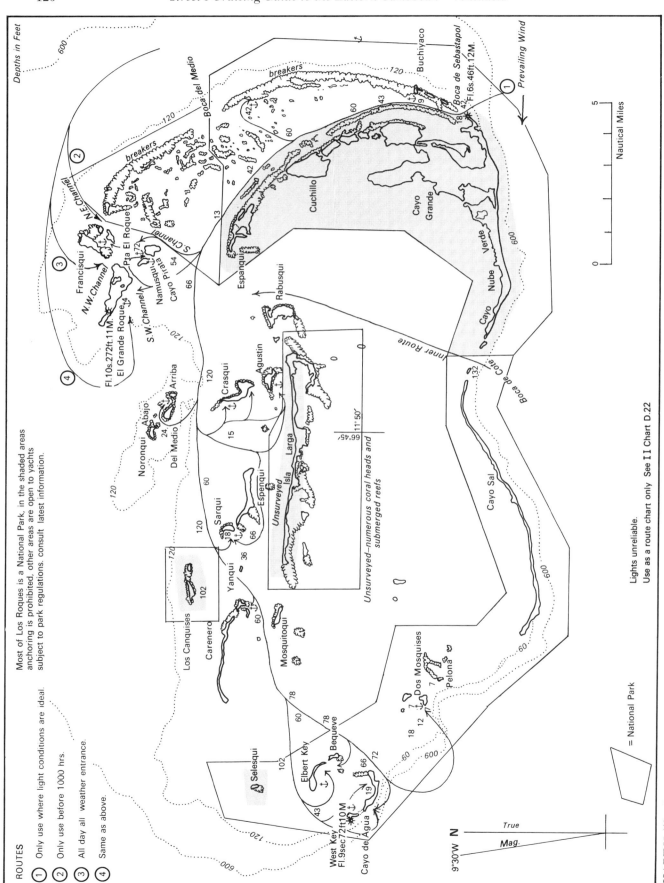

ROUTES

① Only use where light conditions are ideal.

② Only use before 1000 hrs.

③ All day all weather entrance.

④ Same as above.

Most of Los Roques is a National Park, in the shaded areas anchoring is prohibited, other areas are open to yachts subject to park regulations. consult latest information.

Lights unreliable.
Use as a route chart only See I I Chart D.22

☐ = National Park

CHART V–58   Los Roques

west, but on our last trip we encountered a 1-knot set to the west.

The second choice is to approach from the west, where there is a good light on Cayo de Agua as a lead-in. But if you plan to approach the western end of the cay, you should not leave the Caracas area until fairly late in the evening. You need to approach the cays after 1000 in the morning; otherwise, the sun is well in the east and you cannot see to find your way in and anchor. If you decide to approach from the west, I suggest that you anchor either in Cayo de Agua in the northwest anchorage or up behind Dos Mosquises and wait there until the sun is high. This route will give you a much more comfortable trip across from the Caracas area, but it will mean that as you head eastward through Los Roques, you will be beating to windward. Since it sometimes blows from 25 to 30 in Los Roques, you may decide that you don't want to work your way eastward and will find yourself anchored at Dos Mosquises or Cayo de Agua for your entire stay.

There are four different approaches to Los Roques (covered by Chart V-58 and II D-2 and D-22) usable by yachtsmen; a fifth approach is usable only by Venezuelan fishermen entering through Boca de Cote.

There are no buoys, so all navigation is strictly eyeball. Everything must be done when the sun is high, although the northern, southeastern, and western corners are supposed to be marked by lights.

Approach 1. You can sail to the light marking the western end of Los Roques, rhumb-line course about 005° magnetic from Puerto Azul, usually an easy reach. Anchor and spend the day here, and then the following day work your way east into Los Roques, beating to windward or powering all the way.

Approach 2. Head for the southeast corner of Los Roques, whose light supposedly flashes every 12 1/2 seconds. It is 144 feet high and visible for 12 miles, on the western side of the entrance. Remember, though, that Venezuelan lights are *extremely* unreliable. The approach to this entrance can be made only after 0900, when the sun is high enough for eyeball piloting. I am told that it is an all-weather entrance, but in periods of heavy weather, it is only for the stouthearted. Put a crew member in the rigging and pass the sand island to port and the breaking reefs to starboard. Once through the entrance, stand north between the two reefs. There is ample water and the seas will be smooth, having been broken up by the outer reef. You can anchor behind

the little sand island a few miles north of the entrance.

From here, you can explore to your heart's content, as there is a 10-mile barrier reef where you can see lobster and all kinds of fish. (Just remember that you can't capture them, as spearfishing is prohibited.)

Boats drawing 6 feet or less can head approximately 285° magnetic from the entrance, pass between the sand spit and the inner reef, swing around to port, and anchor behind the point. There is not enough water (except for very shoal-draft boats) to continue north inside the inner reef. I am told that just west of this anchorage there's a great beach for finding driftwood.

You can also continue north between the two reefs, following the deep water just to windward of the inner reef, jibe around the north end of the inner reef, and then backtrack to the south. This is best done under shortened sail or slowly under power, as there are some very narrow gaps with the bare minimum of water, and these must be checked carefully. A good place to anchor is immediately inside the northern end of the inner reef, where there is ample water. From here you can explore southward in the dinghy, making sure there is enough depth to anchor or pass.

Sailing northward between the inner and outer reefs has been well described by Pedro Gluecksman:

"The southeast entrance has a steel-frame light. The entrance, called Sebastopol, is at least 20 feet deep at its center. You can notice two channels going in a northerly direction. The channel to port is not navigable, as it becomes obstructed farther north and its entrance is too shallow, unless you have a shallow-draft boat. The channel to starboard is navigable right toward the northern part. You must, however, stick closely to the middle string of reef that separates the two channels. Staying close to the windward side of the separating reef will ensure a deep channel all the way, with no trouble under sail. The wind is usually south of east.

"Coming from the north, the same procedure is used, but you'll be on a close reach. There are times, however, when the wind is very much from the southeast and there's no space for tacking at some locations, particularly at the northern end where the course to be sailed is a true southeast. When venturing off the indicated channel, you will normally find plenty of water, but you must exercise caution, as you might encounter numerous spot reefs. You can anchor just to leeward of the windward reef east of the islands. This is a tremendous experience. The waters are very calm, yet the strong sea swells break just off the reef, which completely dampens the effect of the swells.

"Anchoring at this point is done in the following manner: The bottom shallows from a good 50 feet, all sand, to about 4 feet. We have anchored just off the drop-off, putting our Danforth anchor right in the shallow part with the dinghy. [Make sure it is well buried; I would advise two anchors on the reef set in a Y shape.—DMS]

"In extremely heavy seas, there is still no danger; very occasionally it becomes uncomfortable at this point, but not dangerous. You need anchor only by the bow, as the prevailing trades never change direction enough to give you trouble. At this outward windward reef, there is an opening that may be entered during the day with no particular dangers. Keep to port and drop the hook just as you enter, in the manner previously described. [Again there are plenty of fish, but don't spear any, as you are within the national park.—DMS]"

At Boca de Sebastopol, there is a new light tower southeast of the position of the light tower noted on most charts. While flying around Los Roques in February 1989, however, it appeared that the light tower at Boca de Sebastopol was gone completely. So . . . beware.

Approach 3. The most common way of entering Los Roques is to pass east of them, carry on north, and then ease sheets and run down the northeastern edge of the reef, taking careful bearings on the light on El Gran Roque. Continue sailing northwest until Cayo Pirata bears 220° magnetic; then run down southwest, through the northeast channel into Puerto El Roque.

Approach 4. The last approach is to run off to the west north of Francisqui, then southwest to pass north of El Gran Roque; jibe over and beat up the south coast of El Gran Roque into Puerto El Roque. When making Approaches 3 and 4, the best landmark for taking bearings will be the light towers of El Gran Roque, but it should be noted that at the western end of El Gran Roque there are two light towers, one in use and the other abandoned. Note that both are a mile and a half west of the eastern tip of El Gran Roque. The US chart notes an old lighthouse on the eastern end of El Gran Roque, but we couldn't spot it.

Even though you are forbidden to discard garbage within the national park, it is unfortunate that almost everywhere you see the sign denoting Los Roques as a national park, there is garbage piled up beneath the sign! If you use your head, it is possible to get rid of most of your trash with little damage to the environment. Flatten cans, punch holes into their bottoms, and place them in a bag. Put plastic in another bag and biodegradable garbage in a third. When you are sailing between the islands and you feel you have a clear shot out to the west, you can dump the tin cans to sink in hundreds of feet of water, and biodegradable garbage will break down before it reaches the Central or South American coast. Keep the plastic and nonbiodegradable garbage in a tightly secured bag until you finally reach a port where you can dispose of it properly. If every sailor (I say "sailor" instead of "yachtsman" as all too many boats cruising the Caribbean are owned or crewed by people who are not yachtsmen) would follow the above procedure, the litter on the beaches would be minimized.

There are three areas where anchoring is off limits. First, the entire reef and island complex to the southeast, south from Espanqui (sic) and extending all the way around to Boca de Cote; second, the island of Los Canquises, northwest of Sarqui; third, the small island on the northwest, Selenqui, north of Elbert Key.

Once inside Los Roques, you will find so many anchorages you won't know which to choose. Below are just a few of them:

FRANCISQUI
(Chart V-58; II D, D-22)

This is an excellent stop that provides many anchorages, and I'd be interested to find out how it got its name. We saw a cannon on shore, supposedly salvaged from a French wreck off to windward of the island. Was this one of the ships of Comte d'Estrées's squadron that was wrecked on Ave de Barlovento, on the night of 11 May 1678, en route to seize Curaçao?

The entrance into Francisqui is strictly eyeball navigation. About 2 fathoms can be carried through the southern entrance, which is very narrow—probably 50 to 70 feet. After the narrow gap, there is plenty of water. The best anchorage appears to be in the eastern corner of the harbor.

Sail right up to the beach and throw your anchor ashore, as the beach is very steep-to. Boats drawing 5 feet or less can enter the inner lagoon between eastern and southern Francisqui. Excellent beaches are all around, with crystal-clear water and good shelling.

For those who don't want to go into the lagoon, there is an anchorage in the shallow water west of

Pequeño Francis. A sand bar has built up between Pequeño Francis and Francisqui.

Hank Strauss reports on anchorages:

"The anchorage is close to shore, just inside the northwest point. There's excellent snorkeling around the anchorage, and good fishing. On a holiday weekend, the joint is loaded with sailboats and powerboats from Caracas. When we were there it was Easter weekend, and it looked like Long Island Sound and Cowes Week combined."

Francisqui is always crowded now, because day-trippers have been coming out from Caracas every morning and spending a day on the beach. So it's no place to stop if you want to get away from it all, although they all depart about 1600, leaving the islands relatively deserted until about 0930 the next day.

CAYO PIRATA
(Chart V-58; II D, D-2, D-22)

This cay probably received its name because it would have been a first-rate place for pirates to hide and careen their ships; and the cay's two exits would have made for easy escape in case of attack. Deep water goes right up to the beach in the harbor.

Boats are no longer built on Cayo Pirata (shown as Isla de Rata on the old Imray-Iolaire chart). An anchorage can be had south of Cayo Pirata, but holding is poor, with plenty of coral heads. There is no passage between Namusqui and Cayo Pirata. As long as the wind is east or south of east, an anchorage can be had between the two islands approaching from the north, but according to Daniel Shaw, owner of a Swan 47, the only way to anchor is to run the bow up on the beach and have someone jump ashore with the anchor and bury it. Then back off and drop a stern anchor. Reverse the process when leaving. On *Iolaire*, in February 1989, we discovered this to be true—holding was very poor in the deep water.

NAMUSQUI
(Chart V-58; II D, D-2, D-22)

There is an anchorage to leeward of Namusqui, but it is shoal, with scattered coral heads. West of Namusqui there is an anchorage, but the holding is poor and this area also is full of coral heads. There are rental cottages and a hotel on Namusqui, so it is possible to arrange for some of your crew to sleep ashore if they are so inclined.

EL GRAN ROQUE
(Charts V-58, IV-59; II D, D-2, D-22)

This is the main island of Los Roques, with a small airstrip that connects it to the outside world. Caracas has a private-plane airport in the city, and local businessmen with a boat in Los Roques and a private pilot could live at Los Roques and commute. Information about the village and airport is quoted below from a 1979 letter from Hank Strauss of *Doki*, who has been most helpful with regard to checking existing information and doing original exploration:

"The little airstrip that you mention has weekend traffic of up to sixty planes a day, and believe me that's accurate. They've been flying over our masts from Caracas like I'm living in Long Island on the Kennedy Airport flyway. . . .Virtually no supplies here. The Port Captain's office is in a new Spanish-style building on the little square. No bread, but a Venezuelan substitute (*arrepás*) can be ordered from the house on the starboard side of the street running south from the square. It's like large biscuits, similar to hoecakes, and each one is a potential weight for a lead line. The hotel at the west end of the airstrip is like a scene from *Rain*; it looks like a haunted, rundown grain mill. Dozens of dogs, children, and two tables, which makes for a large, no-menu, excellent meal—fish, lobster, etc. Order in advance. No electricity. Worth the experience."

A Venezuelan chart from a 1984 survey shows the best anchorage on El Gran Roque (see Chart V-59) as Puerto El Roque, to the west of town. When anchoring, bring the old ruins on the hill bearing 049° magnetic and the southeast corner of El Gran Roque bearing 120°. Anchor on the outer edge, on the shelf, in 8 to 9 feet of water. Do not go inside the bearing of 120° unless you draw 6 feet or less. The whole shelf has 7 feet of water or less. We know! *Iolaire* draws 7 feet 6 inches and we were parked!

If anchoring out in deep water, I would definitely anchor in Y fashion—one anchor in shoal water, one anchor in deep water, as you will note that the soundings drop off very suddenly from 10 to 75 feet in a distance of a hundred yards. Your anchor is on the backside of a slope, and it will be very difficult to get it to hold if it is not on the shelf.

The Guardia Nacional is in the new building with the radiotelephone tower on it. They have telephone communications to Caracas that private individuals can use in an emergency. The Port Captain is in the white igloo west of the Guardia headquarters.

Basic food supplies and fuel are available here,

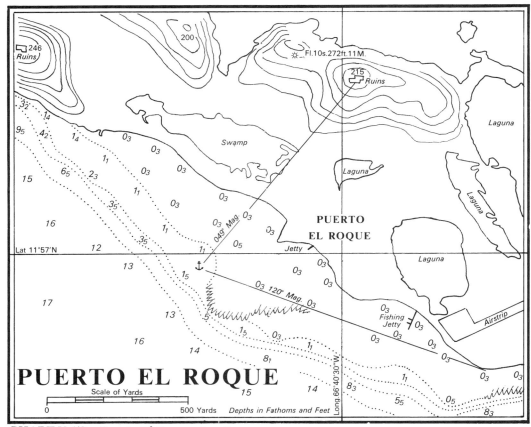

CHART V–59   Puerto El Roque, Los Roques

but nothing fancy. Water evidently is a major problem. There is a distillation unit, but when we arrived in February 1989, the distillation unit had broken down and a navy ship came out to bring water. Everybody was loading water ashore using fifty-five-gallon plastic drums, and obviously this happens fairly regularly, as a number of the launches that pulled up pumped water to their cisterns via a long hose and an electrically driven pump. They seemed well prepared for this situation, so don't expect to find any water.

After Antigua Week 1990, the skipper of *Flying Scotsman* reported that he had discovered fresh fruit and vegetables on El Gran Roque—in the main square of Puerto El Roque. The store is not marked; it's just a matter of poking your nose into every open door until you find the one that leads to a room full of fresh fruit and vegetables.

NORONQUI
(Chart V-58; II D, D-2, D-22)

This is not really one island but rather an archipelago, comprising Noronqui Arriba, del Me-

dio, and Abajo. In this little archipelago, I will categorically state, is one of the finest anchorages I have visited in the entire Eastern Caribbean.

A break in the reef on the north side can be used by powerboats in settled conditions—there appears to be about 5 or 6 feet of water through the gap. Obviously, in heavy weather, the seas break all the way across it. There is really no reason to use the northern passage except for the powerboats exiting the area en route back to El Gran Roque.

Entering from the south is strictly a case of eyeball navigation in ideal conditions. I am told that once inside, there is a perfectly sheltered anchorage, as the reef shelters it from the north and breaks any ground swell coming in. When entering from the south, short-tack up to the southeastern corner of Noronqui Arriba, avoiding the obvious coral reef that is easily visible in good conditions. The proper method of anchoring is to sail right to the beach and as soon as you feel the keel touch, drop the bow anchor. Have someone jump off the bow and haul the anchor up into shallow water and bury it. In the winter, the wind is always from the east, so a stern anchor is not necessary then. But in the summer, the wind can come in from the west, so I would advise anchoring bow and stern then.

Entering from the west is easier, but it's much narrower than the chart shows. Soundings are not very numerous, but I am told there is 14 feet. (Remember that the US chart for Los Roques is on a scale of 1:60,000, and therefore not very detailed.)

The beach on Noronqui Arriba is absolutely fantastic—perfect! The beach on the north side of Noronqui del Medio is excellent except that garbage is washed over the top of the reef and litters the beach. Almost any beach in the Passage Islands, the Virgins, the Grenadines, the offshore islands of Venezuela and the coast that is exposed to the east invariably is littered with plastic, empty beer cans, and the like. Garbage disposal is a problem.

The diving in this area is excellent, as the reef drops off from 3 feet to 50 feet in a vertical wall! Remember that spearfishing is prohibited in the park area, but fishing with a hook and line is allowed.

On the north side of Noronqui Abajo is the wreck of a World War II LSI (Landing Ship Infantry) that might be interesting to investigate. There is also an anchorage on the south side of Noronqui Abajo, off the southwest part of the island, but since the Arriba anchorage is so good, why go anywhere else?

There is a deepwater basin inside the reef at the eastern end of Noronqui, and an excellent anchorage close to the shore behind the island. Make sure your anchor is on shore, as there is a more or less vertical dropoff. The exact depth is debatable. Do not enter from the north, as the northerly swell will be sweeping in, frequently breaking across the entire entrance.

CRASQUI
(Chart V-58; II D, D-2, D-22)

Warning: There is no passage between Crasqui and the offlying island to the northwest. Some old Imray-Iolaire charts show a solid reef between the island and Crasqui when in fact there is 2 or 3 feet of water.

There's an excellent anchorage under Crasqui on the white-sand beach about halfway down the island, off the fishing colony. It's a case of feeling your way in and anchoring at a suitable depth. Over the weekend, Venezuelan powerboats are found moored bow and stern here, others are close-on to the beach, and the area is inundated with water-skiers.

Hank Strauss reports:

"There's an interesting fishing village at the south end, and it's a good anchorage. There's also an isolated anchorage off the northwest end of the island close to a beach which is some miles in length. Just before sundown, large flocks of pelicans, in the hundreds, divebomb the water in rollover, follow-the-leader bomber technique. An anchor has to be set carefully, since the bottom is a thin layer of sand over hard coral."

RABUSQUI AND BURQUI

Rabusqui and Burqui are southeast of Crasqui. We have not visited these two islands, but it appears from the air that you can either anchor to leeward of Burqui or work your way in around to windward of Burqui and anchor behind Rabusqui. This is strictly a case of eyeball navigation in ideal conditions. I advise sending the dinghy ahead. Whether or not you can get access to the big unsurveyed area south of Sarqui by passing east of Isla Larga, I don't know. Do the Venezuelans enter via the gap in the reef east of Isla Larga and the western end of the tail of the reef extending out from Rabusqui? Or do they pass west around Isla Larga and work their way backward through the unsurveyed area? I don't know, but in February 1989, when we were sailing between Crasqui and Isla Larga (also called Lanqui-Larga), I was sitting on the spreaders. I could see a yacht anchored approximately where the anchor shows on the new Imray-Iolaire chart, and a fishing camp on the island. Unfortunately, I did not have my hand-bearing compass aloft with me, so I cannot verify the locations, but I can at least note that there is a fishing camp and an anchorage off the south side of the eastern end of Isla Larga.

ESPENQUI
(Chart V-58; II D, D-2, D-22)

South of Espenqui is an unsurveyed area where there is a long reef extending in an east-west direction. The best passage is north of the reef. South of the reef there is plenty of water, but there are three shoals with deep water between them. The sketch chart and Imray-Iolaire chart positions are approximate and depths are only guesswork; *the estimated depth over the shoals is 9 feet.*

But there is much argument about the location of reefs south of Espenqui. I firmly feel that the reefs are shown as per the new Imray-Iolaire chart dated July 1989 and the sketch chart (i.e., a long, narrow reef extending east-west with three offlying shoals to the south of it and a depth of 8 or 9 feet over the shoals). However, Lloyd Eccelstone of the big cruising yacht *Kodiak* (and many other hot racing boats) feels that the reef extends in a north-south direction. We both agree that if you hug the Espenqui side of the channel, all is clear.

On the south side of Espenqui, toward the eastern end, is a small white-sand beach that might be an interesting stop in calm weather. In February 1989, we saw three boats anchored farther west of the saltpond, but we did not examine this anchorage closely. The western anchorage (off the south end of the western tip) has a beautiful beach, white-sand bottom, and 6 to 7 feet of water. But, as far as I could see, getting into the anchorage could be accomplished only by boats drawing 4 or 5 feet, and with good reef pilots aboard to zigzag through the reef. A crew member definitely is needed on the first spreaders to help you work your way through the reef. Once inside, conditions are perfect.

There is a passage between Sarqui and Espenqui, a full 2 fathoms through the passage, but the passage is narrow and boats should use it only when sailing downwind, as tacking through the passage with the current against you, I think, would be extremely difficult and pointless.

It is reported that the above channel has been sounded via dinghy and is approximately 6 feet deep—for shoal-draft boats only.

SARQUI

(Chart V-58; II D, D-2, D-22)

There once was an airstrip here, and you can see where it originally was located. Why anyone would build an airstrip on Sarqui, however, is beyond me. There is an excellent anchorage in 9 feet of water off the northern tip, just south of the reef that extends west of the northern tip of Sarqui. Favor the northern side of the cove, as the southern side has a fair number of rocks. The bottom is extremely hard sand. It is hard to get the anchor to dig in, but once it is in, it is good holding.

There is also an excellent anchorage under the lee of Sarqui: a white-sand beach tucked right up in the northeast corner. With the island to the east and a reef looking out to the west, it should be a beautiful, calm anchorage with fishing from the boat. It's also a popular spot with Venezuelan sailors, who often end their races here.

ISLA LARGA/ISLA FERNANDO

South of Isla Larga is Isla Fernando, with what obviously is the second largest habitation in the islands. On the edge of Isla Fernando are the biggest piles of conch shells I have ever seen. If you wanted to build a West Indian house with a rubble wall, you could find all the aggregate you needed.

You reach Isla Fernando by rounding the western edge of Isla Larga, staying east of Mosquitoqui. Stay on the Mosquitoqui side of the channel—eyeball navigation in good light only. Then tack up between Isla Fernando and Isla Larga. There is plenty of water but also a few reefs, which can be seen easily in good light and avoided.

We sailed up to La Maseta Fernando, right up to the shoal west of the island, and parked *Iolaire*. When we dropped the anchor under the bow, Nick, our hairy-legged typist, grabbed the anchor and walked it up to shoal water to bury it. If you attempt this type of operation, make sure you wear shoes, as Nick discovered the hard way that there are sea urchins in the area!

Willy Wilson (head of Imray, Laurie, Norie & Wilson), my son Mark Edward, and I explored the area to the east in the dinghy. We went as far as the island that we think has a fishing camp on the far south side, but we ran out of light at that point and had to return to *Iolaire*. Investigating the eastern area of the south side of Isla Larga will have to wait until the next trip.

We could see from the dinghy, and also from the bo'sun's chair at the top of *Iolaire*'s masthead while anchored at La Maseta Fernando, that there is no problem sailing eastward in the unsurveyed area, as long as the light is good.

We have not explored the area south of Isla Fernando, but we do know there is no water between the western end of Mosquitoqui and the offlying reef to the west.

According to the chart and from the air, it appeared that one could sail from Isla Fernando south of Mosquitoqui in 12 feet of water, then head south either east or west of the reef south-southwest of Mosquitoqui. However, from the deck of *Iolaire*, discretion was the better part of valor—it did not look quite deep enough. We were running dead downwind under staysail and mizzen and still doing more than 6 knots. We chickened out and turned north and passed between Mosquitoqui, Yanqui, and Carenero, then swung around Mosquitoqui and headed south. I think this area south of Mosquitoqui deserves exploration when the wind is north or east and not blowing too hard.

MOSQUITOQUI

Warning: There is a big rock due west of Mosquitoqui, just east of the 5-foot spot on the Imray-Iolaire chart.

An anchorage can be had anywhere along the south coast of Mosquitoqui when the wind is in the north. Feel your way in and anchor.

YANQUI

(Chart V-58; II D, D-2, D-22)

Anchoring off Yanqui would be a bit of a project because the bottom drops off quite steeply on all sides. In periods of moderately calm weather, I think an anchorage could be had off its southwestern tip. Work your way inshore and set your anchor almost on the beach. I feel it is worthwhile stopping at Yanqui because at the eastern end of the island there is a natural pool, behind a breakwater buildup of 2 feet of dead coral. The pool appears to be about 2 or 3 feet deep, and swimming here would be like being in a warm, saltwater bathtub!

LANQUI-CARENERO

(Chart V-58; II D, D-2, D-22)

Warning: In the entrance to Carenero (Los Roques), there is a rock in the center of the channel with 2 or 3 feet of water over it, but there is plenty of room to navigate on either side.

Lanqui-Carenero is actually a group of three islands. In the eastern end of this group is, without doubt, the finest little anchorage I have seen, or been in, in my years in the Caribbean. The entire crew agreed that had our trip not been an exploratory one (which meant we had to press on), we'd have stayed here for at least a week. This harbor is perfectly sheltered, and the entrance from the south is 2 fathoms deep. Once inside, there are depths of 4 or 5 fathoms all over, despite the fact that the US chart shows no soundings.

To anchor on the eastern side, sail up to the reef or island until you run aground and then throw the anchor ashore—the wind will hold you off. There is a beautiful, crystal-clear lagoon with an island and a reef to the west and an island to the north and east, with only a small opening to the south—a wonderful place to throw the kids into the rowing dinghy with no fear of their being blown off to leeward and out of the harbor.

The harbor is loaded with conch: Twenty minutes of diving, directly from the boat, provided enough for a big stew. We weren't there long enough to find any lobsters, but many people report that the area is loaded with them. The water temperature was 81°F on the surface, and it will still be more or less the same 5 feet down—quite a change from the cold water (68°F) along the Venezuelan coast. There are heavy mangroves along the shores, so oysters undoubtedly are available if you search.

West of the above-described anchorage is a deep basin with excellent diving around the edges. The water appears clear, but neither Jan de Bosset's exploration from the water's edge nor mine from the aircraft revealed any passage into that area for boats drawing more than about 3 feet.

On the eastern side, the easternmost part of Carenero has another very good basin that does not show at present on our Imray-Iolaire chart.

Apparently there is also another anchorage, which I refer to as the "eastern pool anchorage," on the eastern end of Isla Carenero. This appears to be a completely sheltered anchorage with an entrance from the southeast heading northwest. Once you have passed the reef on the starboard hand, head due north, then round up immediately and anchor. You will have to put the bow up on the easternmost reef, place an anchor, and back off. Then run a stern anchor right across the harbor and put it on the west side of the harbor. There is room for no more than one or two boats. I would not contemplate entering the anchorage except in ideal conditions, when it is not blowing too hard, and then probably only in a 40- or 50-foot boat. We have only seen this anchorage from the air, but it looks superb.

There is no habitation in Carenero cove, but at the western end of the main island, on the southern shore, there is a fairly large fishing village. To the west, it is completely foul with coral heads, making it poor for anchoring but good for snorkeling.

ELBERT KEY

The best anchorage in Elbert Key is southwest of the southern extremity of the island. This anchorage can be reached in two ways: Either swing west around Elbert Key and beat to windward up to the eastern corner, making sure you dodge the 4-foot spot marked clearly on the chart. Alternatively, sail west around Cayo Becqueve, then swing north, passing between the shoals west of Cayo Becqueve and the detached coral reefs to the west. Then head due north, anchoring southwest of Elbert Key, west of the northern tip of Becqueve.

In all these areas, if you just eyeball the situation and stick to the white sand, you will be okay.

WEST KEY

A small island has been thrown up southwest of the light on West Key. On the north side of this island is a small sand beach with an anchorage in 9 feet, shoaling to 8 feet. This is a very small, restricted area, but the beach is the calmest of all the beaches on the west side of West Key and Cayo de Agua. With the light bearing 065° magnetic, boats 35 feet or less could find an anchorage here in calm weather. Obviously, you would have to anchor bow and stern, as there is no swinging room.

CAYO DE AGUA
(Chart V-60; II D, D-2, D-22)

An anchorage can be had on the northwestern tip of Cayo de Agua, between the reef and the sand spit. The sand cliffs, about 20 feet high, should be bearing due east. Work your way inshore as your draft permits; 6 feet of draft can be carried almost up to the beach, 7 feet a little farther out. You can

still carry 9 feet with the end of the southern reef bearing about 200° magnetic. Tucking in behind the reef will get you out of the swell (which I think is caused by the tide that sweeps around and catches you beam-on for three or four hours twice a day). An anchorage can also be had in the area now described and carefully viewed from the top of the 72-foot-high light on West Key. (We have not actually sounded the area—the sketch chart is based on viewing from the tower and an aerial photograph.)

Halfway along the north side of Cayo de Agua, where a reef extends north from the point, there are two anchorages—one to the east and one to the west. For the western anchorage, follow the dotted line westward behind the reef, eyeball-navigate through the coral heads (estimated depth is 9 to 12 feet), and anchor behind the reef. To reach the eastern anchorage on the north side of Cayo de Agua, pass northward around the reef, then turn south and head for the break in the long line of trees on Cayo de Agua. Anchor off the break in the trees in 9 to 12 feet of water. Note that the area along the eastern edge of the shoal that forms Cayo de Agua is littered with coral heads with 3 to 5 feet of water over them. This is not enough to break the swell, so these anchorages on the north side of Cayo de Agua are tenable only when the wind is east or basically south of east. Any north in the wind and these anchorages will be quite rough.

The name Cayo de Agua means "Cay of Water." There are several ponds on the island in which the

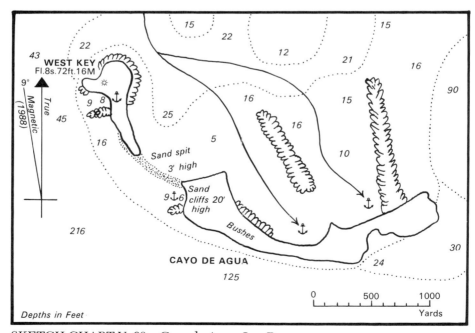

SKETCH CHART V–60   Cayo de Agua, Los Roques

water appears to be brackish, but reputedly there also are various wells where, in years gone by, fishermen would fill their water tanks—hence the name. Cayo de Agua is heavily covered by brush trees, and there is a group of palm trees that is said to be a veritable oasis. An excellent view of the whole area can be had from the top of the tower on West Key, but do not attempt to walk to the tower unless you are wearing a good pair of shoes. The "prickers" will cut your feet.

DOS MOSQUISES
(Chart V-58; II D, D-2, D-22)

Regarding the best approach to Dos Mosquises, I have looked at it twice from the air and have visited the area myself in *Iolaire*, and I agree completely with the Venezuelan yachtsmen who state that the best approach to Dos Mosquises is from the southwest. Come in on a bearing of 060° magnetic on the palm trees on Isla Tres Palmeros. (There are two big palms and one very small one to the west. In between the two big palms I spotted a large stump, and I wondered whether the third palm had blown down.) A bearing of 060° between the two palms leads into the anchorage in a good 10 feet of water. If you draw more than 6 feet, *do not* go north of an east-west line drawn on the northern end of Dos Mosquises. Above this line it definitely shelves to 7 feet—we know, as we parked *Iolaire* for a few minutes. If you run aground, friendly fishermen will help. They came out unasked and helped us. We paid them with a couple of large shots of good Scotch, with which they were quite happy.

With care, one could probably squeeze 7 or 8 feet through the channel between the two islands. Once to windward of them, there is a full 2 fathoms of water. You can anchor there and go swimming on the outer reef without even having to put the dinghy in the water. It is said that there is a gap in the reef, but looking at it from the air and from the bowsprit of *Iolaire*, I could not see a gap even large enough for a dinghy. The windward reef makes an excellent breakwater.

Dos Mosquises has numerous excellent white-sand beaches and an airstrip, which I am told makes for rather hairy landings—but the problem must be related to the wind conditions, as it is a large, hard runway, much better than some on which I have landed! There is an experimental fisheries station where they raise turtles. The anchorage in Dos Mosquises is excellent, with smooth water and shelter from the sea. There is plenty of wind and you're

guaranteed to find no mosquitoes, so I wonder where it got its name.

We have one report that the islands are completely free of fish poisoning (*cicutería*), except in the region of Noronqui. This was news to me, since, as far as I know, there has been no report of fish poisoning south of Guadeloupe!

The area between Dos Mosquises and Punta Salina (or Cayo Sal) is littered with coral heads. With an experienced reef navigator, and in perfect conditions, you could easily pass through this area and then work to windward in the uncharted area.

ISLA PELONA

West of Isla Pelona, the bottom drops off the shelf very steeply. Get one anchor on the shelf and then use the dinghy to put the second anchor out ahead—if the anchor drops off the shelf, it will be hanging straight down in 50 feet of water and the next stop is somewhere down near Aruba! On Isla Pelona are lovely white-sand beaches and a small fishing shack. To windward of the island is a big basin of white sand 6 to 7 feet deep. It is enclosed completely on the northeast, but there are plenty of gaps on the eastern side of the reef. This area would make a good base for boardsailing, and, of course, the diving on the edge of the reef should be excellent.

SOUTHERN EDGE OF LOS ROQUES

Quoting Pedro Gluecksman:

"Southern edge of Los Roques. Cayo Sal: no anchorages possible, since the whole coastline is open to the sea. Nevertheless, about at the center of the southern coast, an entrance to the inner lagoon can be noticed. Some protection from the swells can be obtained here. Fishing at this point has got to be the best in the world. If you don't catch a fish here, it is simply because you don't want to.

"Inner Lagoon: This whole area is shoal, but it is all navigable with a dinghy. Local fishermen with their seagoing vessels called *tres puños* enter the middle section of the southern keys and cross the inner lagoon toward El Gran Roque. I have seen them take a 010° magnetic course from this point and make it across, but I certainly would not advise a stranger to these waters to do so."

I have given here a quick summary of anchorages around the edges of Los Roques. For those who want to get away from it all, there is a vast area—marked "unsurveyed" on the chart—that would be exciting to explore. Let's hope it will be surveyed sometime. Meanwhile, it is a glorious area for the adventurous. If someone could produce a good color aerial photo of the area, it would give indications of water depths, from which a rough sketch chart could be developed. Remember that since the area has not been sounded, eyeball navigation is necessary.

Considering how much yachting is booming in Venezuela, it can be hoped that the Venezuelan Hydrographic Office will one day set some naval officers loose in Los Roques to chart the entire area. This would do yachtsmen a tremendous service and also would be an excellent training program for the hydrographic office.

In addition, I feel that the area would be an excellent bareboat charter spot whose center of operations would be not in the crowded waters of Caracas—with a 70-mile trip at the beginning and end of the charter—but rather in Los Roques. It's only a thirty-five-minute flight from Maiquetía Airport, which has international connections, to the airstrip on El Gran Roque. One of the smaller, 45-foot Venezuelan fishing boats could move supplies from La Guaira to El Gran Roque. All the necessary food supplies, plus luxuries and extras, are available in the La Guaira area.

The boats, of course, would have to be shoal draft, such as those used by charter organizations in the Bahamas. I think the ideal boat would be the aft-cockpit version of the Freedom 40, illustrated in Volume II of *The Ocean Sailing Yacht.* Considering the sailing qualities, or lack thereof, of all too many bareboats, anything other than the Freedom 40 probably would be under power most of the time. Since the Freedom 40 draws only 3 feet with the board up, and will go to windward with the board up as well as a Morgan Out Island 41, she would be able to sail easily in the vast areas of shoal water in Los Roques. You could practically dispense with the dinghy, as in many areas you could usually moor bow-on to the shore.

For those charterers who feel the Freedom 40 is too large, the Herreshoff Meadow Lark, which draws 12 to 14 inches with the leeboards up, would be absolutely superb. With this little ketch, you would be able to moor practically everywhere bow-on to the beach.

Rather than the Herreshoff rig, which has two small gaffs, I think the Meadow Lark would be better equipped with the easy-to-handle wishbone rig of the Freedom 40. In fact, I've just defined the ideal vacation package for my wife and myself: a Herreshoff Meadow Lark with a Freedom 40 rig, and a commission to spend a couple of months exploring each and every anchorage in Los Roques!

Given a fleet of shoal-draft boats such as described above, it would seem to me to be virtually impossible to overcrowd Los Roques with charter boats, for the simple reason that the anchorages are too numerous to count.

Incidentally, another super way to explore Los Roques would be in a large Hobie Cat, with jugs of water, a tent, air mattresses, and a couple of coolers full of food and beer. You could camp out on the beaches and sleep under the stars—idyllic!

Most diving enthusiasts traditionally have headed for the Bahamas on the grounds that the diving there is better than in the Eastern Caribbean. Well, in my opinion, the Los Roques area has it all over the Bahamas. The water is warmer, the weather is better (with no sudden drops in temperature), and the sailing is better, since one is completely protected from the easterly ground swell. Furthermore, transportation to Los Roques is easier than to most parts of the Bahamas, and it probably would not be that much more expensive if a charter company organized things properly.

So let's hope someone with vision and investment capital will do yachtsmen a favor and set up a really good bareboat operation in Los Roques. What a dream-come-true that could be!

Thirty miles to leeward of Islas Los Roques lie Islas Las Aves (Barlovento and Sotavento), two groups of low, uninhabited cays 15 miles apart. Each group has numerous anchorages, miles of shoal water littered with coral heads, superb snorkeling and spearfishing, and innumerable wrecks, both ancient and modern, to explore.

Islas Las Aves

AVE DE BARLOVENTO
(Chart V-61; II D-2, D-22)

This is another group of islands that we would love to spend more time exploring. Although Ginnie Higman of the ketch *Tormentor III* reported in *A Cruising Guide to the Caribbean and Bahamas* that "the solitude is great, but the fishing poor," numerous other people have said that the fishing is superb. I am told that the lobstering is particularly excellent on these islands.

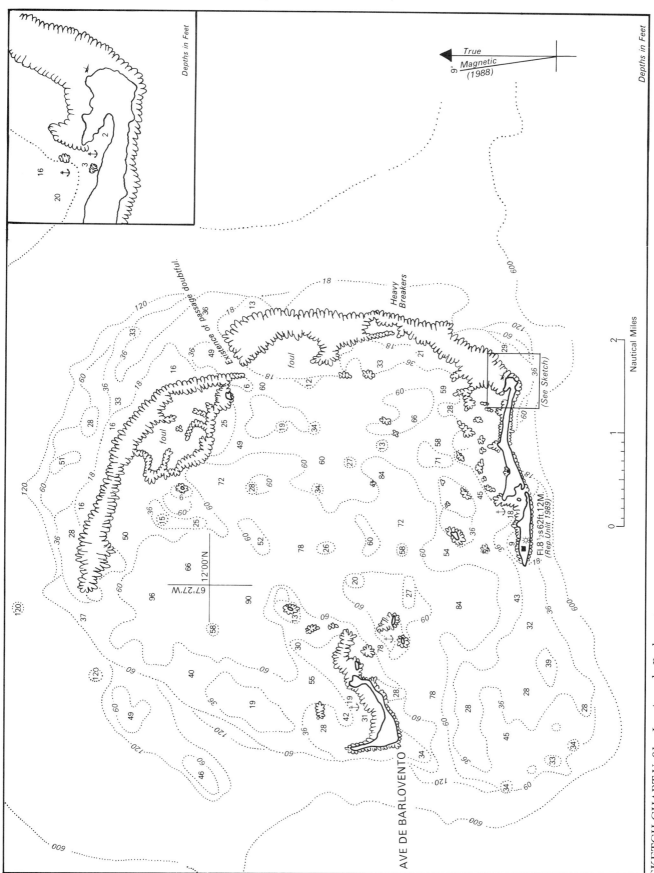

This group must be approached from the south, where there is an easily spotted (Fl8-1/2s.72ft.15m) light tower. Come around the west of the island and then eyeball eastward. The best anchorage is in the cove east of the light. When we were there in March 1989, the old light tower had been cut down and was lying on its side. The beautiful new light tower had been erected, but the light had not been installed. Who knows when that will happen. As stated elsewhere, lights on the Venezuelan coast are noted for their unreliability.

A good anchorage is right under the mangroves in 3 fathoms (see Chart V-61). We explored the mangrove area in the dinghy and discovered that the trees in Ave de Barlovento are the biggest and tallest I have ever seen. Some of those trees must have towered 60 feet in the air and had trunks 12 inches in diameter. I had always thought mangroves grew as bushes, but these certainly were trees! Billy Wray recommends the anchorage under the mangroves, but I would think the mosquitoes would drive you out! Billy also states that a friend of his reports being there and sitting out a bad blow (that later developed into a hurricane). When it was blowing 50 knots outside, it was almost calm among the tall mangroves. If you want to use this anchorage, send the dinghy ahead and sound out the channel.

Those who wish to dive can sail east right up behind the main reef and anchor anywhere suitable. Those who don't want to work so far east can go to the two small cays that lie in a direct line between the western end of the southern Ave and the western Ave (see Chart V-61). Anchor on the shelf of the western island, keeping the other tiny island to the east.

Warning: A shoal has been reported in this area—exactly where the Imray-Iolaire chart shows 9 fathoms (5 feet)! One boat swears it is there and many others claim it doesn't exist, but . . . an isolated coral head?

An anchorage can also be had northwest of the western Ave. Work your way well in, anchor, and make sure your anchor is set. The bottom is sand, loose coral, and miscellaneous rocks, making the holding tricky. You can swim right off the boat, with plenty of fish around the rocks and a white-sand beach ashore. Although this is an excellent anchorage, be careful of the northerly ground swell to which it is exposed.

A big yacht can anchor virtually anywhere it desires, as the reef to the east shelters it from the worst of the swell. Smaller yachts will want to tuck themselves in behind one of the many small islands.

There are at least half a dozen small islands that spring up on top of the reefs.

We spotted a large local fishing boat moored bow-on to the beach on the westernmost of the two small islands east of the large island.

On the north side of the large island, a couple of coral reefs create two huge pools. You might be able to bring a dinghy into the pools, but, more important, you can anchor a dinghy off the lee side of the reef and then wade into the pools, an experience I have heard about secondhand. Looking at them, I can well believe it. The pools are so shallow that the sun heats them up and they become rather like a giant Jacuzzi.

There is an anchorage with a beach on the western side of Long Island, but tuck in as tightly as possible in the northeast corner. All one has to do is look at the western beach to see that it is open to the ground swell—a wonderful, soft sand beach, but you can be guaranteed it will be a rocky and rolly anchorage.

There is no habitation on these islands, but there are the ruins of some very substantial buildings near the lighthouse. We were surprised to discover there was no Frontiere guard (a branch of the Guardia Nacional).

The western end of Ave de Barlovento is a bird sanctuary, a rookery for frigate birds. The island is alive with birds, so the island is well named. It has also been reported (erroneously, it seems) that an airstrip has been built on this island.

There are those who think that somewhere off the windward side of Ave de Barlovento lies a large part of the fleet of Comte d'Estrées, who captured Dutch Guiana in 1696. He fought and lost an action against Dutch Vice-Admiral Binkes off Tobago, then sailed home to France to refit his ships in Brest. He headed back to the West Indies on 7 October 1696 for another attempt at capturing the islands.

D'Estrées seems to have been heading for Curaçao, but on the night of 4 May 1697, his flagship suddenly sailed up on one of the Aves. Before anything could be done, the ships following astern also piled up. At daybreak, seven ships of the line, three transports, and three frigates were stranded on the reef and became total losses. (Jamaica, arming to defend itself against d'Estrées's fleet, was saved by an error of navigation.)

The only problem historically with all this is that no one can agree on the specific island where d'Estrées's fleet piled up. Dr. Daniel Camejo maintains it was Ave de Barlovento. He says the ships were en route from Tobago to capture Curaçao.

Dudley Pope, on the other hand, feels that the correct location is Aves Island in the middle of the Caribbean Sea off Guadeloupe.

The solution to the mystery lies in finding answers to the questions: "Where was d'Estrées's last landfall?" and "Where was the fleet last sighted?" In other words, where had the fleet been between 7 October 1696 and the following 4 May? Somewhere there is a wonderful treasure trove of guns, jewels, artifacts, and other archaeological goodies. But before the divers go down, someone has to come up with the answers to these questions.

Jan de Bosset spent three or four weeks exploring both Barlovento and Sotavento. He feels that the gap shown between the northern and southern reefs in Ave de Barlovento does not exist. In any case, I can't imagine anyone trying to sail a boat through that gap.

AVE DE SOTAVENTO
(Chart V-62; II D-2, D-22)

Las Aves de Sotavento, lying about 12 miles west of their cousins windward, have claimed an impressive number of wrecks: a liquid-gas tanker, a small coastal freighter, a fishing trawler, and the beautiful 65-foot schooner *My Destiny* all piled up here on the northwest reefs in the early 1960s.

At first glance, it is not clear why there should be so many more wrecks here than in Ave de Barlovento, but I think the answer becomes clear with a good look at the chart: The light on Ave de Sotavento flashes every seven seconds, the one on Ave de Barlovento every 8 1/2 seconds, the one on Bonaire every ten seconds, the one on Curaçao every four seconds, and the one on El Gran Roque every ten seconds. In other words, one light can easily be mistaken for another. A ship coming down from the north and headed for, say, Bonaire, which has clear water north of it, might be wrong enough in its DR position so that the light on Ave de Sotavento, nearest island to Bonaire to the east, is homed in on by mistake. The vessel would be hard aground in short order.

Some approach Ave de Sotavento, coming from the east, on the northern side. First you will pick up the wreck of the propane tanker, which looks for all the world like a ship chugging along the horizon. Soon you will see the wrecks of a couple of cargo vessels and trawlers. Pass around the northern end of the reef, which is clearly visible; take bearings on the lighthouse and then head south in the lee of the reefs to smooth water, picking your way to an anchorage. Pedro Gluecksman of *Bayola* recommends anchoring in the lee of Lighthouse Island (see Chart V-63).

On the other hand, Venezuelan fishermen prefer to pass around the southern end of Ave de Sotavento, pick their way east as depth permits, and anchor off Round Island, the small island north of the southernmost island in the group (see Chart V-64). Approaching from the south or southeast, the tall mangroves become visible before you even spot the island.

The anchorage off Customs, except in calm weather, is too exposed—we were practically blown overboard there. Besides, the water is shallow, only 7 feet quite far offshore.

The best anchorage near the main island is in Mangrove Bay. Small boats can tuck themselves into the mangroves, but, as mentioned earlier, I would expect that mosquitoes might be a problem.

Another anchorage used by yachtsmen is at Long Island (see Chart V-65), at the northern end of the group, the first island south of the one with the light. The bottom is poor holding, though, with loose rocks and sand. Anchor on two anchors; then, with a face mask, check that the anchors are set properly. Here there is excellent spearfishing right off your boat, with large parrotfish and plenty of yellowtail and blue runners. We saw no lobsters—perhaps they have been fished out here. But many people report that once you have worked your way into Las Aves and out toward the eastern reef, there is plenty of lobster.

Examine the three sketches of the landings and anchorages on the three northern islands of Ave de Sotavento and take your pick as weather conditions permit.

Ave de Sotavento tends to be the more popular with divers, as the entire area is littered with shoal water and coral heads. You can anchor easily anywhere suitable for your depth, once you have threaded your way through the coral heads.

Ave de Sotavento is also much safer for small-boat exploration than Ave de Barlovento: If the outboard packs up when exploring the latter, it will be impossible to anchor and you'll be blown offshore very rapidly. If your engine quits while in the area of Ave de Sotavento, you can anchor immediately or dive down and tie the painter to a coral head.

Further, if the ground swell is coming in at Ave de Sotavento, it would be quite easy to work well to the east, where you would avoid the ground swell and be able to anchor in shoal water.

Basically, Ave de Sotavento is open and wind

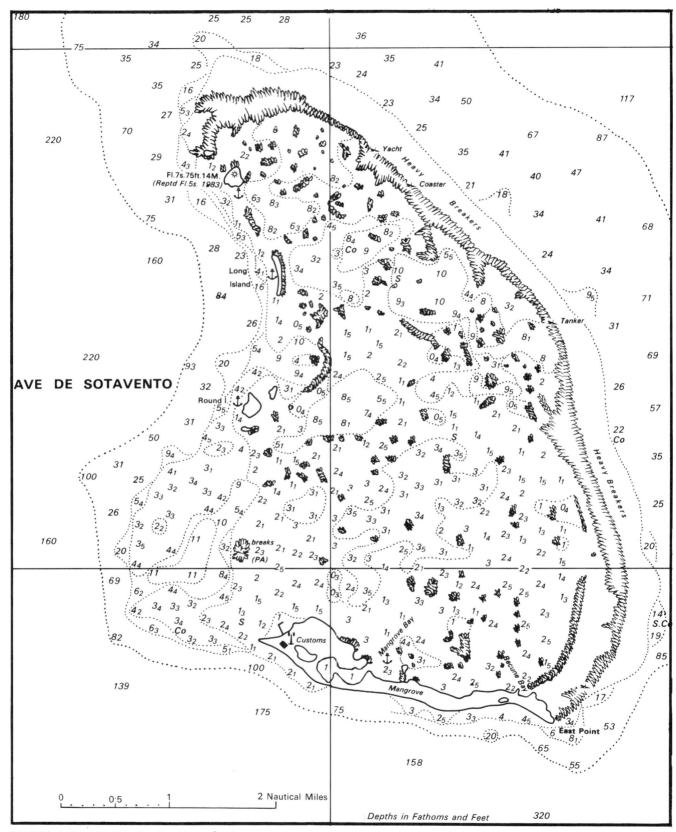

AVE DE SOTAVENTO

0   0·5   1   2 Nautical Miles

Depths in Fathoms and Feet

SKETCH CHART V–62   Las Aves de Sotavento

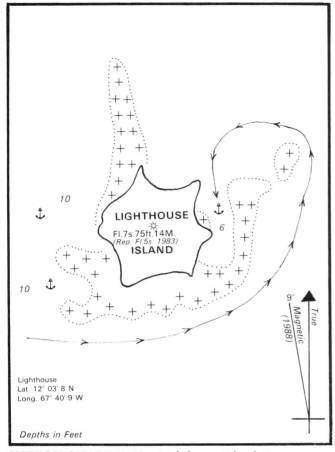

SKETCH CHART V–63 Lighthouse Island, Sotavento

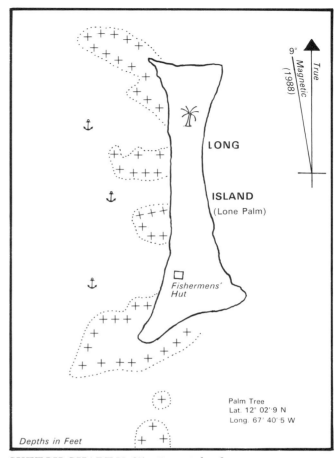

SKETCH CHART V–65 Long Island, Sotavento

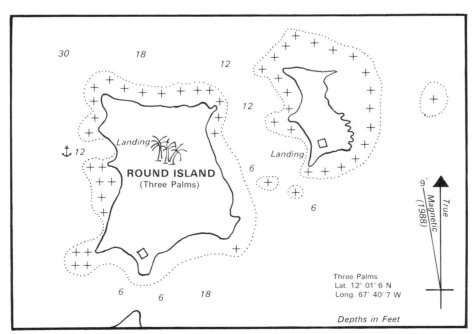

SKETCH CHART V–64 Round Island, Sotavento

swept and a paradise for the spearfisherman and birdwatcher, but not an island for those looking for a quiet anchorage and a big beach. The whole area has superb diving, but a diver would want a good dinghy with an outboard, as a considerable chop builds up between the main reef and the diving areas to the west. There are nowhere near as many birds in Ave de Sotavento as there are in Ave de Barlovento.

There are three officers of the Frontiere based on Ave de Sotavento. They are friendly, have no boat, and love to go spearfishing. The old abandoned tanks on shore now have water in them, so you can sometimes get water on Sotavento, but of course it is a case of lugging it in jugs.

When you have had enough of the solitude in Las Aves, you can sail 35 miles west to Bonaire or 75 miles south-southwest to the civilization and incomparable cruising of the Chichiriviche-Morrocoy/ Tucacas area.

11

Aruba, Bonaire, Curaçao

II D, D-2, D-23, D-231, D-232

Generally, the islands of Aruba, Bonaire, and Curaçao (referred to as the ABC islands) are only visited by yachtsmen coming from or going to Panamá. But they should be a must for yachtsmen finishing a Venezuelan cruise and looking for a jumping-off point while heading north.

Aruba used to be one big oil refinery, but this has changed in recent years. The island is now geared strictly for tourism, and it is worth a visit.

Bonaire rises almost vertically out of the sea and provides superb snorkeling around its shores. Since all spearfishing is forbidden, the fish are so tame they'll practically eat out of your hand. The people of Bonaire, although few in number (or perhaps *because* they are few in number), are among the most charming and helpful of the people we have encountered in the Eastern Caribbean.

Curaçao is the big, civilized island of the group, with excellent free-port shopping, big hotels, gambling, floor shows, yacht clubs, and excellent direct flights to the United States.

The islands originally were settled by the Dutch in the sixteenth century. At the time, Spain and Portugal were briefly united under a single king, who, in an attempt to bring the Dutch to their knees, cut off their supply of salt from the mines and pans of Portugal. Without salt to preserve the fish, the fleets of Holland would have collapsed, so the Dutch came to the New World and settled permanently in Aruba, Bonaire, Curaçao, and Sint Maarten, where they set up salt pans. For a brief period, they also seized the pans in Venezuela at Araya and El Morro de Barcelona from the Spanish.

The ABC islands are now grouped with Sint Maarten, Saba, and Sint Eustatius (Statia) as the Netherlands Antilles, a semi-independent political body still governed by the Netherlands; the Dutch guilder is the legal currency. Mail service is slow in the extreme and cable service is best forgotten (I have three times sent cables from this area, paid the bill, and the cables "ain't reach yet"). Phone service is not much better, but Customs and Immigration procedures are relaxed and simple, and the people are very friendly. So why worry about the less-than-efficient mail, cable, and phone—aren't those what we go to sea to avoid?

Bonaire

(II D-2, D-231)

Bonaire is 45 miles to leeward of Ave de Sotavento, and it is a logical place to stock up prior to taking off north back to the rest of the Caribbean. The course from Bonaire to St. Thomas is 040° magnetic (420 miles); to the western end of Puerto Rico it is 020° magnetic (350 miles). Of course, remember that if you are heading for either of those ports, the current probably is running 1 knot to the west; this, plus the normal drift of a sailboat on the wind, means that you'll probably have to allow for a 20° set. If the wind goes around to the northeast, you'll be lucky if you end up in Haiti. I well remember once when I was delivering a boat from Curaçao to St. Thomas that, although we were steering 050° magnetic, we ended up laying Mona Island; we then had a long slog to windward up the south coast of Puerto Rico.

In 1978, however, it was different. For months we'd been dreading the passage from Bonaire to St. Thomas, figuring it would be four to six days of pure hell—but the gods smiled on us. We left

Bonaire under no. 1 jib, genoa staysail, and reefed main; at the end of twelve hours, we shook the reef out of the main; at the end of twenty-four hours, we eased sheets and breezed home on an easy reach all the way to St. Thomas. In 1989, it was a hard-on-the-wind slog and we ended up in Cabo Rojo, on the western end of Puerto Rico!

Bonaire offers enough food supplies for the voyage to Puerto Rico or even the States. A starboard-tack passage north to the Mona Passage and beyond should be a reach all the way.

Bonaire is certainly one of the nicest islands in the Eastern Caribbean, but it is also about the most expensive one. Just like in Bermuda, money in Bonaire lasts about as long as does an ice cube placed on a black-capped road in the Caribbean at high noon!

As mentioned above, the island was originally settled for salt—along the coast you will notice obelisks that were set up to guide ships coming to the island for salt. However, in that era the island evidently was much wetter than it is today, so salt was not the only important product. The Dutch also raised provision crops, horses and fruit, which they sold to Curaçao and other islands.

The entire island was owned by the government and no settlers were allowed. If you lived in Bonaire, you were either a government employee or a slave. In 1863, the slaves were freed, and by 1868 the government realized that their operation was not all that efficient. Since they were losing money, they divided the island into large estates, which they then sold to wealthy individuals. As years went by, the island went downhill economically and many of the residents emigrated—especially after 1915, when oil refineries were being built in Aruba and Curaçao.

However, about twenty-five years ago, Captain Don Stewart arrived on a schooner of uncertain seaworthiness and ancestry that finally succeeded in sinking. He started diving on Bonaire and has been there ever since—Bonaire being one of the few places where a diving operation can be run without boats. For many years, Don ran his operation from a stretched Land Rover and various diving stages scattered around the island and built down into the water.

Tourism has taken off, and Bonaire is rapidly becoming the diving capital of the Western Hemisphere—the diving is indeed superb. The whole area is a nature sanctuary, so no spearfishing, lobstering, or disturbing the coral. (When Customs boards your boat, they impound your spearguns until you depart.)

The island is progressing rapidly, but, thankfully, the architects have designed the buildings in the traditional Dutch style. Many buildings are restorations. The town of Kralendijk—the capital—is very picturesque, immaculately clean, and charming. Yachtsmen like the island, but the yachting facilities are minimal at best.

One of the nicest things about Bonaire is that they have not yet had to import outside labor. The old Bonaire honesty remains—to the point that nobody locks their cars. Some idea of this can be demonstrated by our experience: While hauled out at the Silver Yacht Club, we were continually surrounded by locals of all ages who were fishing under, around, and close to *Iolaire* as she lay on the dock. For four days, our tools, brushes, and paint lay on the dock, yet not once did so much as a screw go missing. I wish the same thing could be said of all of the Eastern Caribbean islands, where light-fingered ten-year-old boys all seem to be contenders for the Olympic 100-yard dash, even though they could well be carrying your toolbox, 25 pounds of nuts and bolts, and anything else that is not nailed down.

If you spot high land when approaching Bonaire from the east, Los Roques or Las Aves, you undoubtedly are seeing Mount Brandaris (787 feet), on the northwestern tip of the island, or Ceru Grandi (384 feet), which is 10 miles north of the southern tip of the island. The rest of Bonaire is dead flat (10 feet) and extends 10 miles south of Ceru Grandi. If you spot high land on your bow, alter course *drastically* to the south.

The run from Las Aves to Bonaire is always a problem, as you almost invariably run dead downwind. Helmsmen tend to steer high of the course, so you end up north of the rhumb line and have to alter course once you pick up Bonaire. The distance at which you pick up the highlands of Bonaire will affect the degree you will have to alter course to the south.

The lighthouse on the south end of the island, at Willemstoren, is very difficult to spot in daylight, as it is a sand-colored structure that melts into the haze. Why is it not painted in black-and-white stripes?

At night, boats have ended up on the reef when they have mistaken the Boca Spelonk light (flashing every five seconds) for Willemstoren light (flashing every nine seconds). If approaching at night, give the Willemstoren light a good berth, as the light is about a quarter of a mile inland from the point and its offlying reef. Again, remember that the lights are not too reliable, as they are untended.

When sailing between Puerto Cabello or Chichiriviche and Bonaire, or the reverse, the current is variable—it can be as high as 2 or 2 1/2 knots, but in general it is 1 to 1 1/2 knots. However, it can also disappear completely. This happened to us when we were sailing from Chichiriviche to Bonaire in March 1989. I allowed for a 1 1/2-knot current and laid the course accordingly. When we did not pick up the light on the south end of Bonaire, we tuned in to Trans World Radio (800 kHz) and picked up Bonaire well off the lee bow. Since we did not get a really good bearing, we bore off to an approximate course 320° magnetic. The morning sunline gave us our longitude, and when we altered course to 280° magnetic, we finally picked up Bonaire.

Working backward from our landfall against our log, we figured out that we were at least 20 miles east of the rhumb line when we altered course to the west. Yet the next day, when I discussed this with Charlie Interrante, the manager of the marina and slipway in Bonaire, he reported the opposite situation on his previous trip: He fought a 3-knot current and ended up 8 miles west of the island when he made his landfall. Needless to say, it is more pleasant to be to windward of the rhumb line and ease sheets than to be to leeward and have to fight your way against the current.

The radio beacon at the airport in Bonaire is BGB (-.../--./-...), frequency 321 kHz. But pilots who fly in and out of Bonaire say that the radio beacon is so unreliable that they use Trans World Radio (880 kHz; broadcast 0715 to 0100 local time), which is one of the most powerful in the world.

Entry into Bonaire is simple: Collect your passports, ship's papers, and about four crew lists and wander ashore in Kralendijk sometime after you have secured—the anchorage is more or less off the Zeezicht Restaurant. For Customs and Immigration, go to the police station. If Immigration is closed, they will take care of you downstairs, but during normal working hours, the office is upstairs. Customs is the two-story yellow building at the head of the north commercial dock. They are very friendly, very courteous, and very firm. They will most likely insist that you go alongside the dock, where they probably will give you a pretty good search—having made up their minds that they are not allowing any drugs on the island.

When trying to get things done in Bonaire, a very handy man to know is Armando Felix—just ask anyone on the island and they will turn him up. He has built an excellent reputation as an expediter and helper to visiting yachts. His brother, Gabby, is in charge of keeping all the bulldozers and rolling-stock working in the salt factory—if you can keep a bulldozer that continually shovels salt going, you can keep anything going. Consequently, he has developed a reputation as a first-rate mechanic.

As mentioned earlier, air communications to and from Bonaire are good. There are numerous daily flights to Curaçao, and flights to Caracas four to five times a week. The brand-new airport is wide open, cool, and comfortable. We were stranded there for five hours waiting for a delayed flight and, rather than being torturous, it was rather pleasant.

Because of a fiasco that is too long to relate here, I highly recommend that if you need to make any travel arrangements, do not use ALM; use Maduro Travel, a firm that is infinitely better and more efficient. I thought nothing could beat the inefficiency of LIAT and the now-defunct CaribAir, but ALM seems to have surpassed both.

Telephone calls can be made at the telephone exchange or from hotels. One problem is that you cannot make collect or credit-card calls, and the number of overseas lines is limited. Make your calls early in the morning or late at night.

Food stocks vary drastically—according to how recently the supply boats arrived. When we were there, we were able to get enough supplies, but had we wanted to stock for a really long trip, we would have had to wait two or three days for the next small freighter. Everyone in Bonaire is so nice, though, that we wouldn't have minded waiting a week or so.

Captain Don not only runs the diving operation mentioned earlier, but he also runs the Habitat Hotel—nothing very fancy, but extremely good value and well thought of by everyone who has stayed there. Another hotel, Bonaire Beach Hotel, is a gambling hotel. It is expensive, but nothing spectacular.

Evening entertainment in Bonaire is excellent. At least five nights a week, there is entertainment ashore. The Flamingo Beach Club in Kralendijk has an excellent floor show with traditional folk dancing a couple of nights a week. Other nights, other hotels have shows presented by divers—there are lectures and slide shows, and videos are shown.

It's worth renting a car for a day and exploring the Washington/Slagbaai National Park. Bonaire is not the *only* place where pink flamingos are found, but it certainly is one of the *few* places. A taxi ride around Bonaire is worthwhile, as the drivers are friendly and prices are negotiable. You'll see plenty of cactus and some wild parrots.

What makes Bonaire excellent for diving makes it

hell for yachtsmen. It is practically impossible to get an anchor to hold—unless you sail up to shore, send the dinghy ashore with the anchor, dig a hole in the beach, and bury the anchor. This is how we finally succeeded in mooring when I visited Bonaire in the late 1960s on *Boomerang*, a 67-foot Sparkman & Stephens yawl from Venezuela owned by Humberto Contazano.

When I next arrived, on *Iolaire*, we tried anchoring in the same spot. We ran aground and dropped our anchor in 4 feet of water; the wind blew us off, the anchor refused to hold, and we were at sea again.

KRALENDIJK TOWN DOCK AREA
(Chart V-66; II D-2, D-23, D-231)

The chart shows a 1 1/2-fathom spot south of town off the Flamingo Beach Hotel; it is shoal enough to anchor, but holding is very poor and you are likely to drag. Richard Beady of the Flamingo Beach Hotel provides open-air showers for yachtsmen. He likes yachtsmen—he thinks they are amusing and help to entertain his guests. I hope that yachtsmen will not abuse the privilege of these showers by stripping down and washing *au naturel* or washing their clothes in the public showers. Too many sailors visiting Trinidad and Puerto Azul already have ruined the welcome by exhibiting behavior that the local yachtsmen considered unacceptable, and guest privileges in both clubs have been removed. I suggested to Richard that he install a couple of enclosed, coin-operated showers that would enable yachtsmen to strip, lather up, and shampoo in privacy. The coin-operated system would prevent people from using lots of water for washing their clothes.

The best spot to anchor is 150 yards north of the town dock. In 1976, we anchored here and discovered that our neighbor was Ron Roberts, the "Mad Major," aboard *Haida Sea*, his beautiful little wooden Robb 35 that he has all but sailed around the world. I recognized *Haida Sea* because only the "Mad Major" could keep a fifteen-year-old wooden boat looking that good. Ron came aboard, we renewed old acquaintances, and he gave me much valuable information about Bonaire, Curaçao, Aruba, and the problems of beating to windward across the Caribbean. (He once fought his way from Panamá to St. Thomas, singlehanded in *Haida Sea*, dead to windward all the way—an experience he hopes not to repeat.)

As I said, you can anchor north of the Kralendijk town dock, between the north end of the commercial dock and the entrance to the marina, a quarter of a mile to the north. The shelf is very narrow, dropping from 6 or 7 feet close inshore to 30 feet about 50 yards out, then a sheer drop to 300 feet. The shelf is widest off the Zeezicht Restaurant and Bar, which is built over the water. Anchor as close to the bar as possible, but even then it is advisable to run a line ashore and tie it to one of the small jetties, or put out two anchors. This is very convenient, as the bar management is happy to have yachtsmen tie dinghies to their dock. But remember that the holding is not particularly good, as the bottom is only about 18 inches of sand covering hard rock. Plus, when we anchored *Iolaire* there in March 1989 and I swam around to make sure the anchor was holding, I discovered how lucky we were: A few feet away on the starboard side was a great pile of wire that would have fouled the anchor and caused us to drag. On the port side, there was something that looked like a huge canvas cargo sling and a bellhousing off an engine. So don't be surprised if you have to winch up the anchor and start again.

On the second day we were there, we had a great shock when we found ourselves being swung ashore. Despite the fact that we had the awning and the mizzen up and there was a 10-knot breeze out of the east, we were still facing north and south. Obviously, there is occasionally a strong north-south current. We later checked this out with Ray Gingrich, who formerly was in charge of the tugs in Bonaire, and with Charlie Interrante at the marina. Both confirmed that there is a such a current and that it comes and goes, but no one has figured out any schedule.

The next morning, we ran the anchor out astern, dropped it, and felt we were properly moored bow and stern, facing east-west. However, we were not. As mentioned before, the bottom drops off suddenly in a vertical wall. The anchor line chafed through on a coral head, and the line had come free. Luckily, the anchor had not fallen down the hillside, and Don Woods, with the aid of a lung, retrieved the anchor line and tied them together.

Obviously, the proper way to anchor in Kralendijk is to sail in, get your bow anchor as close to the shore as possible, get the second anchor out to the east, then put a third out to the west. Put on a face mask and go down to make sure it is inside the dropoff. Then take the line from the anchor to the west to the bow of the boat, not the stern, and set up a Bahamian moor, but have two anchors out to

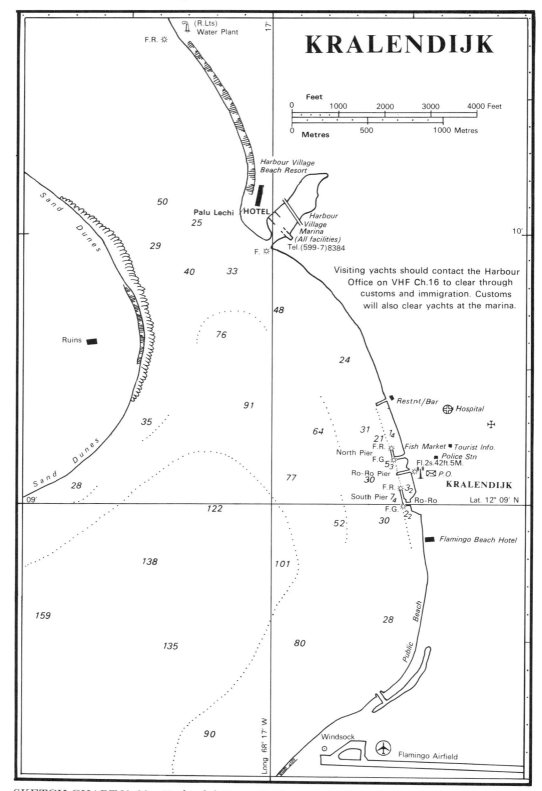

KRALENDIJK

(R.Lts)
Water Plant
F.R. ☼

Harbour Village
Beach Resort

50
Palu Lechi
25
HOTEL
Harbour
Village
Marina
(All facilities)
Tel.(599-7)8384
F. ☼
29

40   33

48

Visiting yachts should contact the Harbour
Office on VHF Ch.16 to clear through
customs and immigration. Customs
will also clear yachts at the marina.

76

Ruins

24

91

Restnt/Bar
⊕ Hospital

35

31   1
64   21   4
F.R. ☼   Fish Market ■ Tourist Info.
North Pier
F.G. ☼   ■ Police Stn
53   3   Fl.2s.42ft.5M.
Ro-Ro Pier
30   ⊠ P.O.

77   F.R. ☼   3
South Pier 7   4   Ro-Ro   **KRALENDIJK**
F.G. ☼   2   Lat. 12° 09′ N
28   30   2

52   30
■ Flamingo Beach Hotel

122

138   101

28
Public Beach

159   80
135

90

Windsock
⊙   ✈ Flamingo Airfield

Ruins

SKETCH CHART V–66   Kralendijk Town Dock, Bonaire

the east in the Y pattern. (For a more detailed explanation of the Bahamian moor, see *Street's Transatlantic Crossing Guide*.)

While anchored off the Zeezicht Restaurant on a morning when it was absolutely flat calm, we spotted what appeared to be an old hurricane ground chain. Needless to say, if you hook your anchor under that, you will never winch it up. You will have to dive to free the anchor. One wonders why the local tourist-oriented government does not stretch the ground chain out straight, secure a big anchor at each end, and secure risers to it. This would provide moorings for visiting yachts, and I'm sure the yachts would be willing to pay a reasonable fee.

If the wind comes in from the west—a rather rare occurrence—move immediately either north inside the marina (where there is 16 feet in the channel and inside) or south to the canals north of the airport. (About 2 miles south of town, immediately north of the airport, are two half-completed Dutch colonial-style buildings. Approximately due west of these buildings is an entrance to a defunct development with about 2 miles of canals; estimated depth is about 7 feet. The canals were dredged for a large holiday project that went belly up when the Venezuelan bolívar was devalued.)

In between the breakwaters, there is approximately 10 feet, but in midchannel there is a 7-foot rock, easily seen when the light is right. Once inside the channel, it shoals to about 7 feet. Proceed with caution.

Water can be obtained by one of several methods: If you only need a small amount of water, take the jugs ashore to the small dinghy dock immediately north of the commercial pier—near the old fish market. Take along a hose and a funnel and walk across the street to the public toilets. All the water you can carry is free. A second option is to go to the Silver Yacht Club (i.e., the marina), but there have been complaints that the water flow there is very slow. A third option is to see the Port Captain. Go alongside the north dock and you can buy metered water from the distillation unit. But here you have to buy the water by the ton, so what won't fit into your tank can be used to wash yourselves, your clothes, and the boat.

If you need gasoline for the outboard, carry your gas can up to the nearest gasoline station. If you need diesel, go to the gas station and let them know how much you want, and then bring your boat alongside the main steamer dock, where a truck will come down and deliver the diesel.

To get your laundry done, find a taxi driver, give him the laundry, and he will take it to one of the laundromats. (Laundromats in Bonaire are places where someone has a washing machine and will do laundry.)

The taxi drivers are very nice, friendly, and expensive—but extremely helpful. We met Nelson, who said, "Never mind the last name, just Nelson." Go to the Zeezicht and ask. They will contact him via his paging system and he will appear out of the woodwork.

Bottled gas is a real problem, as the bottles have to be shipped over to Curaçao and then brought back—an eight- to eleven-day wait. However, you can contact the above-mentioned Nelson, as I demonstrated to him how to fill bottles from a standard 100-pound bottle. (We hoisted his 100-pound cylinder upside down on his porch roof rafter, took our 20-pound cylinder, put it in a big plastic garbage bag, packed 20 pounds of ice around it, cross-connected the two bottles, and got a 90 percent fill. This is a lot easier than sending your bottle to Curaçao.)

KRALENDIJK YACHT HARBOR AREA
(Chart V-67; II D-2, D-23, D-231)

You do not have to anchor nowadays, since there is a channel dredged into the lagoon north of town. There is 16 feet in the channel, about 14 feet inside. In 1989, we found a semioperational marina, with an excuse for showers, intermittent electricity, and water (although the pressure is very low).

The Silver Yacht Club (marina and hauling facility) is an example of a good idea that never really got off the ground, due to the combination of bad planning by a foreign engineer, the caginess of Bonaire fishermen, and the devaluation of the Venezuelan bolívar.

Apparently a Dutch engineer conceived the idea of dredging through to the pond and building the marina and the synchro-lift dock, with a beautiful transfer system—all of which was done. However, the dock faces south-southeast, the wind is out of the east, and Bonaire is famous for the fact that it blows 365 days of the year. The only difference is that some days it blows, and other days it blows harder. Trying to haul boats, especially sailboats, in half a gale creates a major problem.

Further, if the yard were fully operational, ten large yachts could be hauled at the same time. But to service all ten on the slipway, you would need an excellent infrastructure (i.e., shops with machines and electrical equipment for wood, fiberglass, and

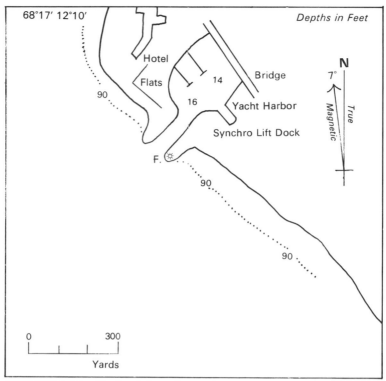

CHART V–67   Kralendijk Yacht Harbor, Bonaire

steel—all well staffed—as well as paint and other supplies). The planning was very poor at the beginning, as these shops were never built. Then, because the shops were not built, it was impossible to attract an outside specialist who could come in, set up shop, and then train the locals.

Because the island is so small, there was—especially in the mid-1970s when the synchro-lift was built—a tremendous lack of skilled labor.

In the first burst of enthusiasm, a fish factory was set up and eleven fishing boats were built. Money was loaned to both operations, neither of which got off the ground. The arrangement with the fishermen was that they would give a percentage of their catch to the banks in lieu of cash. But the fishermen soon discovered that they could sell the fish to Venezuelan fishing boats, then come back to Bonaire with the minimum amount of fish, and explain, "The fishing has been bad, sorry." As a result, the banks never got enough money in repayment of their loans and the fish factory never got enough fish to get going. The fish-factory operation went belly up and the fishing boats were repossessed by the banks and sold.

Fishermen are smart. The same thing happened in both Guyana and Trinidad, and the Venezuelan fishermen also discovered a better way to make money. They buy fuel at 7 cents US a gallon, then

go up to the Eastern Caribbean and sell it at a dollar a gallon—making money hand over fist. Then they fish for a few days, return to Venezuela, and say, "Sorry, the fishing was bad."

The yard did stagger on with the business of hauling Venezuelan powerboats: Yank them out, paint the bottoms, and drop them back in. But with the devaluation of the bolívar, that business also dried up.

At the present time, the synchro-lift dock is, as they say in Grenada, "in a state of disrepair." Its designed capacity is 240 tons, but I doubt if they would be willing to lift more than 100. The transfer cars are in such bad shape that no large boats could be transferred. The whole thing looks like a complete disaster, but actually it isn't. Charlie Interrante and his sidekick Ken, plus a painter, make up for the deficiency of the yard and the hauling system with enthusiasm and good cheer—they do not have much to work with, but they certainly should be given top marks for effort and cheerfulness.

Due to a leak, they did an emergency haul for *Iolaire* in March 1989. We hauled, broke our tails working well after dark, and got it all ready to go in the water the morning before Easter (a holiday)—only to discover a new leak. We spent most of Saturday—their day off—going up and down like a yo-yo. Easter Sunday, needless to say, everyone was off celebrating, and they finally put us in on Easter Monday—again a holiday.

Labor is expensive—St. Thomas wages—and the yard admits that they have no one who can work on wooden boats. They have a lot of experience with steel, some with fiberglass, but none with wood. Needless to say, using a huge lift dock for a small boat is not very economical, and the charge works out to about $12 US per foot, which is not cheap. But it is the only yard west of Caracas where you can haul boats that draw more than 6 feet.

Exactly what the current situation is, no one knows, as in the end of 1989, the developer who was building a new condominium complex immediately north of the lagoon bought out the Silver Yacht Club and prices doubled immediately. Will the services improve? Will the lift dock be rebuilt? Any information from readers will be greatly appreciated.

Unfortunately, marine supplies are few and far between in Bonaire, but there is an excellent building supply and tool store, General Store Bonaire. If you carry all your supplies with you and are prepared to do 90 percent of the work, it will not turn out too badly.

Ashore are some very nice restaurants and friendly bars with plenty of good, cold Heineken. There are two supermarkets with adequate supplies, but, as noted, these will vary according to when the last supply shipment came in. Alongside the main pier are vegetable boats that come over from Venezuela with fresh fruit and vegetables; any currency is acceptable—Venezuelan, Dutch, or US. Enclosed showers are available at the marina—alongside the docks—and there are open showers at the Flamingo Beach Hotel.

During the week around October 15 to 20, the island really jumps: A large small-boat regatta attracts cruising yachts from Venezuela, Curaçao, Aruba, and Sint Maarten, plus Sailfish, Sunfish, Lasers, and other dinghy classes from the entire Caribbean. The bay between Klein Bonaire and Bonaire provides an absolutely superb small-boat racing area.

As in some other locales in the West Indies—the east coast of Puerto Rico, Anguilla, Bequia, and Martinique—the Bonaire fishermen sometimes go out and race. Bonaire has a class of racing sloops that are descended from commercial inshore fishing boats. They are raced with great enthusiasm and energy on certain major holidays.

Richard Beady of the Flamingo Beach Hotel is an enthusiastic sailor and hopes to encourage more of the racing. I suggested to him that he arrange the courses like they do in Anguilla: a dead-downwind start from the beach, to a mark that could be off Klein Bonaire, then a beat back to the finish—which, rather than a line, is a white flag moored about 20 yards off the beach. The winner is the boat that sails by and picks up the flag, which a crew member delivers to the judges on shore. In Anguilla, if it's a close finish, there have been times when the man who picks the flag out of the water is not the man delivering the flag to the judges! Sometimes there is a fight between rival crews in the shallow water between the flag and the judges. Great fun is had by all! Needless to say, cash prizes encourage competition!

There are a few daytime anchorages on Bonaire. One is on the west side of Bonaire south of Punta Wecua. There is a small shelf where, if you can get your anchor to hold, you'll find excellent swimming and snorkeling along the reef north of the shelf. But leave someone on board in case you drag off the shelf. Two places frequented by local yachts for lunchtime anchoring and swimming are Playa Frans and Boca Slagbaai; again, it's a case of sneaking right on in and putting your anchor on the beach.

Also, when visiting the small coves on the lee side of Bonaire and Klein Bonaire, you probably will see mooring buoys. Pick them up; do not anchor!! The buoys have been established by the divers, who do not want anchors to damage the coral. The moorings are sufficiently heavy for daytime anchoring, as the 50- and 60-foot dive boats regularly use them.

LAC BAAI
(Chart V-68; II D-2, D-23, D-231)

Another anchorage in Bonaire that provides a change of scenery is Lac Baai, on the eastern side of the island. The entrance is 5 miles north of Willemstoren (Lacrepunt). Round the point and head north, staying 300 yards off the coast, as it is a lee shore with heavy surf. After 3 1/2 miles, you will pick up seven big heaps of conch shells on the lee bow. Do not steer for them yet, but keep them off the port bow. Continue northward until the conch shells bear in one line. Now ease sheets and steer approximately 315° magnetic. Enter the gap, keeping the land close on your starboard side. As soon as you reach the first heap of shells, turn due west. Then eyeball and swing slowly south of west, carrying on toward shore until the hotel bears approximately south. Swing around and anchor in the southeastern corner of the bay. Once you turn west,

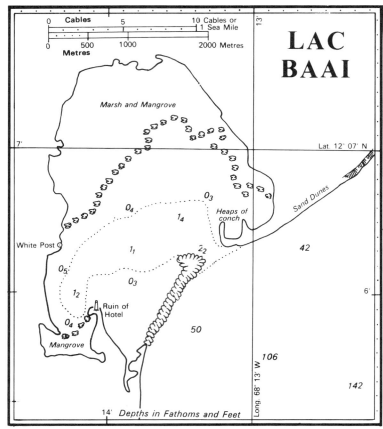

CHART V–68   Lac Baai, Bonaire

you're on your own—strictly a case of eyeball navigation.

The hotel in Lac Baai is now open, but I am told the bay is very rough, since the reef does not completely break the Atlantic swell. It must be remembered that the wind will be blowing extremely hard across the bay. On weekends, it is a popular place for boardsailing.

This bay is not recommended for any yachts drawing more than 7 feet. In the summer of 1979, there was a rusty buoy in front of the reef that had no navigational meaning at all. (This information is courtesy of the dentist, Dr. Fritz Pierebaum, who frequently visits this anchorage. He also supplied the information for the sketch chart.)

KLEIN CURAÇAO
(II D-2, D-23, D-232)

About 6 miles off the southeast corner of Curaçao, this is a favorite place for local yachtsmen when the ground swell is not running. A good anchorage is in the lee of the island, where the fishing

boats are anchored. There are good beaches and few visitors on weekdays; the wind sweeps across the low land, so the anchorage should be cool and free of bugs.

The yacht *Jomy* reports that the island has *no* manned light anymore, and although no one has heard of the light not working, several vessels (including a small tanker) have found their end at the north side of this island. (It is recommended that you *not* fall asleep when you're sailing from Bonaire to Curaçao and passing Klein Curaçao.)

Curaçao
(II D-2, D-23, D-232)

Curaçao developed essentially as a bunkering and refining port for Venezuela (before Venezuela began to build up its own facilities). Even today, it continues to supply vast quantities of oil to the rest of the world. Air pollution is avoided by the ever-present trades that sweep across the island and blow the pollution out to sea. Further, in their usual fashion, the Dutch keep everything as clean and tidy as possible.

When approaching Curaçao at night, you'll see so many lights along the shore that navigational lights are almost impossible to pick out. The loom of the airport beacon is clearly visible, however, so use that as a point of reference. Make sure you stay well to windward of the entrance to the harbor of Willemstad, the capital, as the current can set very strongly to the west. If you are swept to the west of the entrance, you'll have a hard time fighting your way back. We discovered this the hard way, on *Toscana*, in March 1980: The current was setting west at a full 3 knots, and even large ships were having trouble allowing for it.

WILLEMSTAD

(Chart V-69; II D-2, D-23, D-232)

Willemstad is the island's port of entry; offices of Customs and Immigration, and the Port Captain, overlook the harbor, and all are friendly and helpful. One of the first sights you'll see is the pontoon swing bridge, which since 1888 has been handling traffic across the channel from one side of town to the other. Formerly, yachts often had a long wait here, because when traffic was heavy on the bridge, ships had to wait. Now, though, it is only a footbridge and should open on demand. Call Harbor Control, Fort Nassau, on channel 16 and request that the bridge be opened. If you have no radio, heave to or circle under power, blow three blasts, and hope. You cannot lie alongside the bridge, as there is too much surge.

Once the bridge opens, proceed up the channel to the new, high-level, overhead cantilevered aluminum bridge. (It is the second one, actually; the first one collapsed just as it was being finished. Nearly every salvage firm in the southern Caribbean was called in, and they cleaned up the mess in something like forty-eight hours.)

To clear Customs, tie up by the fueling dock. The harbormaster's office is north of the Shell dock. Be prepared: The officials request—and in fact insist—that you surrender your passports to them for the duration of your stay. In that way, they make absolutely sure that you do clear out. I am told it is now legal to anchor in Spanish Water and have the skipper come into town with the ship's papers to arrange clearance.

You can lie here in the center of town and do all your shopping within walking distance of the boat.

Venezuelan fruit boats and the ships entering and leaving the harbor provide plenty to watch.

On the western side of the channel, above the bridge, you can get fuel and water at Maduro & Sons. For meat, fish, and vegetables, go to the new market, above the floating market; it opens at 0500, so go early. Then visit the floating market. North, across the footbridge (east of the floating market) and 100 yards up the road is a fairly good supermarket. Fresh food is also available at Chinese shops called *toko* and Portuguese shops called *frutería*. Block ice is available at the ice factory—Ijsfabriek Kortijn, Kortijn 48 (tel.: 623644). Marine supplies are found at Marine Coast Master, Caracasbaaiweg 202 (tel.: 614476 and 614025). Marine supplies are also available at Vreugdenhil, which is within walking distance of Marine Coast Master, Granaatappelweg 131 (tel.: 614715). For engine work, Curaçao Drydock is best, but also the most expensive. They can haul your boat at NAC, which is inside the Annabaai, but this is also quite expensive. The maximum tonnage is 50. For electric, electronic, and refrigeration repairs, ask at the harbormaster's office or at one of the local yacht clubs.

When eating ashore, be sure to try the very good Indonesian food offered by several restaurants. (Luckily, the phone book is printed in both Dutch and English.)

When you have finished your business in Willemstad, or when you tire of the city's bustle, my advice is to cruise to some of the many attractive anchorages along Curaçao's coast. There are at least a dozen good, interesting spots, which the Curaçao yachtsmen have explored thoroughly. The following description of these anchorages, based on my own observations and those of helpful sailors—such as Dick Nebbling, plus John Vieverich and Myra Rauchbaar of the yacht *Jomy*—starts at the southeast corner of the island and works northwest. All are found on charts II D-2 and D-23; some have detailed charts or sketch charts as well.

FUIKBAAI

(II D-2, D-23, D-232)

This is a suitable anchorage with deep water and a clear, marked channel. The west side is easiest to sail, but beware of moored cargo ships loading phosphate—they sometimes lay hawsers across the western part of the bay, effectively blocking it off.

To get to the other side, swing to starboard on

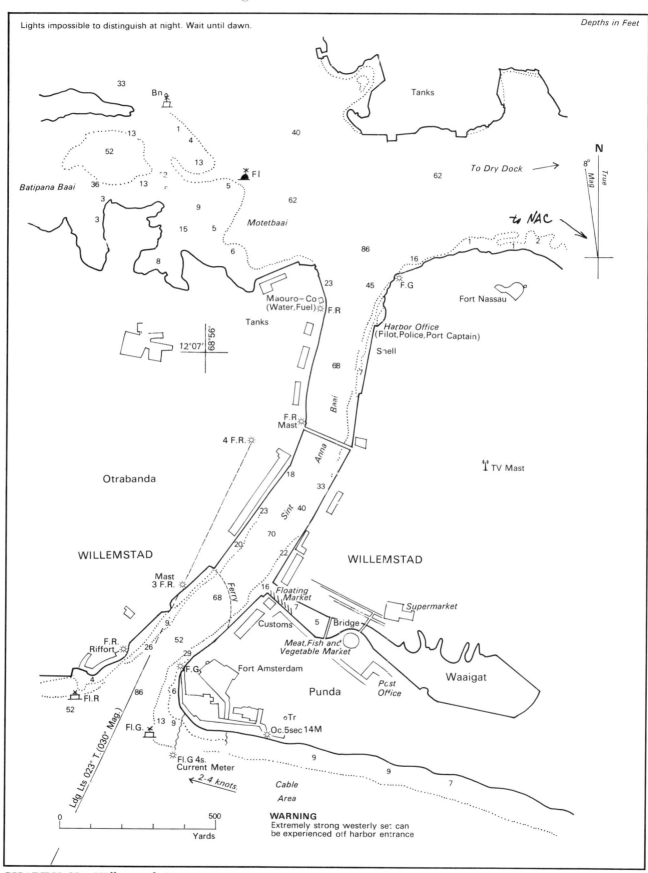

CHART V–69   Willemstad, Curaçao

entering and head southeast past Nieuwpoort. On the northeast side of this bay is Pelican Creek, which is beautifully isolated and alive with pelicans. Dick Nebbling, a local yachtsman, says it is his favorite spot in Curaçao.

SPANISH WATER

(Chart V-70; II D-2, D-23, D-232)

Spanish Water (Spaanse Water) is the headquarters of yachting in Curaçao, roughly 1 1/2 miles northwest of the entrance to Fuikbaai. The entrance to Spanish Water is hard to spot, but if you hug the coast—it's deep water all along—you'll see it. It is not buoyed, but the water is clear enough to eyeball it; favor the east side of the channel.

There are various yacht clubs in the bay (see sketch chart). The Curaçao Yacht Club is hospitable and has slips for forty to fifty yachts, but the docks usually are so crowded that you must anchor off. There is a slipway, but it's basically for club members, who have so many boats that the schedule usually is fully booked. Occasionally a visiting yachtsman, if he waits long enough, can manage to get hauled; size is limited to 30 tons and 6-foot draft.

Club Asiento, formerly owned by Shell and now by the government, has a large fleet of small boats, and this is the club where most of the Curaçao ocean racers lie. (Some of them beat to windward for Antigua Week—that's what I call true enthusiasm—but at least they have a good run home.) They are most hospitable to cruising yachts but have nothing in the way of hauling facilities. They are not very accessible, however, because it is very shallow.

Spanish Water is a pleasant place to stay, but if you don't have a rented car, or make friends with one of the local yachtsmen, it's a long, expensive ride to Willemstad. I understand now that if you moor your boat at Spanish Water and hitch a ride into town with all your papers, you'll be able to clear without the officials actually visiting the boat.

The cruising yachtsman appears to have worn out his welcome with some of the clubs in Spanish Water, probably because an awful lot of people who are sailing around are not yachtsmen and their behavior has ruined the scene for others. I have mentioned this problem several times in this guide (particularly in the discussion of Puerto Azul), and I hope all yacht-club officers will heed my comments about dealing appropriately with visiting yachts.

Curaçao Yacht Club is felt to be the best yacht club for cruising yachtsmen. We hope the "water people" will not ruin the welcome there.

The crew of *Jomy* says a new marina can be found if you pass the Curaçao Yacht Club, keeping the small island on the starboard hand. Before the Jan Sofat Yacht Club, you will find Sarifundy's Marina. It is easy to spot. You can anchor your vessel in front of the marina and let them look after it when you have to leave on business or visit abroad. Prices are very reasonable. Also, it is possible to fill your water tanks, get rid of oil, exchange books, and avail yourself of many more services. The marina is planning to build some hauling facilities and/or docks.

PISCADERABAAI

(II D-2, D-23, D-232)

This is the first anchorage west of Willemstad. The outer bay is not too deep for anchoring, but you can moor alongside the former Hilton Hotel (now the Concorde Hotel) pier. Unfortunately, the wonderful trained porpoises are no longer there—one escaped and the other died of heartbreak.

You can enter the channel into the inner bay, which appears to have 20 feet and plenty of room to anchor. In March 1980, we anchored in the channel 200 yards north of the entrance; it was cool and windy, with clean water, good swimming, and a view of the bay. It would have been an excellent place to explore from a sailing dinghy, had we had more time. The gamblers in your crew can go to the hotel and lose their money. On shore, near the anchorage, is a small beach bar/restaurant with showers.

BLAUWBAAI

There is a nice beach anchorage in the southeast corner of the bay, but it is for daytime use only, and it may be crowded on weekends.

SINT MICHIELBAAI

This place has a very attractive fishing village and a navy beach club—which obviously means it has a very good beach. Sneak in close and anchor off the beach. Go ashore, look at the fishing vessels, make friends with the fishermen, and buy fish for dinner.

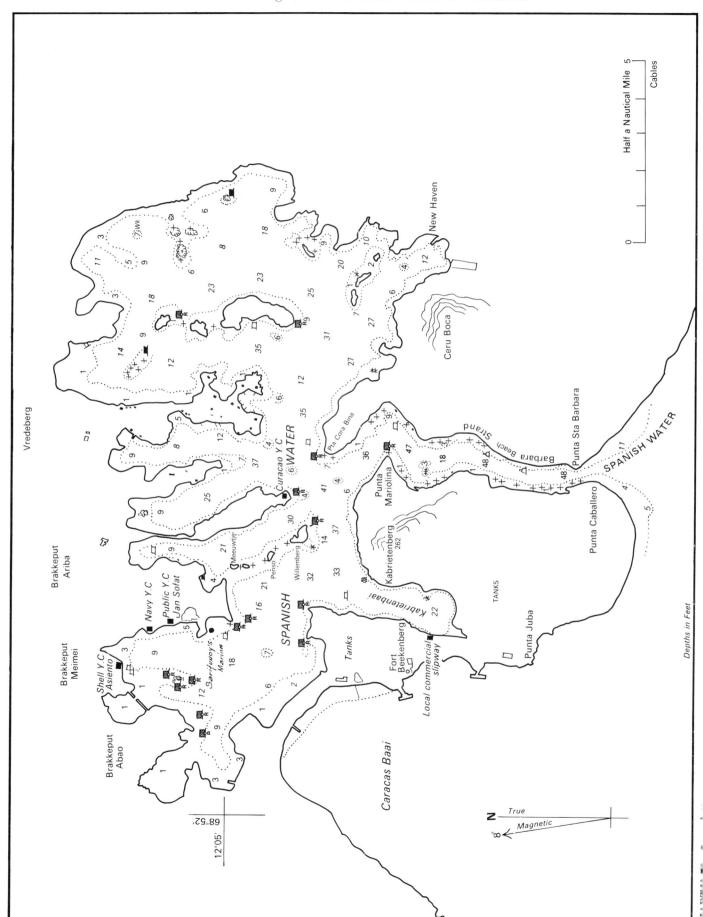

VAARSENBAAI

Here there is a good beach and a fair anchorage. It is the hub of the policemen's weekend retreat and the scene of many Curaçao yachtsmen's parties.

BULLENBAAI

Bullenbaai is easy to spot because of its storage tank farm, said to be the largest collection of oil storage tanks in the Western Hemisphere. Supertankers that draw up to 90 feet come in and offload.When coming from Santa Martabaai or Westpuntbaai and going to the harbor at Spanish Water, you have to fight your way up because of the strong current in front of Bullenbaai. However, the southeast corner of the bay has a good anchorage and a jetty. It used to be a common rendezvous for many Curaçao races, but this is no longer true.

DAAIBOOIBAAI

This is a small anchorage (with a wonderful name). It is an interesting place to go ashore and take a look at the old saltponds. To the north is Portomaribaai, which has only a fair anchorage, but it features an old estate house that is an excellent example of colonial Curaçao architecture.

BOCA GRANDI

Pedro Gluecksman reports: "Not to be entered; very dangerous."

SANTA MARTABAAI

Pedro Gluecksman does not think much of this place, either, but the narrow entrance and outer bay have 15 feet of water, and it looks to me like a good spot for exploring in a small boat. A hotel and real estate development seem not to have gotten off the ground; there would seem to be tremendous potential here, though.

The crew of *Jomy* says you can enter the bay through a narrow entrance; favor the east side of the channel. It is not buoyed, but the water is clear enough to eyeball it. Anchor at the east side and explore the bay with your dinghy. The bottom of the bay is mud. Ice cubes and some other articles can be bought at the Coral Cliff Hotel, overlooking the sea and Santa Martabaai. The hotel has an excellent barbecue on Saturday night. There is also a beach bar. Because the tickets for the beach are very expensive (in 1989, it was about $5 US a person), the beach is not crowded. *Jomy* usually stays in the bay and therefore does not use the beach or the restrooms on the beach. Sometimes it is possible to anchor in front of the dock so you don't need your dinghy to get ashore. At the dive shop on the beach, you can rent dive equipment, Sunfish, and Windsurfers. Until now, they have never asked for payment for using their dock, but this might change in the near future: The hotel has plans to build a marina inside the bay. During Easter weekend, it is very crowded because of the Curaçao Regatta—involving local yachts, Sunfish, catamarans (Hobie Cats and Prindels), and Windsurfers. Foreign boats are welcome!

BOCA SANTA CRUZ

A narrow indentation in the coast with not much room, this is another good anchorage with an excellent beach. I recommend anchoring bow and stern.

PLAJA LAGUN

A good daytime anchorage with a nice small beach.

PLAJA JEREMI

Another good daytime anchorage.

KNIPBAAI

As above. The crew of *Jomy* reports that there are two parts to this anchorage: Groot ("big") Knip and Klein ("small") Knip.

PLAJA ABAO

As above.

WESTPUNTBAAI

This is a good spot from which to head back north to Puerto Rico or St. Thomas. A good anchorage can be found in 4 fathoms off the town, and a few basic supplies can be bought in town. It is likely to be crowded on weekends.

The crew of *Jomy* found that the restaurant overlooking the beach was not very good. If you like fish (or something else), it is recommended that you go ashore (near the fishing boats), follow the road, and go to your left at the road junction. You will find Jaanchi Christiaan's restaurant. Excellent!

Aruba
(Chart V-71; II D-2, D-23, D-231)

This island was originally settled about the same time as Bonaire and Curaçao, but I have been unable to ascertain whether it was a source of salt. What I have figured out is that there was not much happening in Aruba until 1915, when the Americans began to build oil refineries for the oil they were bringing out of Venezuela. But no one has been able to tell me why they built the refineries in Aruba, which doesn't have an especially good harbor, rather than concentrating all their refineries in Curaçao, which has a superb harbor. The oil refineries provided a labor market for the Eastern Caribbean islands. (Grenada's former prime minister Eric Gairy learned his technique of labor organization while he was a young man in Aruba, before emigrating back to Grenada and organizing the agricultural labor and causing all sorts of problems—he served his apprenticeship well.)

In years gone by, Aruba was the first stop for boats fighting their way eastward from Panamá. There was not much of a harbor, and there were no facilities for yachts, but anyplace where you could throw out an anchor and sit in one spot that was not rocking and rolling seemed like heaven. Boats heading west normally took off directly from Curaçao.

With the drop in oil prices, the refineries became uneconomic and were dismantled. Now the island is no longer an oil island but rather a tourist island with numerous hotels. Rob Swain, who made his fortune with the Toys R Us retail chain, decided to invest heavily in Aruba. He built a marina in Oranjestad, the capital, and now is in the process of building a hotel, shopping complex, and casino. The marina, which opened in the fall of 1988, has fuel, electricity, water, showers, hotel, restaurant, and casino—everything the yachtsman desires. (The plan is as shown on the sketch chart.)

Since the marina has been built, there has been very little room to anchor off. It is pretty much a matter of going into the marina if you plan to stop at Aruba.

I have been told you can anchor south of Oranjestad, inside the reef, but I have never discussed it with anyone who has done so. No one I have spoken to seems to know the controlling depth—they have only seen boats doing it. Some boats actually wend their way through the shoal water and reefs to anchor off the yacht club.

Northwest of town, the shelf is narrow, but boats do moor off the hotels. Anchoring is probably similar to anchoring in Kralendijk in Bonaire.

<u>Warning:</u> In late spring and during the summer, the trades sometimes die out, a southwest swell builds up, and there is a light southwest breeze. This will quickly swing boats moored off the beach high and dry unless they are moored bow and stern or on a Bahamian moor. Be forewarned.

Entrance to Oranjestad can be had either via the main channel coming in from the northwest or up the lower channel from the south.

There are no marine supplies on the island—all marine supplies are brought up from Curaçao—but there is a very good hardware store (with no marine supplies). Ice is available only in cubes. There are numerous laundromats, and many restaurants that are expensive but excellent. There are two Asian supermarkets (also expensive) with excellent selections of goods. The phone system is like the one in Bonaire—good, but no collect calls.

(The above information was supplied by Glen Smith and Helena Henderson of the 38-foot Aitken cutter *Hornpipe*.)

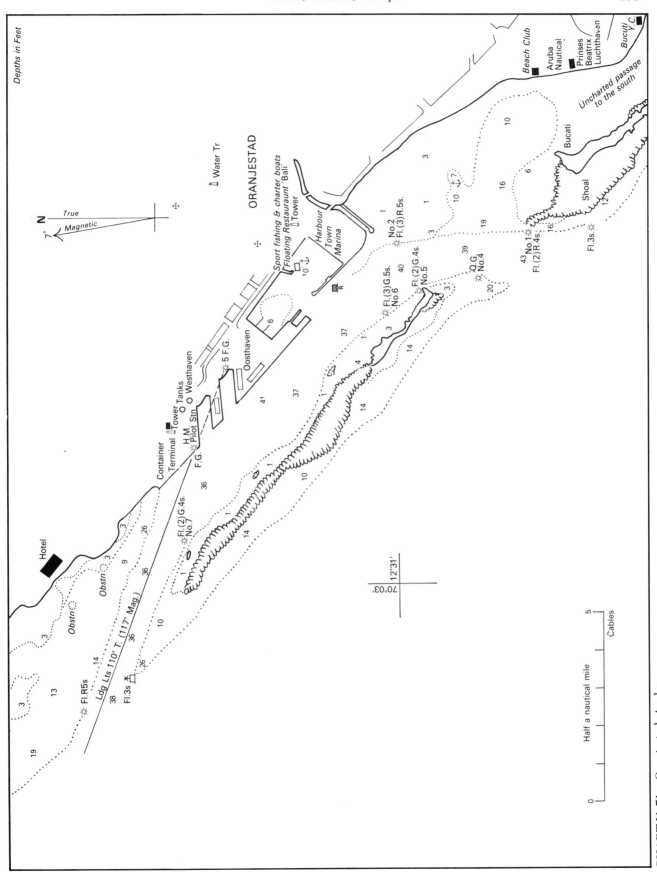

CHART V–71   Oranjestad, Aruba

NOTES

Bibliography

Cruising Guides

Buzby, V. M. *Virgin Island Sailing Directions*. 1952. Privately printed by the Coast Guard Auxiliary in the early 1950s.

Carey, Charles, and E. A. Raiwhold. *Virgin Anchoraging*. A superb collection of aerial photographs.

Chubb, Percy, III. *Cruising Guide to the Windward and Leeward Islands of the Eastern Caribbean*. 1961. Privately printed.

Eggleston, George Teeple. *Virgin Islands*. 1959; reprinted, Huntington, N.Y.: Krieger, 1974. Available at Palm Passage Bookstore, St. Thomas.

Eiman, William J. *St. Maarten/St. Martin Area Plus St. Kitts and Nevis Cruising Guide*. Copyright 1983 by Virgin Island Plus Yacht Charters, Inc. Also covers Anguilla, St. Barts, Saba, and Statia.

Forbes, Al. *Virgin Islands Cruising Guide*. Hollywood, Fla.: Dukane Press, 1970.

Kelly, Tom, and Jack Van Ost. *Yachtsman's Guide to the Virgin Islands*. 1968. Now Van Ost, John R., and Harry Kline. *Yachtsman's Guide to the Greater Antilles*. Coral Gables, Fla.: Tropic Isle, 1979.

Mitchell, Carleton. *Islands to Windward*. New York: Van Nostrand, 1948. Now out of print, this classic yarn of Mitchell's cruise from Trinidad to Nassau on board the *Carib* in 1946 is the first cruising guide written for the area.

Street, D. M., Jr. *Cruising Guide to the Virgin Islands*. 1963. Privately printed. No longer available.

————. *Yachting Guide to the Grenadines*. Hollywood, Fla.: Dukane Press, 1970.

————. *A Cruising Guide to the Lesser Antilles*. New York: Norton, 1964, 1974.

Stevens Yachts of Annapolis, *A Crusing Guide to the Windward Islands*, Annapolis, Md.: 1979. A picture and text guide.

Wilensky, Julius M. *Yachtsman's Guide to the Windward Islands*. 2nd ed. Stamford, Conn.: Wescott Cove, 1978.

General

Fenger, Frederic A. *The Cruise of the Diablesse*. New York: Yachting, Inc., [1926]. A description of cruising through the islands in 1915. Possibly back in print. If not, try the library. A truly great book on the Lesser Antilles.

————. *Alone in the Caribbean*. Belmont, Mass.: Wilmington Books, 1958. A description of cruising through the Islands in a decked canoe in 1911. Another great book on the Lesser Antilles.

Mitchell, Carleton. *Islands to Windward*. Washington, D.C.: National Geographic Society, 1967. A description of the author's second cruise through the islands in 1965 aboard the *Finisterre*.

Robinson, William. *Where the Tradewinds Blow*. New York: Charles Scribner's Sons, [1963]. A collection of stories about various cruises by the editor of *Yachting*.

History

Kay, Francis. *This—Is Grenada*. St. George's, Grenada: Carenage Press, [1971]. An excellent description of Grenada and a must for anyone who loves it.

Lewisjohn, Florence. *Divers Information on the Romantic History of St. Croix*. Hollywood, Fla.: Dukane Press, [1963?].

————. *Tales of Tortola and the British Virgin Islands*. Hollywood, Fla.: Dukane Press, 1966.

————. *St. Croix under Seven Flags*. Hollywood, Fla.: Dukane Press, 1970.

Mann, Zane B. *Fair Winds and Far Places*. Minneapolis: Dillon Press, 1978. Excellent account of a successful executive who chucks it all and runs away to the Lesser Antilles. An honest appraisal of the joys and sorrows involved. Required reading for anyone thinking of doing the same.

Morison, Samuel Eliot. *Admiral of the Ocean Sea*. Boston: Little, Brown, 1942. Superb biography of Columbus with vivid descriptions of the men, ships, islands, and sailing. Voluminous and interesting footnotes.

————. *Christopher Columbus, Mariner*. Boston: Little, Brown, 1955. A condensed version of *Admiral of the Ocean Sea*, and infinitely more readable.

O'Neill, Edward A. *Rape of the American Virgins*. New York: Praeger, 1972. A must for anyone who wishes to understand the problems of the U.S. Virgin Islands.

Thomas, G. C. H. *Ruler in Hiroona*. [Port of Spain], Trinidad, [1972]. Novel of a mythical island, but an all-too-apt description of the typical West Indian situation.

Waugh, Alec. *Island in the Sun*. New York: Farrar, Straus and Cudahy, [c. 1955].

Westlake, Donald E. *Under an English Heaven*. New York: Simon & Schuster, 1972. Provides valuable historical insight into island governments throughout the Lesser Antilles. A must for anyone who wants to understand the islands.

Humor

Wibberley, Leonard. *The Mouse That Roared*. Boston: Little, Brown. Side-splitting description of the invasion of Anguilla, with local island characters very thinly disguised.

Wouk, Herman. *Don't Stop the Carnival*. New York: Doubleday, 1965. A perfect description of St. Thomas in the late 1950s.

Flora and Fauna

Chaplin, C. G. *Fish Watching Guide*. New York: World.

Collins, James Bond. *Birds of the West Indies*. 2nd ed. Boston: Houghton-Mifflin, 1971.

Devas, Father Raymond. *Birds of Grenada, St. Vincent and the Grenadines*. Grenada: Carenage Press.

Groome, J. R. *A Natural History of the Island of Grenada*. Privately printed. Available at Sea Change Book Stores, St. George's, Grenada.

Hargreaves, Dorothy, and Bob Hargreaves. *Tropical Blossoms of the Caribbean*. Kailua, Hawaii: Hargreaves, 1960.

Mognotte, Sony. *Shelling and Beachcombing in the Southern Caribbean Waters*.

Murray, Dea. *Birds of the Virgin Islands*.

Randall, John E. *Caribbean Reef Fishes*. Neptune, N.J.: T.F.H., 1978.

Among the most readable books for those wishing to know about the Eastern Caribbean's colorful past are the novels and nonfiction works of Dudley Pope. His knowledge and research are impeccable. The following are highly recommended.

Dudley Pope: Nonfiction

The Black Ship. Philadelphia: Lippincott, 1964. The story of the worst single-ship mutiny in the Royal Navy. On board the *Hermione*, in 1797, between Hispaniola and Venezuela, the captain and all the officers were murdered.

The Buccaneer King. New York: Dodd, Mead, 1978. The first third of this biography of Sir Henry Morgan gives a wide-ranging introduction to the early days of the Eastern Caribbean.

Dudley Pope: Novels

Governor Ramage, R.N. New York: Simon & Schuster, 1973. Covers the U.S. Virgins and Culebra.

Ramage and the Freebooters. London: Weidenfeld & Nicolson, [1969]. (In the United States, *The Triton Brig*. New York: Pocket Books, 1978.) Covers Grenada and St. Lucia.

Ramage and the Rebels. Describes how the island of Curaçao was handed over to the British—and captured by them when the Dutch changed their mind.

Ramage's Diamond. London: Fontana, 1977. Describes the capture by the British of Diamond Rock, off Fort-de-France, Martinique.

Ramage's Mutiny. London: Secker & Warburg, 1977. Set in English Harbour, Antigua, and then in Venezuela.

Ramage's Prize. New York: Simon & Schuster, 1975. Covers the Lesser and Greater Antilles.

Index

ABC islands, xix, xxx, xxxi, xxxii, 98, 138–53
    see also Aruba; Bonaire; Curaçao
Admiral of the Ocean Sea (Morison), 9
Amazon, 13
Américo Vespucio Marina, 2, 67, 68–71
Anegada, xviii
Anegada Passage, xviii
Angel Falls, xxx, xxxi, 17
Anguilla, xviii
Anse Mitan, xviii
Antigua, xvii, xviii
Araya, 48, 52–53
Aruba, xxx, xxxi–xxxii, 2–3, 98, 101, 102–103, 138, 152–53
Astilleros de Higuerote, 77–79
Ave de Barlovento, 3, 6, 130–33, 136
Ave de Sotavento, 3, 6, 133–36
Avenida 4 de Mayo, 38, 40, 41
Ayacucho, 13, 17

Bahía Bergantin, 66
Bahía Boca de las Piedras, 102
Bahía de Buche, 80
Bahía de Chorro, 97
Bahía de Conoma, 65
Bahía de Juangriego, 45
Bahía de los Piratas, 79
Bahía de Mangle, 45
Bahía de Pertigalete, 65
Bahía Escondida, 32
Bahía Guamache, 42, 43
Bahía Guanta, 65–66
Bahía Hernán Vásquez, 5, 29
Bahía Manare, 63
Bahías Puerto Santos, 30
Bajo Caracas, 64
Barbados, xvii, xix
Barbuda, xviii
Barcelona, xxxii, 65
Barrancas, 17
Bella Vista Hotel, 41, 42
Bequia, xix
Blauwbaai, 149

Boca de Cangrejo, 115, 116
Boca de Cote, 121, 122
Boca de la Serpiente, 9, 12, 15
Boca del Dragón, 8
Boca de Lord, 64
Boca del Río, 37, 39, 42–45
Boca de Palo, 115
Boca de Paparo, 77
Boca de Sebastopol, 122
Boca Grande, 8, 12, 17, 95, 97
Boca Grande o de Navios, 17
Boca Grandi, 151
Boca Paiclás, 95, 97
Boca Palo, 116
Boca Pilar, 95–97
Boca Santa Cruz, 151
Boca Seca, 95
Boca Slagbaai, 145
Boca Suánchez, 95
Bonaire, xxx, xxxi, 3, 5, 6, 98, 101, 138–46
Brazil, 17
Bridgetown, xix
Bullenbaai, 151
Burqui, 125

Cabo Codera, 1, 2, 4, 5–6, 77, 79, 80
Cabo de la Vela, 3
Cabo Negro, 47
Cabo San Francisco, 24, 25
Cabo Tres Puntas, 27
Caicara, 17
Camurí Grande, 4, 82
Caño Grande, 97
Caño Macereo, 17
Cape Verdes, 17
Caraballeda, 4, 84
Caraballeda Yacht Club, 83–84, 84
Caracas, xvii, xxix, xxx, xxxii, 2, 4, 68, 82, 84, 86–87, 119–21
Caracas del Este, 63–64
Caracas del Oeste, 63, 64
Caracas del Sur, 64
Carenero, 77–79, 80, 82, 127

Carenero Harbor, 117
Carenero Yacht Club, 79
Caribbean Yacht Club of Maracaibo, 103
Caribito, 80
Cartagena, Colombia, 2–3, 102
Carúpano, 4, 5, 23, 29–31, 108
Castillo de San Antonio, 58
Castillo de San Carlos Borromeo, 39
Cavafa, 79
Cayo Borracho, 90, 98, 101
Cayo de Agua, 121, 128–29
Cayo del Norte, 97
Cayo Heradura, 111, 113–15
Cayo Los Muertos, 98, 100
Cayo Pelon, 100
Cayo Peraza, 98, 100
Cayo Pescadores, 98
Cayo Pirata, 123
Cayo Punta Brava, 97
Cayo Sal, 100, 129
Cayo San Juan, 101
Cayo Sombrero, 98
Centro Marina de Oriente, 67, 70
Ceru Grandi, 139
Chacachacare, 45
Chacopata, 49
charts, xxiv–xxv
    British Admiralty, xxiv
    Imray-Iolaire, xxiv–xxv
    sketch, xxv, xxvii–xxviii
    U.S. government, xxiv
Chichiriviche, xxix, 3–4, 6, 90, 98–100, 102, 140
    coastal area west of, 101
Chimana del Oeste, 72, 73
Chimana del Sur, 72
Chimana Grande, 72–73
Chimana Segunda, 72
Chuspa, 80
Cienega Ocumare, 88
Ciudad Bolívar, 13, 17, 18
Ciudad Guayana, 13, 17
Club Asiento, 149
Club Nautico de Maracaibo, 103
Club Nautico El Chaure, 66
Colombia, xxix, xxxi, 2–3, 6, 17, 102
Concorde Hotel, 149
Coral Cliff Hotel, 151
Coro, 101–102
Crasqui, 125
Cristóbal Colón, 9, 10
Cumaná, xxx, xxx, xxxii, 58–61
Cumaná Marina, 60–61
Curaçao, xxx, xxxi, 3, 6, 98, 101, 138, 146–52
Curaçao Yacht Club, 149

Daaibooibaai, 151
Dominica, xix
Doral Beach Villas, 70
Dos Mosquises, 121, 129

Elbert Key, 127–28
El Bichar, 48
El Borracho, 73
El Gran Roque, 105, 119, 122, 123–24, 130
El Morro Colorado, 58
El Morro de Barcelona, 1, 4, 68, 71, 73, 82
El Morro de Chacopata, 35, 48, 49
El Morro de Puerto Santos, 4–5, 29
El Morro de Robledal, 45
El Morro development project, 66, 67–71
El Morro Marina, 68, 71
El Morro peak, 68
El Saco, 47, 48
El Valle del Espíritu Santo, 42
Ensa Aricagua, 9
Ensa Cariaquita, 8–9
Ensa Cumaca, 10–11
Ensa de Charagato, 50
Ensa de Corsarios, 6, 79
Ensa El Rincon, 54
Ensa Guinimita, 10
Ensa La Guardia, 44
Ensa Lebranche, 32
Ensa Macuro, 9, 10
Ensa Mapire, 11
Ensa Medina, 28
Ensa Patao, 10, 12
Ensa Río Grande, 10, 11
Ensa Santa Cruz, 65
Ensa Unare, 22
Ensa Uquirito, 10, 12
Ensa Yacua, 9–10, 11
Ensenada Caleta Guarano, 102
Ensenada Cata, 88
Ensenada de Corsarios, 79, 80, 81
Ensenada de Guaca, 32
Ensenada de Morrocoy, 97
Ensenada de Rondón, 79, 80, 81
Ensenada El Placer, 95–97
Ensenada Esmeralda, 31, 34
Ensenada Garrapata, 32
Ensenada Lebranche, 32
Ensenada Manzanillo, 35
Ensenada Medina, 28
Ensenada Mejillones, 26
Ensenada Pargo, 26
Ensenada Tigrillo, 64
Ensenada Uquire, 24–25
Esmeralda, 32–35
Espanqui, 122
Espenqui, 125–26

Flamingo Beach Hotel, 145
Fort-de-France, xviii
Francisqui, 122–23
Fuikbaai, 147–49

Golfo de Cardón, 2, 3, 102–103
Golfo de Cariaco, xxx, xxxii, 4, 38, 53–56, 58

Golfo de Cuaro, 100–101
Golfo de Paria, xxx, 2, 8–18, 24
 north coast of, 12
 south coast of, 13
 tides and currents of, 8
Golfo de Santa Fé, 38, 63, 64–65
Golfo de Tucacas, 101
Golfo de Venezuela, 3, 102–103
Grenada, xvii, xix, xxx, 4, 5, 11, 12, 18, 20, 25
Grenadines, xviii
Guadeloupe, xvii, xviii
Guagua, 61
Guanta, 66
Guide to Venezuela (Bauman & Young), xxxi
Gui Progreso, Mapas de Carreteras de Venezuela,
 18
Güiria, 11–12, 13, 18

Habitat Hotel, 140
Harbor of Chichiriviche, 100
Higuerote, 77, 79–80
Hotel Concorde, 41
Hotel Mario, 100
Hotel Minerva, 60

Indunave Marina, 97–98
Isla Cabra, 107, 108
Isla Caribe, 49
Isla Casabel, 32
Isla Coche, 38, 47–49
Isla Conejo, 108–109
Isla Cubagua, 38, 49–50
Isla Esmeralda, 32
Isla Fernando, 126
Isla Iguana, 107–108, 108
Isla La Blanquilla, 5, 38, 109–11
Isla La Borracha, 73
Isla La Orchila, 117
Isla Larga, 63, 88–90, 125, 126
Isla La Tortuga, 4, 5–6, 38, 77, 80, 111–17
 east coast of, 113
 north coast of, 113
 south coast of, 115
Isla Los Lobos, 48, 49
Isla Los Palenquines, 113
Isla Margarita, xxx, xxxi, xxxii, 1, 2, 4, 5, 17, 18,
 37–47, 49, 50, 72
Isla Patos, 9
Isla Pelona, 129
Isla Picuda Chica, 72
Islas de Arapo, 65
Islas de Aves, xxix, 5
Islas de Píritu, 1, 4, 73–75
Islas de Plata, 65
Islas Garrapatas, 32
Islas Las Aves, xviii, 130–36, 139
Islas Los Hermanos, 5
Islas Los Roques, xviii, xxx, 3–4, 5–6, 71, 119–30
 southern edge of, 129–30

Islas Los Testigos, xxix, xxxi, 2, 4, 5, 105–109
Islas Los Tortuguillos, 114, 115
Isla Testigo Grande, 107
Isla Testigo Pequeño, 107
Isla Venados, 63, 64

Juangriego, 37, 41, 42, 45–47

Klein Bonaire, 145
Klein Curaçao, 146
Knipbaai, 151
Kralendijk, 139, 140, 141–43
Kralendijk Town Dock Area, 141–43
Kralendijk Yacht Harbor Area, 143–45

La Asunción, 37, 41
Lac Baai, 145–46
La Cuevita Marina, 97, 98
La Guaira, 2, 4, 5, 6, 80, 84–86, 87, 130
Laguna Chica, 53–54, 55
 anchorages east of, 53
 anchorages west of, 53
Laguna de la Restinga, 37, 44
Laguna El Carenero, 117
Laguna Grande del Obispo, xxx, 53, 54–55, 56
La Lechería, 68, 71
La Maseta Fernando, 126
Lanqui-Carenero, 127
Lanqui-Larga, 125
Las Aves, xviii, 130–36, 139
La Sola, 5
Las Piedras, 102
La Tortuga, 4, 5–6, 38, 77, 80, 111–17
 east coast of, 113
 north coast of, 113
 south coast of, 115
La Vela de Coro, 101–102
Lesser Antilles, xvii–xix
Lighthouse Island, 133, 135
Long Island, 132, 133, 135
Los Cañones, 53
Los Canquises, 122
Los Frailes, 47
Los Monjes, 3, 102–103
Los Roques, xviii, xxx, 3–4, 5–6, 71, 119–30
 southern edge of, 129–30
Los Testigos, xxix, xxxi, 2, 4, 5, 105–109

Macuto, 82, 87
Macuto Sheraton Hotel, 4, 83, 84
Maiquetía Airport, xvii, xxxi, 86, 130
Maracaibo, 3, 102, 103
Margarita, xxx, xxxi, xxxii, 1, 2, 4, 5, 17, 18, 37–47,
 49, 50, 72
Marigot, xix
Marina Carenero, 77
Marina El Anda, 98
Marina Grande, 86
Marina Mar, 84

Marine Coast Master, 147
Martinique, xvii, xviii, 45, 83
Mejillones, 21
Meliá Marina, 66
Mona Passage, 6
Monjes del Sur, 3, 102
Morne Jaloux, 5
Morrocoy National Park, xxx, 4, 6, 90, 91, 95–98
Morro de Labranche, 32
Morro Taquien, 31
Mosquitoqui, 126, 127
Mount Brandaris, 139
Mustique, xviii

Namusqui, 123
Netherlands Antilles, 138
Nevis, xviii
Nine Palms Bay, 48
Noronqui, 124–25, 129
Noronqui Abajo, 124, 125
Noronqui Arriba, 124–25
Noronqui del Medio, 124, 125
Nueva Cádiz, 49

Oranjestad, xxxi, 152, 153
Orchids on the Calabash Tree (Eggleston), xix
Orinoco, 12–18, 24
Orinoco Delta, xxx, 12–17, 18

Pampatar, 37, 38–40, 41
    amusement center, 40
Panamá, xxxi, 2–3, 102, 138
Panama Canal, 6
Pargo, 5
Parque Nacional Morrocoy, xxx, 4, 6, 90, 91, 95–
    98
Paseo Colón Marina, 66, 67
Pedernales, 13
Peninsula de Araya, 38, 49, 52–53, 68
Peninsula de Guajira, 102
Peninsula de Manare, 63, 64
Peninsula de Paraguaná, 3, 101, 102
Peninsula de Paria, 1, 5, 20–35
    east side of, xxx, 1, 5, 14, 18
    north side of, 4, 5, 21, 22, 23
    south side of, 8, 9
Peninsula de Punta Gorda, 64
Pequeño Francis, 123
Peru, 17
Pigeon Island, xix
Píritu Adentro, 75
Piscaderabaai, 149
Plaja Abao, 151
Plaja Jeremi, 151
Plaja Lagun, 151
Playa Cacao, 26
Playa Colorado, 65
Playa Frans, 145
Playa Grande Yacht Club, 86

Playa Moreno, 41
Plaza Bolívar, 42
Point Salines, 5
Porlamar, 37, 39, 40–42, 108
Port-of-Spain, 5, 8, 12
Posa Companario, 64
Puerto Azul, 2, 4, 82–83, 84
Puerto Azul Club, 82, 83
Puerto Cabello, xxx, xxxii, 1, 4, 6, 88, 90–93, 101
    street plan, 92
Puerto Cabello Marina, 91
Puerto Calera, 4, 84, 86
Puerto Carenero, 77, 78
Puerto Chichiriviche, 99
Puerto Cumarebo, 101
Puerto de Hierro, 10, 11
Puerto de Ocumare, 88
Puerto El Roque, 122, 123, 124
Puerto Escondido, 61
Puerto Francés, 80
Puerto Grande, 13
Puerto La Cruz, xxx, xxxii, 2, 17, 50, 65, 66–67, 71,
    87–88
Puerto La Cruz-Barcelona area, 37–38, 65–66, 72–
    75
Puerto La Guaira, 85
Puerto Maya, 88
Puerto Mochima, 58, 61–63
Puerto Ordaz, 17
Puerto Páez, 17
Puerto Réal, 53, 54
Puerto Rico, xxxi, 2, 6, 138, 151
Puerto San Juan, 101
Puerto Santos, 20, 22, 27, 28–29, 31
Puerto Sucre, 58, 61
Puerto Tucacas, 96
Puerto Turiamo, 88
Punta Arenas, 45
Punta Bobas, 111
Punta Bombeador, 13–17
Punta Cacao, 27
Punta Camurí Grande, 80
Punta Camurí Grande Club, 80
Punta Caraballeda, 83–84
Punta Colorada, 65
Punta Conejo, 48
Punta de la Aguada, 109–11
Punta de Lande, 33
Punta Delgada del Este, 113
Punta de los Negros, 115–17
Punta del Pozo, 45
Punta de Mangle, 42
Punta de Piedras, 42, 43
Punta Don Pedro, 20
Punta El Morro, 40–41
Punta El Muerto, 80
Punta El Tigre, 13–17
Punta Esmeralda, 32–35
Punta Galera, 47

Punta Gallinas, 102
Punta Garcitas, 9
Punta Gorda, 26–27
Punta Guacaparo, 54–55
Punta Guatapanare, 32
Punta Hernán Vásquez, 29
Punta La Caja, 53
Punta La Crucesita, 77
Punta La Cruz, 63
Punta La Hermita, 26
Punta La Playa, 47
Punta Manzanillo, 23, 35
Punta Mejillones, 20
Punta Moreno, 41
Punta Mosquito, 42
Punta Naiguatá, 82
Punta Oriental, 111
Punta Pargo, 20, 25–26
Punta Patilla, 31, 33
Punta Peñas, 9
Punta Pescadores, 13–17
Punta Piedras, 117
Punta Puinare, 72, 73
Punta Ranchos o del Medio, 113
Punta Reina, 73
Punta Río Caribe, 28
Punta Salina, 129
Punta San Juan, 101
Punta Tigrillo, 27, 63
Punta Uquire, 25
Punta Wecua, 145
Punta Zamuro, 101

Rabusqui, 125
Río Caribe, 28
Río Caroní, 17
Río de Santa Fé, 64
Río Grande, 17
Río Manzanares, 58, 60
Río Meta, 17
Río Negro, 13, 17
Río Orinoco, 12–18, 24
Robledal, 45
Round Island, 133, 135

Saba, xviii, 138
sailing directions, 1–6
     east to west, 5–6
     west to east, 2–5
St. Barts, 38
St. George, xix, 5
St. Kitts, xviii
St. Lucia, xvii, xix
St. Martin, xviii
St. Thomas, xviii, xxxi, 138–39, 151
St. Vincent, xix
San Blas Islands, xxxi, 2
Sand Gully Bay, 107
San Juan, xvii

San Juan Bautista, 37
San Juan de Unare, 27–28
San Juan hills, 37
San Pedro, 47–48
Santa Ana, 41
Santa Martabaai, 151
Sarifundy's Marina, 149
Sarqui, 125, 126
Sea of El Morro, 5, 38
Selenqui, 122
Shore Base Yacht Services, 39
Silver Yacht Club, 139, 143–45
Sint Eustatius (Statia), xviii, 138
Sint Maarten, 138
Sint Michielbaai, 149
Soufrière, xix
South Bay, 111
South Fjord, 111
Southwest Cove, 111
Spanish Water, 3, 147, 149, 150
Statia (Sint Eustatius), xviii, 138

Tacarigua, 27
Tarzan Restaurant, 37
Testigo Grande, 2, 105, 107, 108
Testigo Pequeño, 107
Tobago, xix
trade winds, 1–2, 20–24, 119
Trans World Radio, 6
Trinidad, xvii, 4, 5, 8, 11, 12, 13, 25
Tucacas, 4, 6, 90, 95
Tucupita, 13

Unare, 5, 28
Uquire, 5, 21

Vaarsenbaai, 151
Vencemos, 65
Venezuela, xix, xxix–xxxii
     currents and, 1
     Customs and Immigration procedures in, xxxii
     ground swells and, 2
     hurricanes in, 1–2
     mail services of, xxx–xxxi
     obtaining money in, xxxi
     sailing directions for, 1–6
     telephone service in, xxxi
     trade winds and, 1–2, 20–24
     yachting facilities in, xxx
Venezuelan Hydrographic Office, 3, 13
Venezuelan Tourist Board, 18
Vieux Fort, xix
Virgin Islands, xviii, 6
     American, xix
     British, xix
Vistamar, 67, 70, 71

Washington/Slagbaai National Park, 140
West Key, 128, 129
Westpuntbaai, 151–52
Willemstad, 147
Willemstoren, 139, 145

Yanqui, 127

zarpa (cruising permit), 3, 18, 29–30, 39, 77, 84,
    119
Zip Express, 66–67, 70